Teaching Chinese Literacy in the Early Years

The Chinese language is now used by a quarter of the world's population and is increasingly popular as a second language. *Teaching Chinese Literacy in the Early Years* comprehensively investigates the psychology, pedagogy and practice involved in teaching Chinese literacy to young children.

This text not only explores the psycholinguistic and neuropsychological processing involved in learning Chinese but also introduces useful teaching methods and effective practices relevant for teaching within early years and primary education.

Key issues explored within this text include:

- psycholinguistics of Chinese literacy
- neuropsychological understanding of Chinese literacy
- pedagogy of teaching Chinese as a first language
- pedagogy of teaching Chinese as a second language
- teaching Chinese literacy in early childhood settings
- assessing Chinese literacy attainment in the early years

With the addition of two reliable Chinese literacy scales, *Teaching Chinese Literacy in the Early Years* is an essential text for any student, lecturer or professional teacher who is interested in learning and teaching Chinese literacy.

Hui Li is Associate Professor of Early Childhood Education at the University of Hong Kong.

"Dr Li Hui's new publication, *Teaching Chinese Literacy in the Early Years: Psychology, Pedagogy and Practice,* is the first of its kind to examine Chinese literacy teaching and learning from combined psycholinguistic, pedagogical and practical perspectives. Its extraordinary scope and interdisciplinary insights, supported by rich empirical data gathered worldwide and lucid writing, make the volume an essential reading for anyone who is interested in understanding the key issues in development and learning of Chinese literacy in the early years.

– **Zhù Huá**, Professor of Applied Linguistics and Communication, Birkbeck College, University of London

"I strongly recommend this pioneering book which advances our understanding of the teaching Chinese literacy in the early years. The unique aspect of this book is that it not only considers the characteristics of the Chinese language that influence the learning of Chinese and the psychological processes involved in learning to read Chinese, but also gives equal emphasis to pedagogical processes. Classroom-based research in different Chinese societies provides empirical evidence on the efficacy of different instructional approaches on the learning of Chinese in preschools. This book is a must read for those interested in understanding and promoting the reading and writing of Chinese among both native and non-native speakers of the language."

– **Nirmala Rao**, Serena H.C. Yang Professor in Early Childhood and Education, The University of Hong Kong

"This book is a timely and original contribution to the Chinese language education that covers a wide range of topics including teaching Chinese as a second language. It will be a useful reference for scholars, graduate students and policymakers."

– **Linda Tsung**, Associate Professor, University of Sydney

Routledge Research in Language Education

The *Routledge Research in Language Education* series provides a platform for established and emerging scholars to present their latest research and discuss key issues in Language Education. This series welcomes books on all areas of language teaching and learning, including but not limited to language education policy and politics, multilingualism, literacy, L1, L2 or foreign language acquisition, curriculum, classroom practice, pedagogy, teaching materials, and language teacher education and development. Books in the series are *not* limited to the discussion of the teaching and learning of English only.

Books in the series include:

Teaching Chinese Literacy in the Early Years
Psychology, pedagogy, and practice
Hui Li

Pronunciation for English as an International Language
From research to practice
Ee-Ling Low

The Role of English Teaching in Modern Japan
Diversity and Multiculturalism through English Language Education in a Globalized Era
Mieko Yamada

Teaching Chinese Literacy in the Early Years

Psychology, pedagogy and practice

Hui Li

LONDON AND NEW YORK

First published 2015 by Routledge

2 Park Square, Milton Park, Abingdon, Oxfordshire OX14 4RN
711 Third Avenue, New York, NY 10017

Routledge is an imprint of the Taylor & Francis Group, an informa business

First issued in paperback 2018

Copyright © 2015 H. Li

The right of H. Li to be identified as author of this work has been asserted by him in accordance with sections 77 and 78 of the Copyright, Designs and Patents Act 1988.

All rights reserved. No part of this book may be reprinted or reproduced or utilised in any form or by any electronic, mechanical, or other means, now known or hereafter invented, including photocopying and recording, or in any information storage or retrieval system, without permission in writing from the publishers.

Notice:
Product or corporate names may be trademarks or registered trademarks, and are used only for identification and explanation without intent to infringe.

British Library Cataloguing in Publication Data
A catalogue record for this book is available from the British Library

Library of Congress Cataloging in Publication Data
A catalog record for this book has been requested

ISBN: 978-0-415-84129-0 (hbk)
ISBN: 978-1-138-58015-2 (pbk)

Typeset in Galliard
by Graphicraft Limited, Hong Kong

Contents

Acknowledgements ix

1 The psycholinguistics of Chinese literacy 1
   Chinese characters 1
   Chinese literacy 6
   Modeling Chinese literacy 9
   Acquiring Chinese literacy 14

2 The neuropsychological understanding of Chinese literacy 25
   Themes and topics in Chinese reading studies 25
   Neuropsychological understanding of Chinese reading 29
   Neuropsychological understanding of Chinese writing 37

3 The pedagogy of teaching Chinese as a first language 45
   Reading readiness versus emergent literacy 45
   Phonics versus a whole language approach 48
   Chinese traditional versus Western progressive pedagogies 51
   The best Chinese literacy pedagogy 56
   Story-based project approach 61

4 The pedagogy of teaching Chinese as a second language 67
   Learning Chinese as L2 rather than L1 67
   Teaching Chinese as L2 71
   The TPR approach to Chinese literacy 75
   Common pedagogies shared by L1 and L2 classrooms 81

viii Contents

5 Teaching Chinese literacy in early childhood settings — 86

The practice of Chinese literacy teaching in mainland China 86
The practice of Chinese literacy teaching in Hong Kong 90
The practice of Chinese literacy teaching in Singapore 94
Three gaps observed in China, Hong Kong and Singapore 97
The Story Approach to Integrated Learning (SAIL) 106
Appendix to chapter 5: SAIL example: five-day learning activities 113

6 Assessing Chinese literacy attainment in the early years — 118

Summative versus formative assessment 118
Preschool and Primary Chinese Literacy Scale (PPCLS) 122
Primary Chinese Reading Literacy Scale (PCRLS) 126

Appendix 1:   Preschool and Primary Chinese Literacy Scale (PPCLS) — 133
Appendix 1A: Preschool and Primary Chinese Literacy Scale Manual — 135
Appendix 1B: Preschool and Primary Chinese Literacy Scale – Test A — 143
Appendix 1C: Preschool and Primary Chinese Literacy Scale – Test B — 169
Appendix 1D: Preschool and Primary Chinese Literacy Scale – Test C — 190
Appendix 1E: Preschool and Primary Chinese Literacy Scale – Test D — 196
Appendix 1F: Preschool and Primary Chinese Literacy Scale Record Form — 207
Appendix 2:   Primary Chinese Reading Literacy Scale (PCRLS) — 213

References — 226
Index — 251

Acknowledgements

This academic work is a summary of what I have done in the field of early Chinese literacy since 1997. Many colleagues and friends have collaborated in the development and production of this publication and many debts have been accumulated during the past two decades. Without the inspiration and unfailing help from them, I would not have been able to accomplish this work.

First, I must especially mention that this project originated from my PhD study, which was co-supervised by my dearest colleague – Professor Nirmala Rao and Professor Tse Shek Kam. Without their guidance, encouragement, and inspiration during the past decades, this book would not have been possible. I strongly wish to present this publication as a tribute to them.

Second, I very much appreciate the support, assistance, and guidance provided by Professor Liu Aihua, Professor Linda Tsung, Dr. Connie Lum, Dr. Eva Lau, Dr. Eva Chen, Ms Ho Yin Fong, Miss Lilian Chau, and Miss Eileen Chin-mei Wong. In particular, I am deeply indebted to Dr. Ricci Fong for her painstaking work in reviewing, editing, and proofreading the text. I also thank Miss Jingying Wang for her excellent work on the reference list. Their extensive contributions have made this book a far better work.

My sincere gratitude also goes to the participating teachers, principals, and their kindergarteners in Beijing, Hong Kong, Shenzhen and Singapore for the exceptional collaboration and participation in this decade-long project. I also wish to express my sincere thanks to the reviewers of this book. Their insightful and inspiring comments have contributed in numerous positive ways to the publication of this book.

Finally, my deepest gratitude is directed to my family. My mom, my wife, and my sons, Gavin and Kevin, have given me tremendous support for my out-of-town field studies. This book is the best gift I can give to them.

June 4, 2014

Chapter 1

The psycholinguistics of Chinese literacy

Chinese is the only writing system of the few developed before 3000 BC that is still alive, and the language itself is still evolving and its usage expanding (Li and Wu, 1996; Tse and Li, 2011). Chinese is now used by one quarter of the world's population, and is the official language in mainland China, Hong Kong, Taiwan, and Singapore (Li, 2000). Japan and Korea have also used Chinese characters in their written language systems. A large number of Chinese immigrants living in North America, Australia and other areas use Chinese characters as the tool to maintain their mother tongue and Chinese culture. Nowadays learning Chinese as a second language is very trendy throughout the world as China has become the second largest economy, providing enormous working and trading opportunities for people from other countries (Tse and Li, 2011). Hence, there has been an increase in research into Chinese language learning in the past decades, conducted by psychologists and educational researchers. This chapter will provide an overview of the published studies on the psycholinguistics of Chinese language and analyze their educational implications.

Chinese characters

The orthography of Chinese

Chinese is a monosyllabic and tone language which is deeply orthographic, as defined by its transparency and the degree of its letter-to-phoneme correspondence (Cheung *et al.* 2006; Katz and Frost, 1992). Chinese is considered a highly orthographic language, as its written form has a tremendous number of syllables (quantity) and homophones (difficulty) but lacks direct symbol-to-sound rules (transparency). First, it has little transparency in mapping symbols to sounds, as its written symbols (characters) map onto syllabic morphemes rather than individual sounds (phonemes) (Wang and Yang, 2008). There is no direct correspondence between characters and phonemes. This point will be further discussed in the following subsections.

Second, Chinese is highly orthographic as it has a tremendous number of syllables. Chinese is a monosyllabic language, in which most morphemes consist of single syllables and are represented by single characters (Norman, 2000). Chinese characters function as lexical morphemes to convey the meaning of the written symbols (Chen, 1992). There are approximately 56,000 Chinese characters according to Xu (1995) – only 5000–8000 of them are commonly used, while about 3000 are high-frequency characters used in daily communication. L1 Chinese students in Hong Kong and China are required to learn 2500–3000 characters to be literate (Li, 2000), and some Chinese proficiency tests for L2 learners require the acquisition of about 3000 high-frequency characters (Liu and Song, 1992).

Third, Chinese is difficult as it has many homophones. As a tone language, each Chinese syllable can be characterized by four tones in Mandarin and six tones in Cantonese (Tse and Li, 2011). The syllables have the same segmental elements but different tones correspond to different morphemes. There are 1241 syllables representing 7754 commonly used Chinese characters, and 429 of them are used to represent 90 per cent of the Chinese characters (Ni, 1995). This means that each syllable needs to represent many morphemes, and some of them even represent 40 or more different morphemes (Zhou and Marslen-Wilson, 1999). This produces an enormous number of homophones which can cause confusion and can only be distinguished by the large number of strokes (Butcher, 1995). This makes it very difficult for pinyin – the Chinese phonetic alphabet system – to directly and independently present real meanings.

The nature of Chinese characters

The Chinese language is written using Chinese characters, of which there are two forms: the traditional Chinese character (the complex form) and the Simplified Chinese character. The former is widely used in Hong Kong, Taiwan, and other overseas Chinese communities, whereas the latter is used in mainland China and Singapore. To learn the Chinese language, one has to learn these Chinese characters. To become literate in Chinese, one has to acquire 2500 Chinese characters (Li, 2000). This has become the first obstacle to all beginners learning Chinese. In their eyes, Chinese characters are very difficult to learn as they contain few clues as to their sound and meaning. Is this true? Do Chinese characters contain any clues for their sound and meaning? What is the nature of Chinese characters? All these questions have been debated in the past century among Chinese linguists and politicians (see Li, 1998, for a detailed review).

In general, Chinese characters have been defined as being "pictographic", "ideographic" or "logographic", or all three. Siok and Fletcher (2001), for instance, defined written Chinese as "a logographic system", as it uses characters which map onto the morpheme (meaning) while lacking grapheme-phoneme correspondence rules. All these terms, however, are incapable of defining the true nature of Chinese characters (Li, 2000). More precise definitions include its being "morphographic" (DeFrancis, 1984) or "morpheme-syllable" (Coulmas, 1989; Qiu, 1988). This is because each Chinese character does stand for a morpheme, i.e. a meaning unit, but not necessarily a full word. Coulma's and Qiu's definitions have further included the phonetic nature of Chinese characters, in that they stand for a syllable rather than a single sound. In other words, each Chinese character reflects a syllable as well as a morpheme. These two aspects set the Chinese writing system apart from alphabetic ones. That being said, in this book I am going to define Chinese characters as a morphsyllabic writing system – the majority of Chinese characters can either serve as standalone words or be combined with other characters to form a two- or multi-character word. However, Chinese characters are equally spaced, with no indication of word boundaries, and this has made reading Chinese very difficult as word segmentation is needed for lexical access (Shen, 2008).

The structure of Chinese characters

As the basic unit in the writing system, Chinese characters have three levels of orthographic structure; namely, stroke, stroke pattern, and character structure.

1. Each Chinese character is made up of different strokes, and its visual complexity is usually measured by the number of strokes (Cheng, 1982; Seidenberg, 1985), which can vary from one to over 20. The average number of strokes for the 2,000 frequently used characters is 11.2 for the traditional characters used in Hong Kong and Taiwan, and 9.0 for the simplified characters used in mainland China (Chan, 1982). Like the grapheme in the alphabetic system, the strokes do not carry any information on the meaning, but the change of a stroke changes the meaning and the sound of a character (e.g. 失[shi1] "lost" and 矢[shi3] "arrow", 夫[fu1] "husband" and 天[tian1] "sky").
2. Different combinations of strokes make up the stroke-patterns, or the so-called *radicals*. Stroke patterns that carry information about the meaning are called *semantic radicals*, and those that indicate the sound of a character are called *phonetic radicals*. A radical can be an actual character or part of a character. According to Han's (1994) statistical analyses, the Chinese writing system has about 600 stroke-patterns or radicals.
3. At the structure level, Chinese characters have two forms: integrated and compound. The integrated form is an indecomposable and complete single character, such as 王[wang2] "king" and 土[tu3] "earth", which cannot be decomposed into smaller meaningful radicals; whereas the compound form is a decomposable character that comprises two or more radicals. Over 80 per cent of Chinese characters are in the compound form and are ideophonetic (Li, 1998). Each ideophonetic compound contains two components: one is the phonetic radical, and the other the semantic radical. For example, in the character 雾[wu4] "fog", 雨[yu3] "rain" is the semantic radical which gives a cue to the meaning of the character, and 务[wu4] is the phonetic radical which has the same pronunciation as that of the whole character.

Chinese reading has been described as being holistic (Wang, 1981) or part-to-whole (Ho and Bryant, 1997a) with only one orthographic unit (the phonetic radical) encoding or specifying the syllabic pronunciation of the whole character. Some scholars (e.g. Shu, Chen, Anderson, Wu, and Xuan, 2003) tend to believe that Chinese is not a phonologically reliable orthography thus phonological awareness is not necessarily crucial to word reading. Other scholars, however, find that phonological awareness is uniquely associated with word reading across time (e.g. Chow *et al.* 2005), though not always so (e.g. McBride-Chang *et al.* 2011). In addition, Chung and McBride-Chang (2012) suggest that morphological awareness (sensitivity to the morphemes within words) is also critical to early Chinese reading acquisition, as many Chinese characters are homophones.

It is estimated that 80 per cent (Li and Wu, 1996) or 90 per cent (Feng, 1999) of modern Chinese characters are phonetic–semantic compounds. But the phonetic radicals are not fixed phonetic symbols, and some of them are borrowed characters. Therefore, they themselves bear no sound-to-script correspondence. In addition, the historical changes to Chinese scripts have added to the changes in Chinese phonology. In modern Chinese, the representation of the sound of the compound character by the phonetic radical is blurred. Honorof and Feldman (2006) defined the characters whose pronunciations directly match the pronunciation suggested by their phonetic radicals as phonologically transparent, and those that do not as phonologically opaque. Fan *et al.* (1984) found that 26 per cent of phonetic radicals could cue the correct sound of a compound character. Fan (2010) studied the 10 Chinese textbooks used by Chinese L2 beginners and found that only about 10 per cent of the phonetic radicals could reliably cue the sound of the compounds. Because of this, students learning Chinese can only use the phonetic radical to guess the sound of an unknown compound character – this is a random guessing game, because most of the compound characters cannot give any reliable hints, even if they have the phonetic radical. Nonetheless, it would be useful for beginner learners to remember the few reliable phonetic radicals, those which can serve as a prompt to help memorize the sound of the character (Shen and Ke, 2007).

Other scholars believe that about 20 per cent of Chinese characters could be pronounced directly from their phonetic radicals (Leong, 1991; Zhou, 1978). For the first time, Zhou (1978) calculated the efficiency of the phonological indication of the Chinese language system (not just individual characters) by looking at the radicals from the corpus of 8,075 Modern Standardized Chinese Characters. The efficiency of phonological indication in this context refers to the percentage of those recovering accurately the phonology of initials (onsets) and finals (rimes). Zhou found that 1,348 phonetic radicals, or 17 per cent of the corpus, provide an accurate pronunciation for the whole of the character. In addition, a large number of "quasi" phonetic radicals could provide near accurate pronunciation, as they have degraded orthography-to-phonology correspondences over the historical and etymological changes. Therefore, 39 per cent of Chinese characters are pronounceable by new learners. This efficiency of recovering phonology from the Chinese writing system is significant and has many implications for teaching Chinese literacy.

The uniqueness of the Chinese writing system

For children to become literate, the complex Chinese language system often requires years of learning, both at home and at school (Chung and McBride-Chang, 2011; Li and Wu, 1996; Li and Rao, 2000). Chinese has been classified by the U.S. government (specifically, the Defense Language Institute and the Foreign Service Institute) as a "Category IV language", a substantially more complicated language compared to the alphabetic languages (e.g. Spanish and French, categorized as Category I; Everson, 1994). Perfetti *et al.* (2013) summarize two unique features of Chinese writing system which contrast with English: one at the script level, which concerns the visual form of writing; and the other at the mapping principle level.

At the script level, they believe that Chinese departs from the linear layout of most alphabetic writing in having a rectangular layout for its graphic components. Chinese radicals are normally arranged in three ways: side by side, top to bottom, or inside–outside. Even more complex characters can be formed by vertically or horizontally inserting a radical between another two. This Chinese-alphabetic contrast in visual appearance makes Chinese reading very different from English in terms of eye movement and cognitive processing. Perfetti *et al.* (2013) believe that Chinese character reading includes configural visual processing analogous to the configural information used in recognizing faces (Young *et al.* 1987). This configural information, which defines spatial relations (e.g. up-down and right-left) between radicals, contrasts with the denser visual information carried by stroke sequences within a radical. The stroke sequences contain high spatial frequency information, whereas the configural relations among the components contain low spatial frequency information. All writing systems contain a range of spatial frequencies, but Chinese uses configural (low spatial frequencies) information to differentiate its written morphemes. Because of this, visual processes tuned to low spatial frequencies could be especially useful in reading Chinese in a way that they are not for reading alphabetic languages (Perfetti *et al.* 2013).

At the orthographic level, Chinese has very different principle by which the graphic units are mapped onto linguistic units. Differently to alphabetic writing, Chinese writing does not reflect the segmental structure of speech (Leong, 1997; Mattingly, 1987). Perfetti *et al.* tend to believe that a Chinese character contains no representation of phoneme segments, but instead maps to a whole morpheme syllable. But the many compound characters can contain cues to both pronunciation (phonetic radicals) and meaning (semantic radicals). The locations of the phonetic (usually on the right side in left-right configurations) and semantic radicals (usually on the left) are predictable enough to be useful. Chinese children who are learning to read gain implicit knowledge about the function and location of phonetic radicals (Shu *et al.* 2000), and information about these components can help in character identification. However, the phonetic radicals often provide no more than the onset or the rime of the correct syllable, and provide the whole spoken syllable (not counting tone) for less than 50 per cent of compound characters (DeFrancis, 1989; Zhou, 1978). Thus, Chinese is a system of coarse-grain units that provide syllable-level, rather than phoneme-level, mapping (Perfetti *et al.* 2013), with some reliability of the cues for pronunciation.

Chinese literacy

Literacy is a highly valued and uniquely human phenomenon that differentiates humans from animals. But it is almost impossible to achieve a perfect definition of literacy, which encompasses all of its meanings, as the concept itself has been constantly changing and evolving (Li, 2000). The Literacy Dictionary (Harris and Hodges, 1995), for instance, lists at least 38 types of literacy. It is important to define what literacy means and this section endeavors to do this by reviewing literacy studies and seeking a Chinese equivalent for the term.

Literacy as defined in dictionaries

There are two main definitions of literacy, each of which having its own ideological basis. The first definition of literacy is the most conventional and common-sense view of the phenomenon. This definition embraces literacy as a set of skills, consisting almost exclusively of the abilities to read and write in a "basic", mechanical fashion. In contemporary dictionaries, literacy is typically defined as the ability to read and write in a designated language, as well as being the way of thinking about the use of reading and writing in everyday life; "educated" has a subsidiary meaning. In the *Collins Cobuild English Language Dictionary* (Sinclair, 1995, 975), for example, literacy is simply defined as "the ability to read and write".

The second definition of literacy is more recent and represents a challenge to the orthodoxies of the first definition. The new formulation stresses the sorts of social practices in which reading, writing and talking are embedded, and out of which they develop, rather than the private, cognitive *skills* of individuals. Over the two decades or so, a new body of literature delineating a sociocultural approach to literacy has emerged, combining work in linguistics, social psychology, anthropology and education, and accordingly, literacy is conceived as a plural set of social practices as well as a cultural tool (Carter, 1995).

Advocates of the second main definition of literacy, i.e. literacy as a set of socially variable practices within which particular skills are valued (and the rest devalued), argue that schools and teachers should try to give greater recognition to the fact that literacy is socially and culturally embedded. A more pluralistic view of literacy as the capacity to participate in certain events and to perform context-specific tasks is also manifested in such terms as "computer-literacy" and "media-literacy". The term *literacy* is currently extended in another way to mean being competent and knowledgeable in a specialized area, as is the case with IT (information technology) economic literacy, political literacy, and so on.

Literacy as defined in research

The focus of this section is on what literacy studies have said about the definitions of literacy, and how they come to form a definition of literacy for this study. Literacy has become a code word across a range of disciplines for new views of reading and writing. There has been such a growth of studies in this field that we can justifiably refer to this area of research as literacy studies. The history of the term and the field could be seen in the way that titles of key reference books have staked claims to literacy studies. Prior to 1980, few book titles contained the word *literacy*. Even in the early 1980s, there were only one or two books in this field each year. The number nevertheless increased over the decade, and, in 1991 alone, fifteen books were published with their titles beginning with the word "Literacy". One of the first key books in the field was *Language and Literacy: The Sociolinguistics of Reading and Writing* (Stubbs, 1980). The title itself has clearly defined the term "literacy". In 1981, *The Psychology of Literacy* by Scribner and Cole, which at the time seemed a challenging title, claimed much more about the nature of literacy than books titled *The Psychology of Reading*. These books follow different research traditions while sharing a great deal in common. More specifically, all of these academic studies examined particular communities in detail, investigating the different groups in a community and how they used literacy. They compared and identified the differences between groups in a community without making any grand generalizations; rather, they contributed to the specific settings they studied and provided insights for the people who look into other specific situations. Equally importantly, they raised general questions about what literacy means. Part of what followed from these studies was the recognition that literacy is a complex concept.

Such recognition led to new definitions of literacy. Briefly, Scribner and Cole (1981) worked within the traditions of cross-cultural psychology and conducted a study of the Vai people of Liberia, people who have invented a syllabic writing system to represent their own language (Barton, 1994). They provided detailed descriptions of the different forms of literacy, including those that were learned informally and which existed outside the educational system. Through observation of the unschooled but literate adults of the Vai of Liberia, Scribner and Cole (1981) separated the effects of becoming literate from the effects of attending school.

Heath (1983) and Street (1984) had a different starting point; they began with more descriptive social and anthropological methodologies. Street (1984; 1995) studied Islamic villagers in Iran, where he lived as an anthropologist and carried out ethnographic fieldwork. He described how the meaning of literacy depends on the social institutions in which it is embedded . . . [and] the particular practices of reading and writing that are taught in any context depend upon such aspects of social structure as stratification . . . and the role of educational institutions.

(Street, 1984, 8)

Like Scribner and Cole (1981), he defined literacy in terms of practice.

A third study is Heath's work (1983) in the southeastern United States. She used ethnographic and sociolinguistic methods to study people's literacy in three Appalachian communities. When defining literacy, Heath comments, "the concept of literacy covers a multiplicity of meanings, and definitions of literacy carry implicit, but generally unrecognized, views of its functions (what literacy can do for individuals) and its uses (what individuals can do with literacy skills)" (Heath, 1983, 123).

This contrast between what literacy does for people and what people do with literacy has been highlighted by many researchers. Heath's (1983) work has been important in getting others to focus on literacy events, the actual instances of people using reading and writing in their day-to-day lives. Since then, the field of study has proliferated with books and articles almost too numerous to keep up with. However, illustrating the history of literacy studies, a general collection of papers was published in 1985 (Olson *et al.* 1985) and a reader not long after (Kintgen *et al.* 1988).

Literacy defined in Chinese

The term *literacy* does not easily translate into Chinese, and in fact, there is no literal Chinese equivalent of the English sense of the word. In China, officially, literacy is translated into the Chinese word "扫盲" [shao3 mang2][1] whose literal translation is "eradicating illiteracy". Disagreeing with this translation, Stites (personal communication, October 16, 1999) created a new term "识文" [shi2 wen2] meaning "learn to read" as a translation of the English word, but his translation has not been recognized or accepted by any Chinese dictionary. From an ethnographic perspective, Postiglione (personal communication, October 16, 1999) translated literacy into "学文化" [xue2 wen2 hua4] meaning "learning to be culturalized". Which one is better? There is no clear answer. However, in this study, we defined this term in a conventional perspective and used "识字" [shi2 zhi4] as its Chinese equivalent, which means "being able to read and write" or "learning to read and write".

A survey study conducted in the U.S. (Ke *et al.* 2001) found that the most difficult challenge of learning Chinese literacy at all levels was to learn the Chinese characters. Another study of British college students showed similar results (Hu, 2010). Taken together, all the results indicated that learning Chinese characters (memorization and recognition) was the major challenge for beginner learners. This is in line with the U.S. government's decision to label Chinese as a

Category IV language, which means that it would take three times longer for an American learner to reach a proficiency equivalent to that needed for learning a cognate language such as French (Everson and Xiao, 2009).

Why is Chinese so difficult to learn? This should be attributed to the unique features of the Chinese language discussed earlier in this chapter; the Chinese language differs linguistically and culturally from the languages adopted from the Roman alphabet writing system in many ways. Such uniqueness presents a special challenge for learners whose first language uses an alphabetic system (Everson, 2011).

Modeling Chinese literacy

There are many ways and approaches to modeling Chinese reading. Many of these are cognitive activities, such as form-cognizing, semantic-understanding, phonetic-recalling, and the phonetic-form-semantic connecting of certain Chinese characters (Li, 1998). I prefer using Information Processing Theory (Simon, 1979) to frame the cognitive processing of Chinese reading; namely, a chain of information input, encoding, storage, and output activities. The following subsections review the existing psycholinguistic studies based on this framework.

The input stage

As the first stage of Chinese cognition, this process has been thoroughly explored by Chinese psycholinguists with various behavioral and neuroimaging methods. The foci of these studies have been the effects of stroke number, stroke type, components, and structure in the recognition of Chinese.

Stroke-number effect

The stroke is the minimum unit of a Chinese character (Fu, 1991). Solitary characters are composed of strokes; compound characters, though consisting of components in different structural types, can also be decoded into strokes. The number of strokes indicates the degree of complexity of a character, and is thus regarded as an important factor hindering or facilitating the graphic decoding of Chinese characters. It was widely believed that the more strokes there are, the more difficult it is to read Chinese (Yu and Cao, 1992). This stroke-number effect was found in early studies of Chinese reading (Cao and Shen, 1963; Ye and Liu, 1982). However, some studies lent empirical support to the theory that such an effect does not exist (Zhang and Feng, 1992), as Chinese character reading is processed by units of strokes and components, rather than individual strokes (Shen, 1988). Nevertheless, in support of the stroke-number effect, Yu and Cao (1992) classified the retrieving stage into two parallel processing mechanisms: i) the primary and holistic perception of a character, which is the processing unit in reading and represents an entire visual schema; and ii) the secondary and detailed processing of strokes and their connections. The two parallel processing mechanisms compete for the limited attention – the more strokes, the more attention the second processing mechanism will occupy, and in turn, the primary mechanism will need to take a longer response time (RT) to process the character; the fewer the strokes, the less attention the second processing mechanism will take, and the RT of the holistic processing mechanism will be shortened because there is more attention capacity available. To date, it is widely believed that the stroke-number effect in Chinese reading is significant (Peng and Wang, 1997).

Stroke-type effect

For thousands of years, there were eight types of strokes in the Chinese writing system; namely, the horizontal, vertical, left-falling, right-falling, dot, stroke, hook stroke, and turning stokes. This is called "永字八法" (*Yong3 Zi4 Ba1 Fa3*). However, the Committee for Reforming the Chinese Characters (1965) simplified them into five types; namely, the horizontal, vertical, left-falling, dot and turning strokes. Both the horizontal and the vertical strokes are straight lines, whereas the left-falling, dot, and turning stroke are curved lines. In this way, a Chinese character can be classified into either a straight or a curve line according to the classification of its strokes. It was found that straight lines are easier to process than curved lines, and that characters with straight lines are easier to recognize than those with curved lines (Lasaga and Garner, 1983; Yu *et al.* 1985; Yu *et al.* 1997). This is called the stroke-type effect.

Structure and radical number effect

Peng (1982) analyzed the structure of 3000 Chinese characters collected from primary school Chinese textbooks. Each character was divided into four quadrants, i.e. upper-left, upper-right, bottom-left, and bottom-right. The result showed that the bottom-right patterns are simpler than those of the upper-left in terms of the number of junctions. A further study (Peng and Zhang, 1984) found that there are some common patterns in recognizing Chinese characters with different structures, for both adults and children. Specifically, the characters with symmetrical structures are easier and the characters with half-encircled structures are more difficult to recognize. Adults and children share the same strategies in recognizing Chinese characters: the bottom-right quarter is extracted frequently for the characters separated vertically and the upper-left quarter is extracted for half-encircled characters.

Further, it was found that the radicals of Chinese characters also affect reading effectiveness in two ways: i) the radical frequency – some studies (Han, 1994; Taft and Zhu, 1996) found that the high-frequency radicals are easier to process than the low-frequency ones; and ii) the radical number – the more radicals, the longer the RT, at least in processing low-frequency characters (Peng and Wang, 1997).

Two working principles

Two working principles regulate this information input stage. The first is the *global prior to part principle*, which means that the very first step of processing a single character is to recognize its global contour, followed by analyzing its components and their interrelations (Cao and Shen, 1963). Luo *et al.* (1987) found that, in normal circumstances, the response to a global pattern is significantly faster than that to the part elements and believed that the visual information extraction starts with the global processing. But this does not mean that the part-directed processing could not start before the end of the global-directed processing – they can be parallel. This is consistent with the results of Navon's experiments (1977; 1981) which used alphabetic characters as the materials of the study.

The second principle is called the *contour prior to content principle*, which means the contour of a Chinese character is much easier to recognize than its content details. Yang (1987) reported that the first impression of a Chinese character is its square edges and their characteristics – in effect the cognitive processing of the Chinese character starts with the contours rather than the content details. This is not a unique feature of Chinese word processing, but one of the general principles of visual information processing in human beings, as suggested by the theory of Contour Density (Karmel, 1969, 1975; Pang and Li, 1994). The theory suggests that visual cognition is a function of the contour density of visual stimuli, and this has been supported by many empirical studies (Haith, 1990; Hubel and Wiesel, 1959, 1962).

The encoding stage

Encoding is the second stage of Chinese cognitive processing. In the alphabetic writing system, the visual information of a word/character can be decoded into phonic codes through phonetic encoding. But Chinese is such a unique writing system that it calls for a multiple-tasked encoding stage. Many hypotheses have been suggested in understanding this stage.

The graphematic-processing hypothesis

In the 1970s, scholars widely believed that a Chinese character has visual features which were strong enough to be recoded as a holistic picture, so that direct semantic retrieval and grapheme-phoneme transformation were not needed (Sasanuma *et al.* 1977; Sugishita *et al.* 1978). Some even believed that the Japanese merely use the visual figures to recognize Chinese characters without engaging in any phonetic processing activities. This is the graphemic-processing hypothesis. However, Tzeng *et al.* (1978) found that phonological processing was also very important in the lexical retrieval of Chinese characters. Today, Chinese psycholinguists tend to believe that phonological processing is also crucial in Chinese reading, in addition to graphematic processing.

The phonological-processing hypothesis

Tzeng and his team (1977; 1978; 1979) have conducted a series of experiments to examine the need for phonological processing in Chinese character encoding. Their hypothesis was that phonological processing is universal across all languages, and is an inevitable and automatic process. Zhang *et al.* (1993) found an automatic phonetic-activation mechanism in Chinese processing, which lent empirical support to this phonological-processing hypothesis. Zhang and Shu (1989) found a priming effect between the primes and targets which were both phonetically and graphically similar. A large priming effect was also found for the characters which were phonetically similar. It suggests that there are phonological connections in the Chinese reader's lexicon. Xu *et al.* (1999) examined the role of phonology in silent Chinese compound-character reading. Interference in reading was found for phonologically similar characters (homophones) and orthographically similar characters. Recently, McBride-Chang and her colleagues have conducted a series of studies of Chinese preschoolers (Chow, McBride-Chang and Burgess, 2005; McBride-Chang *et al.* 2004; McBride-Chang and Ho, 2000; McBride-Chang and Kail, 2002) and found that phonological awareness at the syllable level (rather than phoneme onset awareness) was particularly relevant in early Chinese reading.

The multiple-processing hypothesis

Peng *et al.* (1985; 1986) found that the phonological processing might not be needed in encoding the meaning of Chinese characters. In addition to the graphic-phonetic-semantic processing of Chinese characters, the graphic-semantic processing is also needed. Wang (1990), Tan and Peng (1991), and Tan *et al.* (2000) have confirmed this dual-processing hypothesis. Now it is widely believed that encoding Chinese characters is a multiple-channel process, involving many activities such as graphic, phonetic, semantic, and orthographic encoding. Recently, Li *et al.* (2012) found that both phonological processing and morphological awareness significantly correlated with character recognition in kindergarten children, and visual skills were not uniquely associated with Chinese character reading in primary students. However, they found that orthographic skills were strongly associated with reading performance in primary but not kindergarten students. This finding suggests that orthographic skills are more important for literacy development as reading experience increases. And this study implies that Chinese encoding develops over time and various processing activities are involved at different stages and to different degrees.

Zhou and Marslen-Wilson (1999) investigated the nature of sublexical processing in reading complex (or compound) Chinese characters in three primed naming experiments. In the first two experiments, they observed the facilitative priming effects for the target characters which were semantically associated with the phonetic radicals embedded in complex characters, but not with the complex characters themselves. In the third experiment, the presence of semantic primes which were related to the phonetic radicals embedded in the complex targets, but not to the targets themselves, was found to increase the naming latencies of the targets. They argued that sublexical processing in reading Chinese is both phonological and semantic. There are no fundamental differences between the sublexical processing of phonetic radicals and the lexical processing of simple and complex characters.

Bai *et al.* (2008) examined native Chinese speakers' eye movements as they read text which either did or did not contain word boundary information. Results indicated that sentences containing "unfamiliar word spaced format" were easier to read, as were "visually familiar unspaced texts." However, participants took longer to read sentences with non-word spacing and sentences containing spaces between every character. The findings suggest that words (as opposed to individual characters) are the key unit in Chinese reading. Wu and Anderson (2007) examined the character identification strategies of Chinese second grade children who were orally reading continuous text. Results indicated that participants used information within the characters as well as contextual information to decode and identify unfamiliar characters. In subsequent interviews, participants also demonstrated high levels of metalinguistic awareness.

The storage stage

Every Chinese character has a certain shape and different degrees of complexity in terms of its strokes. This will affect learners' short-term memory (STM) and implicit memory retention, which has been frequently explored recently.

Conventional information processing theory suggests that STM has a limited capacity for a fixed number of chunks. Yu *et al.* (1985) and Zhang *et al.* (1986) researched three kinds of Chinese materials: one-character words, two-character words and four-character phrases. They found that the STM capacity span decreased slightly with an increase in chunk complexity, that the degree of familiarity of the stimulus materials played only a moderate role in STM capacity, and that the visual STM span is larger than the auditory span. In other words, STM through vision is better than that through auditory input. Yu (1989) examined the effects of Chinese language units of different sizes on STM and long-term memory (LTM) with single-character, two-character words, and four-character idioms as the experimental materials. The study found that the size effect of units existed mainly in STM whereby its capacity would decrease when the units were extended. This size effect, however, did not exist in LTM. Instead, it is the semantic features, such as the closeness of semantic features and definitions, which strongly influence LTM.

Zhang and Yang (1987) found that the STM capacity for characters with fewer strokes (under 4) is larger than for those with multiple strokes (more than 13). This supported the idea that the capacity of STM that is affected by the complexity of the strokes. Later, Zhang and Feng (1990) investigated the impact of three variables of Chinese disyllabic words (word frequency, complexity of strokes, and spoken duration) on the capacity of STM in a serial recall task. They discovered that word frequency and the complexity of the strokes impacted on the capacity of STM, and there was a substantial negative correlation between recognition time and the capacity of STM. Yu (1986) explored the relative efficiency of semantic and phonetic encoding in verbal memory, and found that semantic encoding was better than phonetic encoding in both STM and LTM. Both semantic and phonetic information can be stored in either STM or LTM.

As mentioned above, we do know more about the relationship between literacy development and cognitive development. For instance, a greater morphological awareness (Chow *et al.* 2008) and phonological awareness (Chow *et al.* 2008; Chow *et al.* 2005; Chung and McBride-Chang, 2011; Leong *et al.* 2005) appear to be associated with later reading skills in children. In particular, an awareness of syllables was a good predictor of children's subsequent character recognition (Pan *et al.* 2011; Tong *et al.* 2011), as were rapid automized naming (Chow *et al.* 2005; Pan *et al.* 2011) and homophone awareness (Tong *et al.* 2011). Other researchers have found syntax knowledge to be more important in contributing to children's reading proficiency (Chen, Lau, and Yung, 1993), particularly for younger children (Chen and Wong, 1991). Verbal memory has also been found to be important for children's reading comprehension (Chow *et al.* 2005; McBride-Chang and Chang, 1995).

Acquiring Chinese literacy

Chinese literacy is typically defined in terms of the number of characters known and nowadays the benchmark to be considered literate is 3,000–3,500 characters (Butcher, 1995; Taylor, 1999). The task of mastering such a large number of characters is made more difficult by other features of the written language. These include the large number of strokes needed to keep characters distinguishable, the many separate characters for infrequent items where homographs would cause confusion, the enormous number of homophones, and above all, the poor correspondence between sounds and symbols (Butcher, 1995). There is more involved in acquiring Chinese literacy than psychologically and mechanically mastering reading and writing skills. There are many theories about literacy acquisition and development which set the stage for our understanding in this regard.

Theories of literacy acquisition

Stages of literacy acquisition

The first documented theory of literacy acquisition can be traced back to Gray (1925) who, for the first time, proposed five stages of literacy acquisition: (1) readiness; (2) learning to read; (3) rapid progress in fundamental attitudes, habits, and skills; (4) extension of experience and increase in efficiency; and (5) refinement of attitudes, habits, and tastes. In a similar way, Gates (1947) outlined eight stages as follows: (1) pre-reading; (2) reading readiness; (3) beginning reading; (4) initial independence; (5) advanced primary; (6) transition from primary to intermediate; (7) intermediate; and (8) mature reading. Later, Russell (1961) refined Gates' work and proposed six stages of literacy acquisition: (1) pre-reading; (2) beginning reading; (3) initial stage of independent reading; (4) transition; (5) intermediate or low maturity; and (6) advanced. More recently, Chall (1996) simplified the conceptualization of literacy development into two stages: (1) learning to read; and (2) reading to learn. But Goodman (1986) viewed literacy development from a whole-language perspective, and thus described reading as a psycholinguistic "guessing game" in which the child attempts to reconstruct the text, in the light of his or her own knowledge.

Holdaway (1984) describes four processes that enable children to acquire reading and writing abilities, namely: (1) *observation* of literacy behaviors; (2) *collaboration* with an individual who interacts with the child, providing encouragement, motivation, and help when necessary; (3) *practice*, which gives children opportunities to evaluate their performance, make corrections, and enhance their skills; and (4) *performance*, where the child shares what has been learned and seeks approval from adults who are supportive, interested, and encouraging. It is clear that the process of learning to read is a lengthy one that begins very early in life, and the capacity to learn reading and writing is associated with children's age-related developmental timetables. However, there is no clear agreement on the chronological or mental age, nor is there any consensus on a particular developmental stage that children must reach before they are "ready" to learn reading and writing.

Home literacy

Research in English-speaking countries has stressed the importance of the sociocultural context in which language is defined, learned, and used for literacy development (Morrow, 1997). Parents are considered children's first and most important literacy teachers (Taylor, 1983; Teale, 1986). Parents arrange time and provide resources that socialize children into the practices of literacy. They develop expectations about the literacy development of children, just as they do in other child-rearing tasks (McNaughton, 1995). Although the teaching of literacy is sometimes thought to be the responsibility of the school, parental involvement is also critical to Chinese literacy acquisition (Li and Rao, 2000). This will be addressed in more detail in later chapters.

Preschool Literacy

Children spend considerable amounts of time away from family in kindergartens or childcare centers in preschool years. Preschool literacy is thus affected by many factors, such as the classroom literacy environment, teachers' perceptions and beliefs, teachers' involvement, and preschool literacy facilitation.

Research has consistently found that:

1 reading aloud to children is the most important activity essential for reading success (Bus *et al.* 1995; Morrow, 1988; Wells, 1985);
2 making children feel emotionally secure and helping them to participate actively in reading are typically associated with high-quality book reading (Whitehurst *et al.* 1994);
3 asking predictive and analytic questions in small-group settings produces positive effects on children's reading achievement (Dickinson and Smith, 1994; Karweit and Wasik, 1996).

Furthermore, a preponderance of evidence suggests that meaningful instruction in letter–sound correspondence facilitates the acquisition of reading (Chall, 1983; Perfetti, 1985). Current theorists emphasize the importance of many types of instruction, both formal and informal, that involve young children in literacy activities (Adams, 1990; Dyson, 1988).

Development of Chinese literacy skills

Awareness of Chinese orthography

Wu and Huang (1994) studied the "concepts and functions of literacy", the first stage of Mason's (1980) model, on children from 4 to 7 years, and found that awareness of functional Chinese literacy emerged from the age of 4, an awareness that would keep developing until school age, but the degree of the awareness was not as strong as that in English-speaking children. They indicated that preschoolers should be supplied with more opportunities to acknowledge and understand the function of Chinese characters, which is more important than just teaching them to read and write. Assessing Taiwanese children aged from 3 to 8 years with pseudo-characters, non-characters, and true characters, Wu (1994) further explored print awareness, knowledge of Chinese characters, understanding of reading rules, and the relationships among the three factors. She raised three key findings. First, she found that children from ages 3 to 6 did not have a clear understanding of the function of Chinese characters. Second, 4-year-old children were familiar with the basic reading regulations, but they could not describe the function of Chinese punctuation until the age of 6. And, third, grapheme identification of Chinese characters emerged in 4-year-old children, and there were positive associations among the three factors.

In addition, Chinese characters have internal structures that are relatively predictable, as about 82 per cent of them are compound characters that can be segmented into radicals based on orthographic rules. There are about 190 semantic radicals that carry information about meaning, and 1,100 phonetic radicals that provide information about pronunciation. Many compound characters are combinations of semantic and phonetic radicals (Fu, 1989). The position of some semantic or phonetic radicals is very consistent within a group of characters, whereas the position of other radicals might not be. It is very easy to find this pattern: the semantic radicals always appear on the left side of characters, whereas the phonetic radicals appear only on the right. The complex rules of positional and functional regularities are seldom taught in schools or addressed in textbooks explicitly, but they are very helpful to beginner learners. Some studies found that children's understanding of the conventions used in the Chinese writing system was important in learning to read Chinese characters (e.g. Huang and Hanley, 1995; Li *et al.* 2000). Orthographic awareness has been reported to be essential for Chinese character reading and writing acquisition (Li *et al.* 2006; Peng and Li, 1995; Shu and Anderson, 1998), and a determinant of language impairment (e.g. Ho *et al.* 2004). Nevertheless, it normally takes Chinese children considerable effort and several years of education to acquire comprehensive orthographic knowledge (Cheng and Huang, 1995; Ho *et al.* 2004).

Visual skills

Visual skills are very important in learning to read Chinese, as the language has a large number of visually distinct and complicated Chinese characters and lacks grapheme-phoneme correspondence (GPC) rules (Ho and Bryant, 1999). The effective use of the morphological and morphographic constituents for Chinese character recognition, in terms of the phonetic and semantic radicals and their component strokes, has recently become the focus of research (e.g. Chen *et al.* 1996; Sue and Liu, 1996). Working within the framework of selective visual attention, Chen *et al.* reported that skilled native Chinese readers show a bias toward the phonetic radicals in phonological tasks and a bias toward the semantic radicals in semantic judgment tasks. This suggested that radicals (stroke patterns), rather than stroke numbers, are the important higher order orthographic units for the recognition of Chinese characters. A caveat of the Chen *et al.* study, as readily acknowledged by them, is that their use of the blocking (by item type) experimental design have somewhat weakened their argument for the importance of radicals as functional orthographic units over strokes.

Since radicals (stroke patterns) are made up of a different number of strokes within the geometric forms in the same fixed space region, Chinese character reading is achieved through a two-dimensional path (Huang and Wang, 1992). Huang and Wang suggested that characters are perceived and read through a process of decomposition of the components and their recombination. The order and number of strokes and their intersection all serve a cueing function in activating the constituent parts. They believed that the depth of processing in memory access, and the number and order of strokes, are the main factors influencing the complexity and processing of characters. Further, Shu and Anderson (1997) found that Chinese children are aware of the relationship between phonetic and semantic radicals and that the better readers are those with greater radical awareness. It is nevertheless unclear if the semantic and phonetic radicals of their stimuli were systematically manipulated in the different legal orthographic positions.

Chinese characters have strokes, radicals, and configurations that provide much more visual information than English words (Chen and Kao, 2002). The space of a character is constant, and each character is a salient perceptual unit that differs from others in terms of strokes, radicals, and spatial configuration. As a result, it is reasonable to assume that visual skills (the ability to process two-dimensional visual representations such as shapes, lines, and dots) play an important role in early Chinese reading development. For example, Li *et al.* (2012) classified visual skills in visual discrimination and visual memory ability, which are both culture-free skills and different from orthographic skills. Beginning readers are very impressed by the enriched visual information embedded in each character (Li *et al.* 2012). Some studies have found that visual skills are essential for early learning of Chinese because of its complexity (McBride-Chang, Chow *et al.* 2005). For example, Huang and Hanley (1995) found that visual skills predicted Chinese reading ability among Hong Kong and Taiwanese children, and Ho and Bryant (1999) found evidence for visual skills being associated with Chinese character reading in Hong Kong. Visual perceptual and visual memory skills also distinguished a subset of children with and without developmental dyslexia in Chinese (Ho *et al.* 2004). All these findings jointly suggest that these skills may be important for certain aspects of Chinese reading acquisition.

Zang *et al.* (2013) investigated eye movement behavior in children and adults when reading spaced and unspaced Chinese words. Results indicated that inter-word spacing reduced the amount of time it took to read and also facilitated word identification for both children and adults. The kinds of fixations that occurred differed between children and adults, suggesting that although children's eye movements bear much similarity with those of adults, there are still differences between the two groups.

Phonological awareness

The pioneer studies by Tzeng and his colleagues (1978) indicated that phonetic encoding was involved in processing Chinese. Their findings suggested that the phonemic similarity of characters affected not only short-term retention of unrelated characters, but also the reading of meaningful sentences. More recently, Tan and Perfetti (1998; 1999) have addressed the notion of a "universal" phonological principle, modulated by the depth or shallowness of different writing systems, including Chinese. From convergent experimental studies using forward and backward masking procedures with graphemic and phonemic masks exposed for very brief durations, Tan, Perfetti and their colleagues have sound evidence of phonological involvement "at-lexically" or "lexically" in the recognition of Chinese characters. This notion of the early activation of phonemic information, or at least its strong version, has not gone unchallenged. There is a debate about whether the strong version of "at-lexical" phonological processing of Chinese characters requires independent evidence that a character is not yet recognized when its phonology is activated. Nevertheless, the existing experimental studies suggest that speech sound is implicated in reading Chinese, even though its time course may not be pre-lexical.

What is emerging is the need for a well-developed framework of orthography-to-phonology correspondence (OPC) in Chinese. This aspect is emphasized by Tzeng et al. (1995) in their study using regular, exceptional, and "mixed" (according to the number of "friendly orthographic neighbors") characters with Grade 3 to 6 good and poor Chinese readers in Taiwan. Tzeng et al. found that by about Grade 3, Chinese children were sensitive to the roles of the radicals in reading, and they also utilized much broader orthographic knowledge in pronouncing new Chinese characters.

Several studies, for instance, Huang and Hanley (1995) and Hanley and Huang (1997), provide good examples of how examining the access to the phonological structure of Chinese children has implications for reading. They examined the effect of metalinguistic awareness in spoken words, English and Chinese phoneme deletion tasks and visual skills related to reading in a sample of 137 primary school children aged 8 in Taiwan, Hong Kong and England. One main result of their studies was that when general ability and vocabulary were partialled out, the performance of the Chinese children on the phonological tasks did not significantly relate to their reading level. However, it should be noted that the children in Hong Kong used Cantonese with the traditional Chinese orthography in learning to read, whereas the ones in Taiwan used *Zhuyin Fuhao* (the Taiwan version of pinyin) to derive sound from the characters.

The studies mentioned above are important in showing that early phonological skills are instrumental in learning to read Chinese. But as Ho and Bryant (1999) demonstrated, reading researchers have put too much emphasis on the significance of phonological skills and have neglected the importance of visual and orthographic skills in learning to read. They noted that visual skills, rather than phonological skills, are more important in learning to read Chinese, and the possible links to reading Chinese still need to be further explored.

Many studies have jointly confirmed the strong link between phonological awareness and character recognition in Chinese children (Ho and Bryant, 1997; Hu and Catts, 1998; Huang and Hanley, 1997; McBride-Chang and Ho, 2000; McBride-Chang and Kail, 2002; Shu et al. 2008; Siok and Fletcher, 2001). A recent study explored the nature of phonological awareness in Chinese and found that syllable and rime awareness increased gradually and steadily across preschool years without instruction, whereas phoneme awareness did not (Shu et al. 2008). Different levels of phonological awareness may develop at varying rates and contribute to Chinese reading ability differently with age. Different results across studies may be accounted for by the variations in instruction. In mainland China, for example, the majority of kindergartens do not teach children to read Chinese. Children have to learn pinyin in the first eight weeks of primary school and then pair this script with characters that are linked to orthographic units.

Shu and her colleagues have studied the effects of learning pinyin in early reading development. They (Shu *et al.* 2008) found that the awareness of phonemes increases rapidly when children receive pinyin instruction – children who had experience of pinyin outperformed their counterparts who had not received any instruction in pinyin (Cheung *et al.* 2001). Shu *et al.* (2006) found that phonemic awareness is particularly important in explaining reading impairment among fifth- and sixth-grade Beijing students. All these findings tend to support the current teaching practice in Chinese Primary 1 classes: all the Year 1 students have to learn pinyin in the first month of their first school year.

Chinese literacy acquisition: patterns and sequences

Common sequences

The present study found that a common sequence of Chinese literacy skills development could be identified for children across Beijing, Hong Kong, and Singapore. This is inconsistent with the Western findings (e.g. Hall, 1994; Strickland and Morrow, 1989; Teale and Sulzby, 1986), which indicate that literacy does not emerge in a systematic, sequential manner. This might be related to the great orthographical distinctions, the different definitions and components of literacy between Chinese and Western languages such as English. Moreover, this inconsistent finding might also be related to the fact that the literacy scale we used in this study was different from that used in Western studies. However, further research is warranted to investigate emergent Chinese literacy and examine these hypotheses.

Among the four Chinese literacy abilities tested in this study, grapheme/semantic association (GSA) and visual/auditory discrimination (VAD) were the ones that emerged very early in life and developed rapidly. This is consistent with the findings of Li and Wu's (1996) classroom observation in Beijing kindergartens. They found that some 3-year-olds who had not been taught to read Chinese characters could, in fact, understand some characters. The character "停" [ting2] (stop), for example, was familiar to many children before it was formally taught to them in preschools. Li and Wu explained that the children had many opportunities to read this character in their daily life (such as parking, taking the bus, or playing) and they learned the associations between the grapheme (停) and the meaning (stop) from their repeated experiences. Li and Wu believed that this is the typical phenomenon of emergent Chinese literacy in early childhood. In accordance with this, and consistently, the present study also found that most Beijing preschoolers who had not had any Chinese literacy education did attain significantly higher scores in a GSA test. All these findings indicate that Chinese children substantively acquired Chinese literacy prior to school entry, which is consistent with Western findings (Hall, 1994; Teale and Sulzby, 1986).

Character recognition was found to emerge between ages 4 to 5 and character utilization appeared very late in the preschool years. Stevenson and Lee (1990) found that many Chinese parents attempted to teach their children to read. The most frequent activity was to teach preschoolers some common characters in Chinese and to recognize their own name. They reported that Chinese parents also tried to teach their children to read some words, but fewer of them (less than 30 per cent) sought to teach their child to read sentences (Stevenson and Lee, 1990; Stevenson *et al.* 1999). Ho and Bryant (1997a) reported that Chinese children in Hong Kong normally started learning to read Chinese at the age of 3 – they learned to read single Chinese characters in their first preschool year, and multiple-character words and short phrases in the second and third preschool years.

Hence, as a natural consequence of their literacy instruction, grapheme/ semantic association and visual/auditory discrimination emerged very early in young children. Character recognition emerged at about age 4 to 5, and character utilization appeared later.

Patterns of Chinese literacy development

Three patterns of Chinese literacy development were found in our previous study (Li, 2000):

The Beijing pattern

Beijing children had the slowest rate of Chinese literacy development among the three samples from Beijing, Hong Kong, and Singapore. There was considerable within-subject variability and some children (around 20 per cent) reported no changes in PPCLS scores after a one-year interval. The years from the ages of 2.5 to 3.5 and from the ages of 4.5 to 5.5 were identified as the critical periods for Chinese literacy development. One possible interpretation for the lower developing rate of Beijing preschoolers is that they are formally forbidden from having systematic training in Chinese reading and writing in kindergarten. Yet, the differences between the age groups and the great variation in within-subject changes might be due to the fact that in the majority of Beijing preschools reading (but not writing) Chinese characters has been surreptitiously undertaken in the first (about age 3) and last school years (about age 5), whereas no teaching of reading is conducted in the second preschool year (about age 4). The teaching of reading Chinese characters was widely carried out in the first year in the name of being an "educational experiment" whereas, during the last preschool year, most preschools taught Chinese reading (but not writing) "to prepare children for entering primary schools" (Liang *et al.* 1997). So, some of the children had received direct instruction in Chinese reading before the administration of the PPCLS, whereas others had not. Therefore, it might not be surprising that the age of children was found to be significant in explaining the 18.5 per cent variance of the PPCLS scores in the Beijing sample. In addition to the age of children, other variables such as home and classroom literacy education (whether or not parents utilize a specific approach to teaching literacy), were found to significantly contribute to the prediction of Chinese literacy attainment among Beijing preschoolers.

The Hong Kong pattern

Hong Kong children had the fastest rate of Chinese literacy development during their preschool years. Within-subject changes varied greatly and the average increase in literacy attainment during the one-year interval is significant. It could be due to the fact that Hong Kong children were immediately immersed in reading, reciting, copying, and writing Chinese characters upon entering the nursery class of preschool. Most (73.7 per cent) of the Hong Kong parents taught their child to read Chinese characters at home. They maintained a "high speed" of development in Chinese literacy during the whole preschool stage and their average increase in literacy attainment was tremendous. Notably, the present study also found that 26.3 per cent of the parents did not teach their children to read at home and 48.1 per cent of them did not teach their children to write. This might explain why the within-subject changes in the PPCLS scores varied so greatly.

The Singapore pattern

The Singaporean children fell between those from Hong Kong and Beijing in terms of the rate of their literacy development and their final achievement in Chinese literacy. The within-subject changes varied narrowly, but some (13.5 per cent) of the children had no changes in their PPCLS scores during the one-year interval. The time between ages 3.5 to 5.5 was identified as the critical period of Chinese literacy development. This is due to the fact that English literacy education was normally given the first priority in the majority of Singapore preschools, whereas Chinese literacy education was typically introduced in the second school year. This bilingual education policy in Singapore, widely believed to be successful, has been challenged. More and more Chinese children are becoming "native" English speakers and readers, at the cost of losing the ability to read and write their mother tongue.

Could they learn English and Chinese equally well, at the same time? Or should they learn their mother tongue language at the cost of learning English? Answers to these questions have the potential to inform the language education policy of the government.

Error analysis in Chinese literacy development

Li (2003) found that semantic-processing errors were common among Singaporean preschoolers and that they had notable difficulties in grasping the meaning of

Chinese characters. One possible interpretation for this finding is that Chinese is learned as the second language by Singaporean preschoolers and that they have inadequate opportunities and few resources to practice reading and writing Chinese, a logographic language that has a complicated and difficult orthography.

It is commonly believed that Chinese characters are learned like logograms because the script-sound associations are not systematic enough to help with reading (Baron and Strawson, 1976). Accordingly, it has been argued that Chinese characters, especially simple characters that are pictographic in origin, are directly encodable as abstract or even concrete images that are themselves representations of meanings. This is called the direct-image hypothesis (Liu, 1995). Until the early 1990s, the general consensus regarding the phonological processing in visual grapheme/semantic association has been that phonology plays no role in recognition, or that character meaning is accessed prior to phonology. This view is labeled the identification without-phonology hypothesis (Tan and Perfetti, 1998). This view has conflicted with their previous studies (Perfetti and Zhang, 1991; Tan and Peng, 1991), which proposed an identification-with-phonology hypothesis which assumed that phonological codes provide early sources of constraint in recognizing characters, and phonology may influence meaning activation (Tan and Perfetti, 1999).

The present study, however, addressed itself to the debate between the identification-without-phonology and the identification-with-phonology hypothesis from developmental and sociocontextual approaches. We found significant societal, but no age, differences in the percentage of response errors among the three communities. In each community, all three types of error were found in children's reading, regardless of whether there was a dominant one or which one it was. These findings indicated, at least, that phonological, graphical, and semantic processing occurred during the reading of Chinese characters in preschoolers, and the dominance of different error types simply reflected the different patterns of Chinese reading that may further reflect varying sociolinguistic contexts.

For example, the dominance of phonetic-similarity errors clearly demonstrated that Chinese children in Hong Kong do rely on phonological processing in reading Chinese characters, although graphical and semantic processing are also involved. This pattern of Chinese reading in Hong Kong was supported by other similar findings reported in a longitudinal study, which suggested that phonological awareness skills at the age of 3 could significantly predict the performance of children in Chinese word reading (Ho and Bryant, 1997a). This indicated that phonological training in early preschool years might be helpful to children's acquisition of Chinese literacy.

Our longitudinal studies, and those of others, have come to several conclusions: (1) there was a common sequence of Chinese literacy development among Beijing, Hong Kong, and Singaporean preschoolers. Grapheme/semantic association and visual/auditory discrimination emerged during ages 3 to 4, whereas character recognition and character utilization appeared later; (2) three distinctive patterns of Chinese literacy development were identified among the children in Beijing, Hong Kong and Singapore; (3) phonetic-similarity and semantic-similarity error were identified as the common errors made by Hong Kong and Singaporean children, respectively, whereas non-significant common errors were found in Beijing children; and (4) teachers' qualifications, and the home and classroom literacy index, were found to be significant predictors of the longitudinal development of Chinese literacy, even after controlling for the children's age.

The abovementioned patterns, however, might be shaped by many socio-contextual influences such as language policy, language education, early childhood curriculum, Chinese literacy pedagogy, teacher qualification, classroom size, parental expectation, and so on. The following chapters will further explore the policies, psychologies, pedagogies, and practices of early Chinese literacy in various Chinese contexts.

Note

1 Note that in this section and all others in this book, Pinyin will be used for the Romanization of Chinese words. In addition, for all words that are not proper nouns (people, place names, book titles), the Mandarin tone markings will be indicated at the end of each syllable with a numeral from 1 to 4.

Chapter 2

The neuropsychological understanding of Chinese literacy

On many fronts, Chinese is different from English and other alphabetic languages. The neuropsychological mechanism involved in reading Chinese might thus be considerably different. Reading scientists have been pondering whether reading Chinese shares the same neuropsychological processing involved in reading English, and some (i.e. Perfetti and his team) are looking for a universal processing mechanism across languages. Recently, many scholars have tried to understand Chinese reading and writing behaviors using new technologies, such as ERP, fMRI, eye movement, and MEG. Very promising as well as controversial findings have been reported and many hypotheses have been made. This chapter will review the existing studies to advance our neuropsychological understanding of Chinese reading and writing.

Themes and topics in Chinese reading studies

There are many studies on the neurobiological basis and mechanisms of Chinese reading, but few were conducted on young children (e.g. Chow *et al.* 2005; Pan *et al.* 2011). This is caused by the limitations of new technologies. For instance, fMRI scans the human brain very precisely, and thus requires highly self-regulated participants. The youngest cooperating sample for fMRI could be about 4 to 6 years old as reported by current studies. Although Hong Kong children start to learn reading and writing Chinese from 3 years old, most children in other Chinese communities are supposed to learn reading and writing during primary school years. The existing neuropsychological studies, therefore, were mostly conducted on older children, of primary school age (e.g. Meng *et al.* 2005). In fact, the easiest target would be adults who are literate and highly self-regulated as the measures used to examine brain activity (e.g. fMRI, ERP) can be more challenging, especially when young children are involved. It is thus understandable why most of the neuroimaging studies have focused only on adults (e.g. Shen *et al.* 2012). Generally speaking, the following themes and topics have emerged in this field.

Research themes

Many studies into brain activity during Chinese reading have been conducted in the past decade, with a focus on the brain circuits in normal and impaired Chinese reading. A unique morphemic language, Chinese has many distinct linguistic characteristics that are absent in alphabetic languages (please refer to Chapter 1 for more details). Reading scientists tend to believe that the Chinese writing system demands different cognitive procedures and learning strategies, and the neural circuits involved in processing Chinese might be correspondingly altered, instead of following a universal mechanism across all language systems (Perfetti *et al.* 2006). This conventional belief runs counter to the universal reading mechanism proposed by Perfetti (2007) who later on tended to believe that all the languages might share some common brain networks. Universality versus specificity has been the most important theme in this field.

Another important theme is about learning Chinese as L1 (Yang *et al.* 2012; Meng *et al.* 2005). It should be noted that the majority of the studies did not explicitly distinguish between Mandarin and Cantonese, referring to the language simply as "Chinese". The lack of differentiation is not necessarily a concern, since Mandarin (the official Chinese language) and Cantonese (the Chinese dialect in the Guangdong province and Hong Kong) share many similarities. However, further studies may be needed to investigate the nuances of how Chinese impacts the brain.

The third theme is about learning Chinese as L2. Learning to read Chinese seems very challenging to Westerners who are used to an alphabetic script, as Chinese has such a difficult orthography. Reading scientists generally believe that the brain networks responsible for Chinese reading are universal, but recent neuroimaging studies have suggested that alphabetic writing systems and logographic writing systems might engage different networks in the brain. It will be interesting to investigate whether L2 Chinese learners are using different brain networks to those that are being used by L1 learners.

Research topics

There are many valuable topics in this field of research. Among them, two have emerged as the most important and topical ones.

Is there a universal neurological network for reading across languages?

To explore this question, Dehaene and his colleagues (2007) used fMRI to examine brain activity in Chinese and French participants as they read their native languages. They found that reading in Chinese and French both activated a shape-recognition region in the brain's posterior left hemisphere – the visual word-forming area (VWFA). Although both the VWFA and Exner's area were indeed activated in French and Chinese participants, there were cultural differences. For example, the effects of gestural direction were stronger for the reading of Chinese. The researchers found that both Chinese and French participants used the visual and gestural systems while reading their native language, but with different emphases that reflected the different demands of each language. Given that Chinese is different from alphabetic languages, it makes different demands on reading and the supporting brain networks. It is widely believed that learning to read accommodates the demands of a writing system through the specialization of brain networks that support word identification, and Chinese is no exception. This specialization increases with reading development, leading to differences in the brain networks for alphabetic and Chinese reading.

Tan and his team (2005b) found that readers of Chinese placed great emphasis on the order and direction of the writing strokes, which steered them to use other brain networks involved in the motor skills required for writing. Motor processing was universally used for writing and it involved a region of the brain known as Exner's area. Perfetti *et al.* (2013) suggested that this region could also be activated in reading to interpret the gestures and, therefore, developing the gestural system more in education might help young children improve Chinese reading. So far, however, the motor decoding aspect has been rather neglected in Chinese reading education.

The universal path of development encompasses a wide range of subthemes. One of these subthemes is the increased value of control functions that allow readers to handle the specific demands of varied reading-related tasks, allowing attention to be directed toward orthography, phonology, or semantics. Another subtheme is the establishment of a basic network that connects the posterior areas that handle graphic inputs to linguistic (phonological and meaning) areas, allowing the rapid stabilization of word identity. These connections, despite some variations in their neural anatomy, reflect the universal mapping of writing to language, which is fundamental to all authentic writing systems. Specific features of the writing system must be accommodated and this leads to specialization. With better skills acquired, reading procedures increasingly accommodate to the demands of the writing system so as to function efficiently. As a result, we see some specialization in the reading network. This trend in specialization should be seen in all combinations of language and writing systems, and may be itself a biologically instantiated reading universal.

In sum, more work has to be done to unpack the neuropsychological mechanisms involved in developing Chinese reading. Are there any unique brain activities in the processing of Chinese reading and writing? Is there a unique brain mechanism underlying Chinese reading and writing? How do young children acquire Chinese reading and writing while developing their brains in the early years? Does reading and writing Chinese shape the form and function of young children's brains? There are more questions than answers. Very recently, Perfetti *et al.* (2013) suggested that there are partly universal and partly writing-system specific reading procedures. Nevertheless, this does not mean that Chinese reading shares the same brain networks with those required for English reading.

What is the role of the LMFG in Chinese reading?

Interestingly, recent studies of Chinese reading have consistently revealed a significant role for the left middle frontal gyrus, which seems to be the most important brain area for reading logographic Chinese. Siok *et al.* (2004) compared brain activities between Chinese dyslexic and normal readers and found that Chinese dyslexics had functional disruption in the LMFG at brain area (BA) 9 and BA46. But English dyslexics' biological deficit was often found in the left temporoparietal and occipitotemporal regions (e.g. Hoeft *et al.* 2006; Paulesu *et al.* 2001). In addition, they also found that the parietal regions (mainly the intraparietal sulcus and BAs 7 and 40) played a much larger part in Chinese reading than in English reading, and the dysfunction in these regions became the marker of Chinese dyslexia. These findings indicated that the reading of Chinese and of English might engage very different brain networks.

In particular, there seems to be an orchestration between the prefrontal and parietal networks during Chinese reading. Stronger activities in both the middle frontal cortex and superior parietal cortex were involved, even in a simple task like Chinese word naming (Kuo *et al.* 2001). In a study investigating the neural system of Chinese reading via semantic decision and homophone decision tasks, activations in the LMFG and the right prefrontal (BAs 46/45) and parietal (BAs 7 and 40/39) areas were also found (Tan *et al.* 2001b). The stronger right lateralization in the prefrontal and parietal regions for reading Chinese might be related to the squarish shape of Chinese characters that required a more elaborated analysis of spatial information. The co-activation of the LMFG and the left-lateralized parietal regions in tasks demanding phonological and semantic processing was also found by Booth and colleagues (2006). Siok and her colleagues (2008; 2009b) repeatedly found that Chinese dyslexics showed weaker activations in the LMFG than normal readers. And the Chinese dyslexics exhibited weaker activations in the left intraparietal sulcus during a physical size judgment task. Moreover, higher activations were observed in the left middle and inferior frontal gyrus, as well as in the left parietal region (including the inferior parietal gyrus and supramarginal gyrus), in the course of Chinese character reading, especially when reading low consistency characters (Lee *et al.* 2010). Tan and Siok and their colleagues tended to believe that the LMFG, especially BA 9, plays a very important role in reading Chinese.

A recent meta-analysis reviewed the past fMRI studies of Chinese character processing in three main categories; namely, phonology, orthography, and semantics (Wu *et al.* 2012). They found a common neural mechanism comprising the LMFG, the left superior parietal lobule, and the left mid-fusiform gyrus, which might be crucial in Chinese orthography-to-phonology transformation. All these studies jointly indicated that activities in the prefrontal and parietal regions could be interconnected when performing normal and fluent Chinese reading. And the LMFG and the parietal regions are likely to be engaged in orthography-to-semantics mapping, orthography-to-phonology transformation, addressed phonology, and possibly in the working memory, all of which appear to be involved in reading Chinese. In particular, the working memory and executive functions encompassed by the LMFG are presumed to be useful and very crucial in reading Chinese characters (e.g. Siok *et al.* 2004, 2008). The following sections will further discuss these state-of-the-art topics in Chinese literacy research.

Neuropsychological understanding of Chinese reading

Psychologists, especially psycholinguists, have been exploring the neuropsychological underpinnings of reading Chinese since Tzeng, Hung, and Wang (1977) took the lead in investigating the importance of phonological awareness in reading Chinese. Over the past three decades, enormous efforts have been devoted to understanding the roles of visual, phonological, semantic, and morphological skills in reading Chinese. This section will systematically review the existing literature.

The roles of visual, phonological, semantic, and morphological skills

The Chinese writing system has some unique and interesting visual, phonological, semantic, and morphological features. In the past decades, psycholinguists have conducted many studies seeking to understand the roles of visual, phonological, semantic, and morphological skills in reading Chinese. This subsection will review these studies with a focus on the roles of phonological awareness, visual-orthographic processing skills, and other skills.

The importance of phonological awareness

Tzeng *et al.* (1977) found that participants' performance was impacted upon when phonemic similarity was included in the test materials, affecting how they processed the Chinese characters during reading. Perfetti and Zhang (1991) tested native Chinese speakers on a number of character identification tasks and found that character identification was not mediated by phonemic processes, although the identification of a written character immediately activated its pronunciation. They suggested a general orthography-independent principle of reading, which means that printed word forms routinely and automatically arouse phonological representations as part of their identification.

Ho and Ma (1999) studied Chinese dyslexic children's ability to use phonological strategies, with a focus on whether phonological strategies could improve their reading performance. They found that a five-day, intensive training in phonological strategies could improve dyslexic children's reading performance significantly.

Siok and Fletcher (2001) investigated Chinese reading acquisition in mainland Chinese primary school children. They specifically examined the role of phonological awareness and visual-orthographic skills. Results indicated that: (a) visual skills predicted reading success at lower grades; (b) pinyin knowledge and the ability to discriminate homophonic characters predicted reading success in Grades 2, 3, and 5; and (c) onset-rime awareness, but not phonemic awareness, predicted Chinese reading. They suggested that Chinese reading in primary school years moves from a logographic phase to an orthographic-phonological phase and that the relationship between phonological awareness and reading success depends on the nature of the writing system. Gottardo et al. (2001) tested English-Cantonese bilingual children (English = L2) on their phonological, syntactic, and orthographic processing skills and reading ability. They found that phonological skill in both English and Cantonese correlated with English reading, indicating that there may be cross-language transfer of phonological processing in L2 learning. Meanwhile, Feng et al. (2001) used an error disruption paradigm to examine how spelling errors impacted on participants' reading of Chinese and English texts. Participants from China and the U.S. read native language texts that had some spelling errors. Evidence of early phonological activation was found for the American participants, but not for the Chinese participants. However, results indicated that phonology could help participants recover from spelling error-related disruption across both languages.

Meng et al. (2005) examined the impact of auditory, speech, and temporal processing on Chinese school children's reading development. Children's auditory processing skills correlated with their reading fluency, phonological awareness, word naming latency, and the number of Chinese characters learned. They also looked at dyslexic children and found that deficits in auditory temporal processing and linguistic processing have an impact on reading development. Meanwhile, Chow et al. (2005) conducted a longitudinal study to examine the relationship between native language (Chinese) phonological processing skills and early Chinese and English reading abilities in Hong Kong preschool aged children. When considering all the potential predictors, only phonological awareness emerged as a significant predictor of Chinese and English reading ability.

Zhang et al. (2013) examined the relationships between socioeconomic status (SES), early phonological processing, vocabulary, and reading in Chinese children. They found SES was associated with children's phonological skills and vocabulary. Conversely, early phonological and vocabulary abilities independently mediated the effects of SES on children's reading achievement by the end of Grade 3.

All of these studies unanimously concluded that phonological awareness and processing skills are very critical for reading Chinese in children as well as in adults.

The importance of visual-orthographic processing skills

The written form of Chinese is markedly different from that of alphabetic languages, as different characters can look broadly, orthographically similar, with minor differences in strokes or radicals. The closer association between the visual symbol of Chinese and its meaning makes orthographic analysis more decisive in the reading. For example, an ERP study of Chinese dyslexic children found a deficit in orthographic processing (Chung et al. 2012). The difference in the radical positions of pseudo-characters (orthographically correct) and those of non-characters (orthographically incorrect) did not have a positive impact on the participants' performance during a character decision task. This implied that failure to process orthographic information might be a marker of Chinese dyslexia.

The importance of other skills

Chen and Wong (1991) examined the reading proficiency of primary school children (third, fourth, and fifth grades) to see if there was any connection between reading and other cognitive skills. They found that *knowledge of syntax* and *lexical coding* were the most effective in predicting the reading proficiency of the third graders, though not so for that of the fourth and fifth graders. Context use was found to be the best predictor for the older participants. Later on, Chen et al. (1993) examined how feature analysis skills, syntax knowledge, and semantic analysis skills contribute to children's reading proficiency. Visual processing skill did not emerge as a good predictor. Phonological access skill was a good predictor for pre-third graders' reading proficiency, but not for the older children. Semantic analysis skill was less relevant to the younger children, but became more important for children in third grade and above. Syntax knowledge remained consistently important across all grade levels.

McBride-Chang and Chang (1995) examined the impact of four components on reading comprehension among 100 Chinese elementary children: visual memory, verbal memory, metacognition about reading, and print exposure. All four components were substantially associated with reading comprehension and could reliably distinguish the good readers from the poor ones. After controlling for the effects of verbal intelligence, verbal and visual memory abilities predicted unique variance in reading comprehension. The distinctiveness of each memory skill underscores the existence of two unique memory processes in Chinese reading.

Zhou and Marslen-Wilson (2000) conducted four experiments and found that, in reading Chinese, semantic information in the lexicon was activated at least as early, and just as strongly, as phonological information was activated. Liu et al. (2002) examined the use of parafoveal character previews in Chinese readers. Preview benefits for targets were found for graphemically similar characters and for homophonic characters. In addition, the parafoveal preview of characters that were graphemically similar led to benefits when the characters also shared a phonetic radical with their comparison targets. Results indicated that Chinese character processing involves orthographic information from the phonetic radicals as well as phonological activation.

Perfetti et al. (2005) proposed the lexical constituency model as a general framework to examine word reading across different writing systems, including the Chinese writing system. The model contains three interrelated constituents –

orthographic, phonological, and semantic. Together, they constitute the "universal reading processes" across languages. Meanwhile, Leong et al. (2005) examined the impact of orthographic knowledge, phonological sensitivity, and word identification on language performance for Chinese elementary school students at a later point in time. Results indicated consistency in word identification and phonological sensitivity, substantial effects of word identification on orthographic knowledge and phonological sensitivity, and larger variations in the growth of orthographic knowledge.

Later, Ren and Yang (2010) used eye-tracking techniques to examine how the inclusion of a comma may impact on the reading of Chinese text. They found that fixation times were shorter when a comma was included, which means inclusion of commas may facilitate word identification. Li et al. (2012) examined whether presenting Chinese characters belonging to a single word simultaneously would lead to more efficient reading, using a variation of the moving window paradigm. Results showed that word knowledge has an impact on how characters are processed.

Tong et al. (2011) conducted a two-year longitudinal study to examine the relationships between various reading-related cognitive tasks, Chinese word reading, and Chinese word dictation in preschoolers in Hong Kong. The study found that homophone awareness, visual skills and syllable awareness were related to Chinese word reading across time. Visual skills and syllable deletion were associated with Chinese word dictation.

Pan et al. (2011) found that syllable awareness and rapid automized naming (RAN) at age 5, and invented spelling of pinyin at age 6, independently predicted later recognition of Chinese characters when the children were older. RAN, but not phonological sensitivity, also predicted reading fluency; phonological awareness predicted Chinese dictation, but not RAN; and, finally, vocabulary knowledge emerged as a predictor of all the Chinese literacy skills tested. On the other hand, Chung and McBride-Chang (2011) found that executive functioning skills were good predictors of Chinese-speaking children's early reading performance. However, at the delayed post-test, they found that morphological and phonological awareness – rather than executive functioning skills – were consistently associated with literacy skills in Chinese children.

Yang et al. (2012) tracked the eye movements of Chinese readers as they read sentences containing a character that was either a single-character word or the first character of a two-character word. The single-character target word was manipulated to be either a plausible or implausible standalone word, while the two-character word was always plausible. Results indicated that although the manipulation had little effect on the processing of the two-character word, it did impact on the reading of the single-character word, suggesting that semantic integration in Chinese reading may be occurring at the word level instead of the character level.

Shen et al. (2012) tracked the eye movements of a sample of non-native Chinese speakers (i.e. American, Korean, Japanese, and Thai) as they read Chinese sentences that either contained un-spaced text, word-spaced text, character-spaced text, or non-word-spaced text. They found that reading word-spaced text was the easiest, with the least amount of disruptions, and that un-spaced text required longer reading time than character-spaced text. Of the different types of texts, non-word-spaced text would lead to the most disruptions. Native language appeared to have little consistent effect on participants' reading.

All these studies reviewed indicated that orthographic knowledge, phonological sensitivity, memory abilities, visual skills, vocabulary knowledge, and word identification are all important in reading Chinese and should not be neglected.

The brain network of Chinese reading

How is Chinese reading processed in the human brain? What kind of brain network is involved in reading Chinese? Are there any differences in the brain network involved in Chinese and English reading? These questions have been challenging reading scientists for decades. In the last century, scholars had to use behavioral approaches to observe Chinese reading to "guess" how it goes through in the human brain, as there were no reliable measures to "observe" brain activity. Since the early 1990s, however, the advancement of neuroimaging techniques, including positron emission tomography (PET), even-related potentials (ERP), and functional magnetic resonance imaging (fMRI), have given researchers greater powers with which to map language onto the intact living human brain. The changes in neuronal activity associated with a cognitive or a motor task are accompanied by focal changes in cerebral blood flow (Fox *et al.* 1986), cerebral blood volume (Fox and Raichle, 1986), and blood oxygenation (Bandettini *et al.* 1992). Therefore, measuring hemodynamic responses underlying neuronal events, such as with fMRI, can help to localize brain activation with high spatial and temporal resolution.

Since 2000, many functional neuroimaging studies have been successfully conducted on the Chinese language and important findings have been obtained to elucidate the brain mechanisms of visual character recognition (Chee *et al.* 2001; Y. Chen *et al.* 2002; Fu *et al.* 2002; Kuo *et al.* 2001; Li *et al.* 2004; Liu and Perfetti, 2003; Tan *et al.* 2000, 2001b, 2003; Xiang *et al.* 2003), Chinese tone and intonation perception (Gandour *et al.* 2000, 2003b; Klein *et al.* 2001), consonant and vowel processing (Gandour *et al.* 2003c; Siok *et al.* 2003), passive Chinese speech production (He *et al.* 2003; Tan *et al.* 2001a), syntactic and semantic analysis of sentences (Luke *et al.* 2002), and bilingualism (Chee *et al.* 1999; Chee *et al.* 2000; Klein *et al.* 2001; Pu *et al.* 2001; Tan *et al.* 2003).

Among all these neuroimaging researchers, Tan and his team have been especially successful in Chinese functional neuroimaging studies. Their main research interest is to use neuroimaging (fMRI and PET) and cognitive techniques to investigate the neuroanatomical and cognitive mechanisms underlying Chinese language processing, learning, memory, and attention. The studies conducted by Tan and his team have shown that the left middle frontal gyrus (BA 9) responsible for verbal working memory critically mediates Chinese character recognition, whereas the left posterior temporoparietal regions critical for English reading are less involved in Chinese reading (Tan *et al.* 2003). They found that Chinese-speaking dyslexics have a different pattern of brain activity than English-speaking dyslexics: the left middle frontal gyrus, rather than the posterior brain regions, is the cause of reading disorders in Chinese. This finding suggests that possibly a person who is dyslexic in Chinese reading would not be dyslexic in alphabetic language reading, and vice versa. And the implication is that different interventions may be more or less suitable depending on the language involved. They also found that the neural systems for Chinese and English reading are shaped by learning experience of the two written languages and that activity levels in the left middle frontal cortex serve as the neurobiological marker for Chinese dyslexia (Siok *et al.* 2003). Their work on the functions of the left middle frontal gyrus in Chinese reading is widely cited and reported.

Chen and his team's work (Chen *et al.* 2002) in studying the brain network for Chinese reading is highly significant and classical. They examined the patterns of brain activity associated with the different cognitive mechanisms needed for reading, contrasting pinyin (alphabetic) and character scripts. They found that reading both types of scripts activated a common brain network including the inferior frontal, middle, and inferior temporal gyri, the inferior and superior parietal lobules, and the extrastriate areas. In particular, reading pinyin led to a greater activation in the inferior parietal cortex bilaterally, the precuneus, and the anterior middle temporal gyrus. Reading characters, however, activated the left fusiform gyrus, the bilateral cuneus, the posterior middle temporal, the right inferior frontal gyrus, and the bilateral superior frontal gyrus. These results suggest that reading Chinese invokes a common language area, but reading characters as opposed to the alphabet may lead to the activation of different specific areas.

Indeed, Cao and colleagues (Cao *et al.* 2010; Cao *et al.* 2009) found that Chinese adult readers, when compared with children, showed more involvement of the brain areas that support the specific demands of Chinese writing. These areas include the bilateral visual-orthographic regions (both the middle occipital gyrus and the fusiform gyrus), the inferior temporal gyrus, the superior parietal lobules (SPLs), and the left frontal areas (anterior frontal and dorsal IFGs). This suggests that with increased reading experience comes increased specialization in accommodating both the visual demands of Chinese characters (bilateral visual-orthographic areas) and their syllabic phonological mapping demands (superior parietal lobule).

The unique role of left middle frontal gyrus

The left middle frontal gyrus (LMFG) is a brain area that is widely believed to play a central role in cognitive control and coordination in general (Miller and Cohen, 2001; Perfetti *et al.* 2013). Many brain areas are located in the LMFG, including BA 8, 9, 10, 45, and 46. These brain areas in the LMFG are engaged in a wide range of high-level brain functions including the generation of color and action words (Martin *et al.* 1995), preparations for truth-telling and deception as well as the execution of deceptive responses (Ito *et al.* 2012), semantic incongruence processing and error monitoring (Balconi and Vitaloni, 2012), and perception, response selection, executive control, working memory, episodic memory and problem solving (Duncan and Owen, 2000).

The prevalent view of Chinese reading research is that the LMFG is more strongly activated in reading logographic Chinese than in reading alphabetic scripts such as English. Siok, Tan, and their colleagues (Siok *et al.* 2008) have found that this region could serve as a useful marker of Chinese dyslexia, as it exhibits both functional and structural aberrations of the dyslexic brain. The association between the LMFG and Chinese reading has been consistently corroborated by different groups of researchers with the use of multifarious experimental task paradigms. Various processing skills relevant to the LMFG, ranging from phonological, visual, orthographic, morphological, radical, rapid naming to handwriting, have been found to be associated with Chinese reading.

Cao and his team (Cao *et al.* 2010) conducted an important neuroimaging study to examine the developmental differences in phonological and orthographic processing of Chinese among the 9-year-olds, 11-year-olds, and adults using fMRI of rhyming and spelling judgments on two-character words. The spelling task showed greater activation than the rhyming task in the right superior parietal lobule and the right inferior temporal gyrus, and there were developmental increases across tasks bilaterally in these regions in addition to those in the bilateral occipital cortex, suggesting their increased involvement, over age, in visuo-orthographic analysis. They also found that the rhyming task showed greater activation than the spelling task in the left superior temporal gyrus and there were developmental decreases across tasks in this region, suggesting reduced involvement over age in phonological representations. Besides this, they found a developmental increase in the difference between conflicting (i.e. rhyming words spelled differently or non-rhyming words spelled similarly) and non-conflicting words in the left inferior parietal lobule, suggesting greater engagement of the systems for mapping between orthographic and phonological representations. Finally, they found developmental increases across tasks in the anterior (BA 45, 46) and posterior (BA 9) left inferior frontal gyrus, suggesting greater reliance on the controlled retrieval and selection of posterior lexical representations. This finding tends to support Tan's hypothesis about the central role of BA 9 in Chinese reading processing.

Another possible role of the LMFG in Chinese reading is the processing of the visual-orthographic form of characters. Non-alphabetic Chinese orthography, which lays more emphasis on visual-orthographic information and less on phonemic processing, might explain the neural network including the LMFG for Chinese readers, marking an obvious contrast with the brain activation pattern for the alphabetic counterparts (Siok *et al.* 2004). Korean and Chinese characters, for instance, share comparable kinds of character form and both provoke the activation of the LMFG, which therefore serves to support the identification and fine discrimination of these character forms, or, more holistically, subserve the intensive visuospatial analysis of characters. The function of the LMFG in Chinese orthography is further supported by Liu *et al.* (2007) study in which stronger activation in the LMFG was observed for character conditions relative to fixation and English word conditions. In addition, Tan and his colleagues (Tan *et al.* 2001b; Tan *et al.* 2003) also proposed that the LMFG might be responsible for phonological and semantic analysis. But since the intricate character forms make Chinese reading likely to involve automatic visual-orthographic analysis, the LMFG might serve the function of mediating the coordination and integration of different features altogether. This is possibly one of the working memory functions, which is to operate multiple resources simultaneously and make use of the greater processing load.

As Wu *et al.* (2012) remarked, a growing body of neuroimaging evidence has shown that, due to its unique linguistic features, Chinese character processing recruits differential activation from alphabetic languages. They applied a meta-analytic approach to summarizing the previous findings and examining the neural networks for orthographic, phonological, and semantic processing of Chinese characters independently. In particular, they used the activation likelihood estimation (ALE) method to analyze eight studies in the orthographic task category, eleven in the phonological, and fifteen in the semantic task categories. They found converging activation among the three language-processing components of the LMFG, the left superior parietal lobule, and the left mid-fusiform gyrus. They suggested that a common sub-network was underlying the character recognition process: the left inferior parietal lobule and the right superior temporal gyrus were specialized in phonological processing, while the left middle temporal gyrus was involved in semantic processing; functional dissociation was identified in the left inferior frontal gyrus, with the posterior dorsal part used for phonological processing and the anterior ventral part for semantic processing; bilateral involvement of the ventral occipito-temporal regions was found in both phonological and semantic processing. The results provide a better understanding of the neural networks underlying Chinese orthographic, phonological, and semantic processing. They also consolidate the findings of the additional recruitment of the LMFG and the right fusiform gyrus for Chinese character processing, as compared with the universal language network that has been proposed for alphabetic languages.

As a result of this, Ip (2013) explored the determining functions of the LMFG in Chinese reading, with a focus on the pivotal functions of working memory in the case of Chinese reading. She conducted four different fMRI tasks involving the working memory component but varying in processing skills. Tasks 1 and 2 focused on executive functioning skills, whereas Tasks 3 and 4 focused on visual-orthography and phonology skills, respectively. She tested 19 normal-reading Chinese university students in this neuroimaging study and found that all four tasks commonly triggered activity in the LMFG at BA 9. An important finding is that the working memory's involvement in the executive processes is critical to the participants' Chinese reading ability. She attributed this to the linguistic features of Chinese, in which the higher-level executive control on top of simple storage is likely to be needed in simultaneously manipulating the different components – phonology, visual-orthography and semantics – in processing Chinese characters. In the follow-up behavioral study on Grade 4 children, she incorporated the same working memory task with executive functioning and further substantiated the relationship between this kind of working memory and Chinese reading performance.

Although current studies have jointly verified the unique role of the LMFG in Chinese reading, Perfetti *et al.* (2013) tend to believe that the LMFG may serve more general functions across writing systems. They suggested that a frontal control function might be more often needed in Chinese than in English. The developmental pattern for the LMFG in Chinese has also been found in English linguistic tasks in a region that is close to LMFG, the left dorsal IFG (inferior frontal gyrus). A similar pattern was also found in neuroimaging studies on nonlinguistic tasks, such as partial working memory, executive attention, music processing, and others, which all involve the dorsal prefrontal area. But these frontal areas do not function in the same way in all tasks. Accordingly, Perfetti *et al.* (2013) proposed that the LMFG and other frontal areas might be serving a broader cognitive function to accommodate the special demands of Chinese writing that are also shared by other cognitive tasks. The abovementioned Chinese neuroimaging findings have been regarded as the cross-linguistic evidence to support a universal reading mechanism.

In conclusion, reading Chinese characters results in the activation of the left fusiform gyrus, the bilateral cuneus, the posterior middle temporal, the right inferior frontal gyrus, and the bilateral superior frontal gyrus. BA 9 plays an important role in Chinese reading, which really depends on Chinese writing. Chinese characters themselves play an important role in shaping the brain networks involved in Chinese reading and writing. When writing in pinyin, the impact of the Chinese language on the brain is found to be similar to that of alphabetic languages overall. Additionally, because reading Chinese can activate different brain regions, we can presume that the learning of Chinese reading and writing will have an impact on the brain development of children – though the nature of this impact needs further study.

Neuropsychological understanding of Chinese writing

Learning Chinese starts with writing practice and this has been a well-established tradition for more than one thousand years. Chinese characters, especially the traditional ones, however, are very difficult to write, as they have very complicated patterns and many strokes. Learning to write is not only very challenging for

L1 learners in Chinese communities, but also very difficult for L2 learners from other cultures. Learners may challenge this tradition but experienced teachers tend to insist on carrying it on. Many educators have challenged this cultural heritage and pedagogical reforms have been conducted in many Chinese communities, but very few have been successful. Why? Why is writing so important in the learning of reading Chinese? Is learning reading through writing really necessary in acquiring Chinese literacy? These questions have been challenging the central role of writing in Chinese reading, and this will be further discussed in this subsection.

The role of writing in Chinese reading

Handwriting is a kind of visual-motor coordination skill, which is partly independent of the writing system and is uniquely important for the reading of the Chinese logographic system. A close relationship between handwriting and letter recognition and perception has been found in a series of alphabetic studies conducted in the past decade. For example, Longcamp *et al.* (2003) found that the motor processes of handwriting might be implicitly and automatically evoked during passive letter viewing, while the same part of the left premotor area (BA 6) was involved in handwriting when alphabetic letters, but not pseudo-letters, were passively viewed. This finding was verified by a similar follow-up study with a group of left-handed participants (Longcamp *et al.* 2005). But these studies did not rule out the possible influence of participants' familiarity with real letters relative to pseudo-letters – the BA 6 activity might be relevant to the familiarity instead of the letter recognition. Therefore, Longcamp and his colleagues (Longcamp *et al.* 2008) conducted a training study which found that handwriting could influence and facilitate the later recognition of letters and graphic shapes that had been handwritten before. Other researchers, James and Gauthier (2006) and James and Atwood (2009), produced similar findings – that the motor regions were engaged in letter perception as well as the letter-specific visual regions which were also activated in handwriting. All these findings jointly indicated an inextricably intertwined relationship between handwriting and letter perception, both of which activate the sensorimotor systems.

In Chinese young learners, however, other capabilities like visual skills and motor skills (e.g. handwriting skills) might even contribute more notably to their reading performance. Tan *et al.* (2005b) found that the ability to read Chinese was strongly related to a child's handwriting skills, and that the relationship between phonological awareness and Chinese reading was much weaker than that reported in alphabetic languages. This has challenged the long-held concept that phonological processing is of the greatest importance in reading in all kinds of writing systems. It also implied that different underlying cognitive mechanisms are engaged in Chinese reading and alphabetic reading, and further implied that the brain processes involved might differ as well.

Tan *et al.* (2005b) made a theoretical speculation about the unique role of handwriting in the reading process of Chinese. They assumed that the linguistic differences between Chinese and alphabetic languages lead to learning differences, which accordingly results in different processing mechanisms for Chinese and English words – reading in Chinese depends on writing whereas reading in English does not. Their argument is that the learning strategies modulate the cognitive system – the learning-to-read strategy used by English children emphasizes the sound structure of speech, whereas Chinese children learn to read by repeatedly copying Chinese characters. This strategy is driven by the language-specific characteristics of Chinese words. As a logographic language, the basic writing units in Chinese are characters, which correspond to a syllable and, usually, a morpheme. The visual-spatial configurations of the characters are rather complex, involving the spatial arrangement of strokes in a two-dimensional square in complicated ways. There is no visual-sound correspondence at the segmental level, and there are many homophones in Chinese. Therefore, Tan *et al.* (2005b) proposed that the role of handwriting in Chinese reading development is mediated by two, possibly interacting, mechanisms: (1) the orthographic awareness facilitates the development of coherent, effective links among the visual symbols, phonology, and semantics; and (2) the establishment of motor programs leads to the formation of long-term motor memories of Chinese characters.

Recent studies (e.g. Chan *et al.* 2006; Tso *et al.* 2011) have further confirmed the potential participation of motor processing in visual word perception, indicating that learning strategies play an important role in inducing this participation. Guan *et al.* (2011) study also supported this finding by suggesting that handwriting strengthens word recognition and the association between orthography and semantics, and further proposed that pinyin typing (where pinyin closely resembles alphabetic processing) enhances phonological representations and the association between orthography and phonology. However, the handwriting of characters and that of pinyin might subserve different neural networks (Cao *et al.* 2012) and the latter might not have the same positive impact as the former on reading. One recent study (Tan *et al.* 2013) found that pinyin typing hindered the Chinese reading development of children as this kind of practice interfered with the visual-orthographic analysis of characters and, subsequently, impeded the formation of graphical representations in the long-term memory. The written Chinese characters are perceived as sequences of strokes, thus another study (Cao *et al.* 2012) explored the writing-on-reading effects in motor and pre-motor areas when English speakers learned Chinese characters through writing them. In brief, character handwriting skills and visual-orthographic processing skills, rather than phonological processing alone, may have a more crucial role in Chinese reading acquisition.

Recently, Perfetti and his team (Cao *et al.* 2012) compared training in character writing with training in pinyin (an alphabetic system) writing. Brain activation patterns suggested that character writing training produced a brain network that was more similar to that of native Chinese speakers: greater activation in the bilateral fusiform gyrus, the bilateral SPLs, the left inferior parietal lobule (IPL) and the LMFG (Cao *et al.* 2010). Greater activation in the bilateral fusiform gyrus and SPL suggests that writing provides a more native-like accommodation to the visual-orthographic features of Chinese characters. Greater activation in the left IPL and the LMFG suggests accommodation to the demands of the Chinese mapping system, although both areas play a role in alphabetic reading as well. The behavioral data showed that writing enhances character reading and the neuroimaging data suggested that writing promotes an accommodation of the brain's reading network for Chinese toward more writing-system specificity.

Because of this, Perfetti *et al.* (2013) speculated that the need for a high-quality, character-specific orthography can be partly met through writing as well as through reading experience. Writing characters, which is intrinsic to traditional Chinese literacy, strengthens orthographic representations, forcing attention on spatial relationships and detailed stroke sequences. With writing, character memories can add sensory-motor components, as practiced stroke sequences lead to neuro-motor patterns associated with characters. In fact, the sequential stroke memory can serve as an additional support for character recognition (Flores d'Aracis, 1994).

The hypothesis that handwriting (an output process) mediates Chinese reading (an input process) is also in line with the simulationist framework developed from the motor theory of speech perception (e.g. Liberman *et al.* 1967). The core assumption of this framework is that one must internally "run" or "simulate" the corresponding production process in order to understand a physical stimulus. This notion has been verified with the recent discovery of mirror neurons in both monkeys and humans. Research using both single-cell recording and functional neuroimaging observed that a specific population of neurons in the premotor cortex were activated both by the performing of an action and the viewing of an action performed by others (e.g. Gallese *et al.* 1996; Kohler *et al.* 2002). This finding lends empirical support to the hypothesis that the recognition of an action might entail the same production processes that are associated with this action (e.g. Gallese *et al.* 1996; Caramazza and Mahon, 2006; Mahon and Caramazza, 2005; Mahon and Caramazza, 2008; Martin *et al.* 2000). This notion could be used to understand the unique role of writing in Chinese reading. Chinese learners can activate the premotor cortex when performing the action of handwriting as well as viewing the characters they write. Therefore, through handwriting practice, young children can better acquire stroke assembly rules and memorize each individual character's intricate graphic form for future reading. The structure of a character can be better analyzed and identified by means of repeated handwriting so that orthographic awareness can also be facilitated (Tan *et al.* 2005b). The following section will further analyze the effects of writing on orthographic representation in Chinese.

The effects of writing on orthographic representation

The abovementioned studies have confirmed the unique role of handwriting in the reading of Chinese, and it is therefore very reasonable to imagine that the visual recognition of word stimuli involves the simulation of producing such visual stimuli – writing. The extreme hypothesis would be that reading depends on writing, which means successful reading has to go through some kind of writing process. A weaker one could be that the writing process influences or modulates the reading process in some manner, but it is not a necessity in reading. And finally, the other extreme hypothesis is that the writing process is activated but does not influence reading at all. Moreover, there might be a distinction between the developing system and the mature system. For instance, being able to write might be necessary in learning-to-read in young children but not necessary in the adult system. Although Tan *et al.* (2005) opted for the strong version of the hypothesis – reading depends on writing in both developmental and adult systems – to explain the developmental data and the adult imaging data, these empirical findings do not necessarily support a strong version of the reading-through-writing hypothesis.

In a series of studies on adult learners of Chinese, Perfetti and his team (Guan *et al.* 2011) tested the effects of handwriting as part of the process of learning to read characters. Across various conditions in different studies, the results were that writing characters from memory (following a brief exposure) improves later measures of character recognition, especially lexical decisions and character meaning decisions (Cao *et al.* 2012; Guan *et al.* 2011). Once again, as was the case with comparative behavioral research, the effect is partly universal as well as partly writing-specific. The reading network becomes specific to a writing system, showing increased involvement of the regions that support the reading procedures and decreased involvement of the other regions. The universal aspects are present in regions of the reading network that show similar changes with age across writing systems. Whereas the mapping between orthography and phonology is at the syllable level in Chinese and at the phoneme level in English, there is a mutual need in both systems to map graphic units to spoken language units. The activation of the brain region that may be associated with a more general mapping function, the left IPL, shows age-related increases in both writing systems (Booth *et al.* 2002, 2004; Cao *et al.* 2010; Cao *et al.* 2009). This developmental increase in the involvement of the left IPL is especially detectable when the task is difficult; for example, when the words share similar orthography but differ in phonology or when they differ in orthography but share a similar phoneme. It is possible that the left IPL can be thought of as supporting word-specific mapping processes in both Chinese characters and English words. Given the IPL's wide-ranging role in memory, its activation during reading may reflect memory demands that are shared by character reading and alphabetic reading under certain conditions.

A very recent study tends to confirm the hypothesis that learning to write Chinese characters influences the brain's reading network for characters (Cao *et al.* 2013). They sampled the students from a college Chinese class who learned 30 characters under character-writing conditions and 30 characters under pinyin-writing conditions. They collected fMRI data after the learning and found that different networks were used for reading Chinese characters and English words, indicating the accommodation to the demands of the new writing system through short-term learning. In addition, they found specific effects of character writing in greater activation (relative to pinyin-writing) in the bilateral superior parietal lobules and bilateral lingual gyri in both a lexical decision and an implicit writing task. These findings implied that character writing could help establish a higher quality representation of the visual-spatial structure of the character and its orthography. They also found a greater involvement of the bilateral sensorimotor cortex (SMC) for character-writing trained characters than pinyin-writing trained characters in the lexical decision task. This finding suggested that learning by writing could invoke greater interaction with sensorimotor information during character recognition. Furthermore, they also found that recognition accuracy was highly associated with the activation in the right superior parietal lobule, right lingual gyrus, and left SMC, which indicated that these areas could support the facilitative effect of character writing. Finally, they found character-writing training facilitated the connections with semantics by producing greater activation in the bilateral middle temporal gyri, whereas pinyin-writing training facilitated the connections with phonology by producing greater activation in the right inferior frontal gyrus.

In conclusion, Chinese writing encourages high-quality, whole-character representations, even when the components can support identification. Chinese writing has an interesting compensation for its limited decomposability. The validity (usually but misleadingly called "regularity") of a phonetic component as a cue to the character's pronunciation increases with decreasing character frequency (Perfetti *et al.* 1992). Chinese children who are learning to read gradually take advantage of the phonetic component of characters (Chen *et al.* 2003), and this serves them well when they encounter low-frequency words, just as English readers are facilitated by decoding when they encounter a low-frequency regular word. Neuroimaging studies have extended empirical support to the traditional approach to learning Chinese literacy: reading depends on writing. Although a challenging task for young Chinese learners, writing does help them to recognize and remember Chinese characters. Pedagogical reforms could be conducted to increase the interesting facets of writing as well as to decrease its difficulty, rather than disposing of Chinese writing – writing itself, in fact, could be made more interesting and innovative.

The relationship between working memory and Chinese reading

In Chinese, a single character represents a whole spoken syllable and a meaning unit. This means that the orthography, phonology and semantics have to be processed simultaneously to achieve reading success. This is a challenge to the human brain and needs greater manipulation and coordination of different features in the reading process. It is widely accepted that different processing component skills, such as phonological and orthographic skills, are all integral to successful reading in Chinese, but there is likely something at a higher level that is coordinating all the processing component skills, and this might be one of the most critical factors contributing to Chinese reading performance. Working memory, defined as the higher cognitive processes that supervise and control other cognitive processes (Angel et al. 2011), is therefore a plausible candidate.

Working memory is really needed to successfully complete the tasks of Chinese reading, and it is involved in phonological, visual-orthographic, radical, morphological, and rapid naming tasks (Ip, 2013). One of the examples is the phonological oddity task, which is often used to examine Chinese readers' phonological awareness (e.g. Ho and Bryant, 1997b). Performance in this task, however, is consistently found to be correlated with Chinese reading performance (e.g. Siok and Fletcher, 2001). This correlation may be caused by the involvement of working memory, as the participants need to retain the set of words in their mind and make a judgment by comparing the words and manipulating their respective sounds. The association between phonological awareness and Chinese reading performance might be mediated by working memory, which plays a pivotal role in Chinese reading. This has been verified by some studies conducted with Chinese dyslexic children, who demonstrated poorer performance than normal achievers in phonological working memory tasks (e.g. Chung et al. 2011, 2013; Ho et al. 2000; Leong et al. 2008; Stevenson et al. 1982; Zhang et al. 1998). While other kinds of deficits, like rapid naming deficits, might possibly serve as a marker for dyslexia, phonological memory deficit, in which dyslexic children performed worse than their normal counterparts, was found to be an even more prominent problem (Ho and Lai, 1999). The importance of working memory, however, has not been highlighted in Chinese reading studies, as there was no standardized paradigm to measure working memory.

The LMFG is the region that underlies both Chinese reading and working memory – it has been identified as a crucial area for both processing different kinds of working memory tasks and reading in Chinese. In Baddeley's (2003) review, the neural mechanisms for Chinese reading fit almost perfectly with the anatomical localization of working memory. He (2000) has conceptualized working memory as a multi-component system with a control system as the central executive and two slave storage systems – namely, the phonological loop (for verbal-auditory input) and the visuospatial sketchpad (for visuospatial input) – plus an episodic buffer that connects the two systems with long-term memory and the central executive. The brain areas depicted to subserve these major systems (i.e. central executive, phonological loop, visuospatial sketchpad, and episodic buffer) in this working memory model include the bilateral dorsolateral prefrontal, inferior frontal, parietal and occipital regions. Coincidently, the phonological processing of Chinese characters also involves four systems – the left dorsolateral prefrontal system, the left ventral prefrontal system covering the superior aspect of inferior frontal gyrus, the dorsal aspect of the left inferior parietal system, and the bilateral ventral occipitotemporal system including portions of the fusiform gyrus and the middle occipital gyrus (Tan et al. 2005a).

Although Tan and colleagues did not examine the role of working memory, it seems highly likely that working memory and Chinese reading share similar processing components and largely overlapping brain activities (especially those in the LMFG). In this vein, training young children's working memory or the rote learning of Chinese characters might have positive effects on the development of reading.

In summary, recent neuroimaging studies of Chinese reading and writing have yielded empirical evidence for the neural networks that are both universal and partly specific to Chinese language and writing systems (Perfetti and Tan, 2013). The LMFG plays an important role in Chinese reading, and BA 9 is widely believed to play a central role in Chinese reading processing. In addition, the writing of Chinese is critical in the learning of Chinese reading, in both L1 and L2 learners. Handwriting is a powerful procedure for establishing written word-form knowledge in both L1 and L2 learners – writing is an integral part of Chinese literacy, and should not be ruled out of Chinese literacy pedagogy. The working memory is also very important.

Chapter 3

The pedagogy of teaching Chinese as a first language

Literacy is normally introduced to children at school, but occasionally informal literacy lessons are conducted at home. In Imperial China, for centuries, boys born into scholarly or wealthy families were given early literacy at home from the age of 6 or 7. In contemporary Chinese communities, however, literacy is taught in the early years, either in preschool or at home. Hong Kong, for example, allows 3-year-olds to learn the reading of Chinese in kindergarten. The Chinese teachers in Hong Kong kindergartens have been criticized for being too skills-oriented and teacher-directed and have therefore asked to implement a whole language approach and emergent literacy in kindergartens (Ho and Bryant, 1997a; Law, 1999). However, they still believe that explicit instruction might be productive and necessary in early literacy learning, especially in Chinese contexts (Li et al. 2008; Tan et al. 2005). What is the best pedagogy for teaching Chinese literacy in an L1 context? In this regard, there are many conflicting views, and these have been disturbing literacy educators as well as scholars (Li, Rao, and Tse, 2012; Li, Wong, and Wang, 2011). This chapter is dedicated to addressing these controversies and exploring the best pedagogy for teaching Chinese literacy as a first language in varying Chinese cities such as Beijing, Hong Kong, and Shenzhen.

Reading readiness versus emergent literacy

Reading readiness versus emergent literacy – these are the two distinctly conflicting views about which is the best pedagogy for the teaching of literacy in the early years (Smith, 1992; Strickland, 1990). The two views present disparate perceptions of literacy acquisition, and therefore imply different pedagogies for early literacy teaching. These controversies about the best ways to foster children's literacy acquisition are not new, as they are originated from the heated debates of the 1920s (Chall, 1992). This is also relevant to the well-known "reading wars" that will be elaborated on, with more details, later in this chapter. The "reading wars", however, have settled down in 1990s through the work of American reading scientists and an eclectic theory of reading development has been compromised and accepted by both sides (Li, 2000). Few studies, however, have been conducted in Chinese communities to compare the effects of a reading readiness program versus an emergent literacy program on early Chinese literacy attainment.

Reading readiness

Early studies on reading readiness initially stressed the importance of waiting until a child is ready to learn to read before providing any type of instruction, but contemporary research has eventually shifted to a stance in which being ready has become synonymous with the learner's having the prerequisite skills for formal literacy instruction to be undertaken (Crawford, 1995). There are six fundamental assumptions from the reading readiness perspective:

1   the visual-perceptual processes involved in reading and writing are centered around the unit sound relationships;
2   children need to be 5 or 6 years old before they learn to read and write;
3   literacy instruction should be systematic and sequential;
4   to behave in a literate way, children must acquire the prerequisite skills;
5   direct, systematic instruction is the best method for teaching reading; and
6   teaching literacy is an unemotional, value-free process.
(Crawford, 1995; Hall, 1987; Harris and Sipay, 1985;
Mason, 1992; Reutzel and Cooter, 1992)

Accordingly, reading readiness instruction should include activities to develop auditory discrimination, visual discrimination, memory, general concept development or vocabulary, listening skills, visual-motor skills, letter-name knowledge, letter-sound relationships, and word recognition (Alexander, 1988; Crawford, 1995; Durkin, 1987; Harris and Sipay, 1985; Sippola, 1994; Strickland, 1990; Teale and Sulzby, 1986).

However, research during the 1980s and 1990s has gradually led many reading researchers to critically examine the above assumptions and this has resulted in a departure by some educators from the traditional readiness philosophy (Crawford, 1995; Reutzel and Cooter, 1992; Teale and Sulzby, 1986). Nevertheless, the readiness view of literacy development is still dominant in Chinese communities. The government documents in mainland China take the readiness view that physical and neurological maturation alone prepare children to take advantage of instruction in reading and writing Chinese. For example, until children reach a certain stage of maturity (i.e. about age 6 or 7, when they enter primary school) they are not allowed to learn the reading and writing of Chinese characters (Li and Rao, 2000).

Emergent literacy

For many years, the classroom experiences of many early childhood educators, as well as the results yielded by researchers such as Durkin (1966), have indicated that the reading readiness paradigm might be theoretically and practically inappropriate. Accordingly, Clay (1966) suggested a new term – emergent literacy – to label the alternative view of literacy acquisition, which gives legitimacy to children's early, nonconventional reading and writing behaviors. Emergent literacy is widely used to symbolize a way of thinking about early literacy development; it means that educators create a literacy-enriched environment to engage young children in a variety of literacy and language experiences (Frerichs, 1993; Harris and Hodges, 1995; Madison and Speaker, 1994; Sippola, 1994; Teale, 1986; Teale and Sulzby, 1994).

For several decades, considerable efforts have been devoted to investigating the nature and process of emergent literacy. Research has consistently indicated that the following characteristics are common to emergent literacy:

1. children acquire literacy prior to school entry, within the home and family (Hall, 1994; Teale and Sulzby, 1986);
2. literacy emerges not in a systematic, sequential manner, but as a natural response to the printed language and early literacy experience (Hall, 1994; International Reading Association, 1986; Strickland and Morrow, 1989; Teale and Sulzby, 1986);
3. children control and manipulate their literacy learning in the same way as they control and manipulate all other aspects of their learning about the world (International Reading Association, 1986; Teale and Sulzby, 1986); and
4. literacy is a social phenomenon that is influenced by sociocultural factors (Hall, 1994; International Reading Association, 1986).

It would appear that reading readiness has been considered to be a good concept, used in an inappropriate way. However, it is built upon a logical analysis of literacy skills from an adult perspective rather than upon a developmental perspective and current research overwhelmingly indicates the need to reconceptualize reading readiness. The emergent literacy perspective, on the other hand, reveals a great deal about children's literacy development during the first few years of life. Emergent literacy is useful as a blanket term that characterizes the manner in which young children learn more and more about the culturally elaborated writing system that is used around them. Furthermore, such insights offer valuable information into achieving the objective of universal literacy, which also includes Chinese literacy.

Since the 1990s, the concept of emergent literacy has been advocated in Hong Kong by many teacher educators (i.e. the Hong Kong Institute of Education, HKIEd). The scholars and teacher educators in HKIEd have tended to use this concept to reframe early literacy activities and to replace traditional literacy ideas. The initiative has also received support from the educational authorities that were not satisfied with traditional Chinese literacy pedagogies. As a result, many kindergartens have tried out "emergent literacy" and found this idea interesting as well as challenging (that is, not easy to do with early Chinese literacy). There is no scientific evidence to support the hypothesis that emergent literacy is better than reading readiness. From our perspective, literacy could be emergent from the very early years but readiness is also critical to literacy acquisition. Chinese literacy could be a mixture of "emergent" natural literacy activities and post-readiness learning ones.

Phonics versus a whole language approach

Over the past century, views on early literacy teaching have varied from one extreme to another, without ever reaching a point of consensus. Particularly in the past two decades, the debate has escalated into the "reading wars", a large-scale battle between advocates of phonics and whole language approaches (Chall, 1996; Goodman, 1998; Snow *et al.* 1998; Reyhner, 2008). Phonics advocates have called for the explicit and systematic teaching of literacy skills (Adams, 1990; Chall, 1996), whereas whole-language proponents have highlighted the importance of literature-based reading, construction of meaning for purposeful functions, the naturalness of reading acquisition, child-centeredness, and teacher empowerment in reading instruction (Goodman, 1998; Weaver, 1998). So which is better, the phonics or the whole language approach?

The phonics-centered approach

The phonics-centered approach is often associated with skills-based, direct instruction (Stahl and Hayes, 1997), which dates back to a behavioral model of teacher-led learning (Rosenshine and Stevens, 1984). Emphasis is placed on the desired product of teaching (outcome-oriented) rather than on the learning process itself (process-oriented) (Reyhner, 2008). Chall (1996) concluded that direct instruction was more effective than indirect instruction for most children, particularly those from families of low socioeconomic status (SES) and those with reading difficulties. Some recent comparisons of direct and indirect instruction show that systematic phonics instruction leads to higher word reading and spelling achievement (Ehri *et al.* 2001). However, the rigor and reliability of the research on which these findings are based have been questioned (Grunwald, 2006; Reyhner, 2008).

The Chinese phonetics approach refers to teaching beginner learners Chinese literacy with pinyin. In China and Singapore, Primary 1 students or even kindergarten children are taught pinyin in the first month of their literacy lessons. As a Chinese reading tool, pinyin is a Chinese system for transliterating Mandarin Chinese using the 26 Latin letters. The pronunciation of most of the letters is similar to that of their Latin counterparts, but there are notable differences. In Chinese, each character corresponds to one syllable, which corresponds to a part of an English word, or an entire word. Chinese syllables consist of three elements: initial sound, final sound, and tone. The initial sounds are consonants and the final sounds contain at least one vowel. Some syllables consist only of an initial sound or a final sound. In Mandarin Chinese, there are 21 initial sounds:

Table 3.1 List of the initial sounds in Mandarin Chinese

	Unaspirated	Aspirated	Nasal	Voiceless fricative	Voiced fricative
Labial	b	p	m	f	
Alveolar	d	t	n		l
Velar	g	k		h	
Palatal	j	q		x	
Dental sibilant	z	c		s	
Retroflex	zh	ch		sh	r

Table 3.2 List of the final sounds in Mandarin Chinese

Category	Final sound
6 simple finals	a, e, i, o, u, ü
13 compound finals	ai, ao, ei, ia, iao, ie, iou, ou, ua, uai, üe, uei, uo
16 nasal finals	8 front nasals: an, en, ian, in, uan, üan, uen, ün
	8 back nasals: ang, eng, iang, ing, iong, ong, uang, ueng

The final sounds in Mandarin Chinese are shown in Table 3.2. There are 6 simple finals, 13 compound finals, and 16 nasal finals. There are seven special syllables in Mandarin Chinese: er, hm, hng, m, n, ng, ~r. The initial and final sounds make a total of 56 basic sounds. Combinations of initials and finals alongside the special cases result in <u>413 possible combinations</u>. Applying the <u>four tones</u> of Mandarin Chinese to this, we can get a total of about 1,600 unique syllables in Mandarin Chinese.

Chinese is a tone language, thus every character should be pronounced with the correct tone. In transliterated Chinese, tone markings are written over the central vowels in most syllables. Some syllables have no specific tone, and no sign is put above the vowel. There are four tones:

1   the 1st tone is marked with a line "ā", indicating a high, even and constant tone;
2   the 2nd tone is marked with a rising line "á", which symbolizes a rising tone that grows stronger;
3   the 3rd tone is marked with a hook "ǎ". This tone is first falling and fading, then rising and growing strong; and
4   the 4th tone is marked with a falling line "à", which denotes a quickly falling and fading tone.

In unstressed syllables, the tone may be hardly noticeable. In such cases, no marking is put above any vowel, and this could be regarded as "tone zero". Tones will not always remain the same when you pronounce a sequence of tones and, under certain circumstances, tones could be changed to make the utterance sound more smoothly. This has made learning Chinese more difficult for learners. Phonics training with pinyin is thus a necessity in early literacy teaching. This is why all the Primary 1 students in China have to acquire the pinyin system in the first month of their first school year.

The whole language approach

The whole language approach, on the other hand, is an approach to teaching reading that focuses on getting meaning through text and teaching reading, writing, and other subjects together. It focuses on child-centered learning, in that children are empowered to direct their own learning at their own pace in acquiring reading skills and are free to make choices, and their interests are central to the curriculum (Goodman, 1989; Weaver, 1994). Some studies have demonstrated the positive effects of these programs on print awareness and word reading acquisition among young children (Reutzel *et al.* 1989), while other studies have not revealed significant differences in reading skills and reading readiness when reading achievement tests were used as a criterion (Stahl and Miller, 1989; Reyhner, 2008). Problems associated with the whole language approach include a lack of structure – which has traditionally been supplied by the scope and sequence charts, lessons and activities, and the extensive graded literature found in basal readers. Further, the approach places a heavy burden on teachers to develop their own curriculum, which may not be easy to implement (Reyhner, 2008).

It is now widely believed that both sides of the debate contain reasonable elements, and that multiple approaches to reading instruction provide children with a solid foundation for proficient reading and writing (Snow *et al.* 1998). On the one hand, through understanding the relationships between sounds and spellings, children improve their abilities to read and spell, and also learn the meanings of multisyllabic words. An enriched language environment, with play and activities, could also help children build their phonological, phonemic, syllabic and lexical awareness which is needed for early literacy. On the other hand, the whole language approach roots literacy development in children's literature, which provides the environment of authentic texts. It is a literacy philosophy which emphasizes that children should focus on meaning. According to this philosophy, language is a natural phenomenon and literacy is promoted through natural, purposeful language use. Language is viewed as an authentic and natural real-world experience, and language learning is perceived as taking place through meaningful reading and writing situations. So, reading skills versus meaningful reading, which is more important?

Problematic, however, is the "either/or" position regarding the phonics and whole language approaches. In fact, young children need a balance of both approaches in learning to read and there is substantial evidence to support the position that the two sides can coexist and complement each other. Pressley and colleagues (1998) found that the most effective classrooms, in terms of students'

Department, 1999). Later, the *Guide to the Pre-Primary Curriculum* (Education Department, 2006) was issued to incorporate the best Western pedagogies into teachers' practice (i.e. the child-centered approach, the project approach, and the whole language approach).

Coincidently, both Hong Kong and Mainland China have gone through the same pedagogical reforms in the past decades. And they shared the same ultimate goals and reform agenda, although they are supposed to have different governance under the umbrella of "one nation, two systems". Unfortunately (or fortunately?), this reform was not so successful, as the imported Western pedagogy did not work well in Hong Kong and Mainland China kindergartens. Instead, a significant policy-practice divide was found by many Chinese researchers, which will be further discussed in Chapter 5.

Western pedagogies in Chinese classrooms

There is no uniform Western pedagogy in educational literature. Western pedagogy in this book refers to those developed and used widely in "Western" countries (relative to China and Asia) that emphasize children's individuality, child-initiated activities, and learning through play (Li, Rao, and Tse, 2012). It favors a child-centered approach (teaching philosophy), integrated teaching (teaching strategy), inquiry-based learning and learning through play (learning approach), small class or group learning (classroom organization), child-initiated and process-oriented activities (teaching activities), and so on. The Project Approach, Reggio Emilia, High/Scope, and emergent literacy are a few well-known examples of this kind of pedagogy/program.

As shown in the above review, a remarkable paradigm shift from traditional Chinese pedagogy to Western pedagogy has occurred in the ECE reforms in China, Hong Kong, and Singapore (Ng and Rao, 2008; Rao and Li, 2009; Zhu and Zhang, 2008). Most of the recommended practices are rooted in Western views of early pedagogy and many are not congruent with traditional Chinese beliefs about early learning. With little guidance about how to best incorporate Western ideas into their daily teaching practices, Chinese teachers have found many challenges and difficulties in directly adopting these borrowed approaches (Cheng, 2001; Li, 2002; Li and Li, 2003; Liu and Feng, 2005; Zhu and Zhang, 2008).

Cheng (2006) interviewed three Hong Kong kindergarten teachers who had tried adopting High/Scope and project approaches and found that their school-based pedagogical reforms were not successful. She highlighted the difficulties of making pedagogical shifts and took stock of local contextual constraints, which included the examination-oriented education system, parental expectation of academic achievement, the tradition of direct instruction and rote learning, and the overloaded curriculum. These constraints are difficult – if not impossible – to eliminate in Hong Kong through simple pedagogical alterations (Cheng, 2006). The researchers therefore urge reflection on how the "new" approaches can be incorporated into Chinese communities (Li, 2002) and on what are the factors impeding the process (Hu, 2002).

In Hong Kong, for example, Western pedagogical models such as High/Scope, Project Approach and Reggio Emilia have been adopted with great passion by local kindergartens (Rao *et al.* 2010). However, classroom observations found that the Project Approach was transformed into a kind of teacher-directed "project work" rather than a child-centered exploration (Li, 2002; Rao *et al.* 2010). This finding suggests that as long as there is a discrepancy between the tenets of these Western pedagogies and those of traditional Chinese pedagogy, the efforts of transplanting or directly adopting the pedagogies will not be successful. Instead, adapted or localized implementation might be more workable.

In fact, there are many discrepancies between Western and Chinese pedagogies in terms of their ideas about teaching philosophy, teacher-student relationships, learning strategies, good student characteristics, and teacher qualities (Hu, 2002; Wong, 2008; Zhu and Zhang, 2008). These pedagogical differences have been shaped by the distinctly different cultural values and social beliefs which might have their own definitions of the *best* teaching practice (Wong, 2008). Adding to the failed attempts are the socio-contextual factors which have further constrained the adaption of Western practices: overcrowded and crammed classrooms, huge class sizes, untrained teachers, unrealistic parental expectations (of early trilingual education), examination-oriented systems, and social competition for survival arising from commercialization pressures (Hu, 2002; Li *et al.* 2008; Tang and Maxwell, 2007). All these influences have made the introduction of Western methods not as straightforward in Chinese communities as many reformers presumed (Li, 2007b; Rao *et al.* 2009; Zhu and Zhang, 2008). Thus, a number of researchers have called for thorough examination of "westernized reforms" in Chinese communities (Lee and Tseng, 2008; Li, 2002; Tobin, 2007; Zhu and Zhang, 2008).

Meanwhile, many Western educators have also begun to rethink their pedagogies and to ponder the value of direct instruction in early literacy learning (Evans *et al.* 2000; Sénéchal and LeFevre, 2002; Whitehurst, 2001). The most effective early pedagogy is now defined as a blend of direct instruction and a holistic, independent learning approach (Siraj-Blatchford *et al.* 2002). This is especially true in Chinese contexts (Li *et al.* 2008; Tan *et al.* 2005) where classroom practice is intensely influenced by Chinese traditions alongside distinctive features of Chinese language learning. McBride-Chang (2004) found that children's learning of reading skills was more rapid when they received direct instruction; and, Tan *et al.* (2005) found that Chinese reading development profited from writing skills training, rote learning, and copying exercises. However, McBride-Chang (2004) concluded that it is hard to draw general conclusions about the effectiveness of different Chinese literacy pedagogies as language, character script, and teaching systems vary across Chinese societal groups. It is suggested that classroom-based studies of varying Chinese contexts are urgently needed if the relative effectiveness of different pedagogies is to be evaluated.

Defining Chinese literacy pedagogy

We found a remarkably common pattern of Chinese literacy pedagogy in Hong Kong, Shenzhen and Singapore: whole class teaching mode, direct instruction, lecturing with questioning, no play, shared reading and writing, reading aloud, teachers' talk focusing on the curriculum not on discipline, language and content knowledge as the foci of instruction, whole-class and individual interactions, frequent use of neutral feedback to probe children's thoughts and learning, the use of positive feedback, no student resistance in the classroom, with short oral answer and sustained oral text being the dominating learning outcome (Li, Rao and Tse, 2011; Li, Rao and Tse, 2012; Li, 2013). These findings are in line with those found by Wu *et al.* (1999), Liu *et al.* (2005), Li and Rao (2000, 2005) and Rao *et al.* (2010) and they deserve more elaboration and investigation.

Although the "reading wars" have almost stopped and a balanced approach has been widely promoted, direct instruction is still dominating Chinese literacy pedagogy and is highly valued by parents and teachers. This preference for whole-class, direct instruction might reflect the selective, dynamic, and changing influences of the hybrid of three cultural threads: Confucian, Socialism (in China), and Western culture. While the influence of the Socialist culture is evident in practical aspects of literacy teaching – such as organization, administration, and learning goals and content – Confucian and imported Western cultures have had a joint but mixed influence on the ideological and philosophical bases of reading pedagogy, including the views on young children, the views on learning and development, and the views on appropriate teacher-child relationships (Wang and Spodek, 2000; Zhu and Wang, 2005; Hu, 2002). Meanwhile, teachers have started to use questioning, individual interactions, positive feedback to encourage child-initiated learning and theme-based explorations, as these are believed to be beneficial to enhancing child-centered learning in Western culture. It is widely accepted that sociocultural influences such as parental expectations, teachers' traditional beliefs, an examination-oriented education system and cultural values have profoundly shaped the early Chinese literacy pedagogy (Lee and Tseng, 2008; Li and Rao, 2000, 2005; Li *et al.* 2008; Rao *et al.* 2010; Tang and Maxwell, 2007).

Psycholinguistically, the orthographical differences between Chinese and English may also be associated with the differences in early literacy pedagogies. For example, recent neuroscientific studies have verified that language does affect patterns of brain activation (Tan *et al.* 2008) and Chinese children's brains are structurally and functionally different from those of English-speaking children (Siok *et al.* 2008). Over the past four decades, it has been widely found that phonological training is the key to early reading acquisition and this finding has provided scientific support to the advocates of phonics approaches. They take for granted that the central role of phonological training should be universally evident, across languages and nations. However, this prevailing view of the central role of phonological awareness is largely based on studies using

Western (alphabetic) languages. Chinese language, on the other hand, uses logographic characters which denote meaning rather than phonology. Tan *et al.* (2005b) found that, in Chinese, reading development depends on writing skills training. They suggest two possibly interacting mechanisms to explain the central role of logographic writing. First is orthographic awareness, which facilitates the development of coherent, effective links among visual symbols, phonology, and semantics. The second involves the establishment of motor programs that lead to the formation of long-term motor memories of the Chinese characters. These two mechanisms require rote learning and copying exercises. This finding may eventually be able to explain why Chinese kindergarten teachers should never abandon direct instruction, rote learning and copying exercises. These teacher-directed activities are, instead, crucial to the success of early learning in Chinese reading and this finding might challenge the prominent progressive and constructivist views that have been well established in the field.

Practically, there are some "have-to" situations for this pattern such as the large class size, teacher-centered classroom setting, untrained teachers, and the competition for survival arising out of commercialization (Hu, 2002; Li *et al.* 2008; Tang and Maxwell, 2007). Liu and Feng (2005), Ng and Rao (2008) and Zhu and Zhang (2008) argued that teachers' beliefs, qualifications and professionalism might be associated with the success of formulation and transformation of early childhood pedagogies in Chinese communities. These factors may become formidable in limiting and shaping the pattern of early Chinese literacy pedagogy and will be discussed in the following section.

The best Chinese literacy pedagogy

What is the best Chinese literacy pedagogy? Which is the most effective pedagogy? These questions have been of interest to many Chinese literacy educators. This section will review existing educational psychology studies to figure out the most effective literacy teaching approaches, and discuss issues with regard to the best pedagogy.

What is the most effective approach

Chow *et al.* (2008) explored different literacy training methods, and found that children in the dialogic reading condition attained higher vocabulary knowledge over a 12-week interval, while children in the dialogic reading (DR) + morphological training (MT) condition improved in Chinese character recognition. Results in the DR condition support the notion that DR only supports children's oral language skills but not their reading and writing skills. The DR+MT condition focused on metalinguistic training and oral language and yielded greater growth in character recognition ability. A trend towards improvement in receptive vocabulary was also observed. These findings suggest that:

1 DR can only facilitate young children's oral language skills;
2 MT facilitates children's reading, by promoting an awareness of lexical morphemes; and
3 the mixture of DR and MT methods is the most effective literacy training program.

In other words, a mixture of phonics and a whole language approach should be the most effective literacy pedagogy.

Palmer *et al.* (2010) examined the nature of oral reading fluency, the cognitive load required for ELL to have fluency in L2 oral ready, and the age/stage of L1 literacy development at which it is most efficacious to introduce children to L2 reading and writing. An eight-week intervention conducted by a bilingual tutor led to the ELL showing significant growth in English language proficiency and reading fluency. However, growth in Chinese literacy slowed down, and even declined slightly. Print acquisition, on the other hand, exceeded oral vocabulary development. These results suggest that direct instruction may be necessary for literacy development. Alongside this, oral proficiency should occur before formal reading instruction, and, finally, the home-school connection can be important. These findings carry many educational implications:

1 direct instruction is critical to Chinese literacy acquisition;
2 reading readiness is a necessary prerequisite to formal literacy activities, and is very important to emergent literacy; and
3 both home and school literacy activities are important.

A very important study was recently conducted to solve the "nature-nurture controversy" in Chinese literacy acquisition. Chow, Ho, Wong, Waye, and Bishop (2011) investigated the etiology of individual differences in Chinese language and reading skills in 312 Chinese twin pairs. Participants were measured in Chinese word reading, receptive vocabulary, phonological memory, tone awareness, syllable and rhyme awareness, rapid automatized naming, morphological awareness and orthographic skills, and the Raven's Coloured Progressive Matrices. Their two key findings were similar to those found in English speakers. First, the genetic influences on word reading, tone awareness, phonological memory, morphological awareness and rapid automatized naming were found to range from moderate to substantial. Second, the environment influences on receptive vocabulary, syllable and rhyme awareness and orthographic skills ranged from moderate to substantial. These findings indicate that teaching and education plays a relatively more important role than genetics in Chinese literacy acquisition. One of the implications is that we have to teach young children to make them literate, whereas play on its own cannot nurture literacy.

In brief, these important studies have together described the most effective methods of Chinese literacy teaching. In the first instance, reading readiness should be observed, as it is the prerequisite to the success of Chinese literacy teaching. The most effective approach should be a fusion of direct instruction and emergent literacy, a blend of phonics and the whole language approach, and a collaboration between home and school.

Balancing Chinese traditional and Western progressive pedagogies

In previous studies, we (Li, Rao, and Tse, 2012) found that Chinese teachers commonly believe in the balanced approach, which is a mix of conventional training of early reading and writing skills, child-initiated activities, and tests to fulfil parental expectations and to promote school readiness. Their common practices include: the early teaching of Chinese reading and writing, direct instruction, copying exercises, reading aloud, nursery rhymes and storybooks as learning materials, using specific teaching approaches and having teaching plans, teaching with a theme approach and with the whole class, assigning homework and involving parents. This finding indicated that there were both consistencies and discrepancies between Chinese teachers' beliefs and practices. Although they were cognizant of the importance of child-initiated learning and other progressive and constructivist ideas, they subscribed to the importance of direct instruction for literacy learning and gave children many copying and reading exercises. This Chinese type of discrepancy between teachers' beliefs and practices was widely and repeatedly reported by Liu and Feng (2005), Ng and Rao (2008), and Zhu and Zhang (2008) in varying studies of early childhood teaching in Hong Kong and on mainland China.

While many Western literacy educators have been promoting a balanced approach, between direct instruction and child-initiated whole language learning, Chinese communities have typically launched a top-down movement to transform the teacher-directed learning into a child-centered and holistic paradigm (Hu, 2002; Rao, 2002; Rao *et al.* 2010; Zhu and Wang, 2005; Lee and Tseng, 2008). The education reform proposals in Hong Kong and China have recommended a shift from an instructivist to a constructivist approach to teaching and learning (Ng and Rao, 2008; Zhu and Zhang, 2008). New concepts and approaches such as the project approach, developmentally appropriate practice (DAP), emergent curriculum, emergent literacy and whole language, have been widely promoted by Chinese teacher educators and policy makers since the late 1980s (Zhu and Zhang, 2008). Early childhood practitioners have been forced to adopt these progressive ideas and Western practices in Chinese classrooms but, in the end, the transplant of the borrowed pedagogies has not been successful (Li and Li, 2003). Li (2002) has articulated six factors which impinge on the success of these Western-based ideas in Chinese classrooms: class size, teacher quality, resource availability, parental expectation, the examination-oriented education system and the sociocultural environment. Further, it was found that "even though teachers could discuss the new 'Western' thinking about language learning, they still used the traditional methods to teach children language" (Zhu and Zhang, 2008).

This dissonance between Chinese teachers' stated progressive beliefs and their use of traditionally endorsed practices has urged researchers to reflect on the factors which impede the implementation of "new" approaches to instruction in Chinese communities (Hu, 2002; Liu and Feng, 2005) and the cultural appropriateness of these European-American pedagogies (Li, 2007; Rao *et al.* 2010; Zhu and Zhang, 2008). European-American and Chinese pedagogies were found to conflict in several important respects, including teaching philosophy, teacher-student relationships, learning strategies, students' features and teacher qualities (Zhu and Zhang, 2008). There are problems associated with deploying pedagogical innovations developed in another sociocultural milieu, without making well-informed pedagogical choices that are grounded in an understanding of local cultures and sociocultural influences (Hu, 2002; Li, 2007; Li and Li, 2003; Tobin, 2007; Zhu and Zhang, 2008).

Previous research has looked at early literacy learning in different Chinese communities (Li and Rao, 2000; Li and Rao, 2005) and found that, despite the sociolingual, curricular and instructional differences, the Chinese parents and teachers in Beijing, Hong Kong and Singapore place a high value on the early learning of literacy. Direct instruction in kindergarten or at home significantly contributed to the prediction of young children's Chinese literacy attainment. Tang and Maxwell (2007) found that direct instruction dominated Chinese teachers' practices because of some "have-to" situations (e.g. the large class size and the competition for survival arising out of commercialization) and Chinese parents' strong preference for knowledge-based learning and direct instruction. Reiterating the cultural conflicts, Lee and Tseng (2008) and Tobin (2007) urged a critical re-evaluation of the taken-for-granted practice of directly implementing the DAP and child-centered approaches in Chinese early childhood settings. With an in-depth cross-cultural comparison of two lab kindergartens in Hong Kong and Canada, Wong (2008) concluded that cultural values and social beliefs might be the most influential factors on the *best* practice in early literacy programs.

Furthermore, Li *et al.* (2008) found that direct instruction of literacy skills was well received by the Chinese parents and teachers in Hong Kong and China, and had significantly contributed to later literacy attainment at primary school, whereas whole language activities did not. They believe that the complicated nature of Chinese orthography might make direct instruction particularly valuable in Chinese literacy acquisition. These findings, however, have warranted an in-depth investigation to provide an authentic account of the ongoing debates on theories, teaching practices, and educational reforms.

Recently, we (Li, Rao, and Tse, 2012) conducted a cross-national study to investigate the actual practices in three Chinese communities that have different sociolingual and educational contexts: Shenzhen, Hong Kong and Singapore. These three cities form a spectrum of cultural openness and "westernization" (from the most open, Singapore, to the least open, Shenzhen), although they share the same "westernized reform" in early childhood education (Li, 2007b). The case study of these three communities provides an ideal opportunity for understanding the complicated dynamics involved in assimilating or adapting Western ideas into traditional Chinese classrooms. The present study observed and analyzed 18 early childhood classrooms in the three localities. We asked the class teachers about their respective teaching practices to see how these ideas were actually turned into practice. Whole-class direct instruction was found to be the predominant Chinese pedagogical mode. This indicates that Chinese traditional pedagogy still dominates Chinese kindergarten classrooms. We also found slight societal differences in classroom practice, which reflects the spectrum of openness and westernization of the three cities. The findings suggest that the direct transplant of Western pedagogies into Chinese classrooms should be avoided because culture, language, parents, teachers, resources, education system, and other sociocontextual factors play very important roles in shaping Chinese literacy pedagogy. The distinctive orthography of the Chinese language, for example, determines to a considerable extent the boundaries of pedagogical reforms. Cultural values, teacher and parent expectations, and the established educational system should be considered very carefully when one is seeking to change literacy practices in the early years. Cultural traditions and social values are both resources and limits, and such awareness is important for improving pedagogy in the age of globalization (Tobin, 2007). Early childhood educators around the world should seek to learn from and influence one another, but the transnational circulation of best practice should not be one way. And questions such as whether the adaptation of Western pedagogies is needed and what the potential merits of these pedagogies are in different cultures should be carefully addressed before making the decision to change.

The results of our studies (Li, Rao and Tse, 2011, 2012; Li, Wong, and Wang, 2011) have clear implications. One of them is the framework of "3CAPs": Culturally Appropriate Practice, Contextually Appropriate Practice, and Child Appropriate Practice. Cultural appropriateness should be seriously considered when nations are engaged in importing pedagogical innovations developed in other sociocultural milieus. In addition, our studies highlight the fact that sociocultural perspectives can help educators provide early childhood teaching that recognizes and empowers linguistically and culturally diverse young learners. In fact, there are multiple realities of early childhood, multiple perspectives on early learning, and multiple learners in the early years. Using the Euro-American norms to unify the learning of young children under varying contexts is an absolutely impossible mission, as different contexts have their own definitions and standards of quality and early learning. Successful early childhood pedagogy should be culturally, contextually, and linguistically appropriate. And individual differences should also be included. The *best* pedagogies could be adapted or assimilated into another society but could never be directly transplanted. Again, the best Chinese literacy pedagogy should be a balance of East and West, a mix of direct instruction (formal) and emergent literacy (informal), a blend of phonics and of whole language approaches, and an integration of home and school literacy. The middle way is the best way, says Confucius.

Story-based project approach

Young children and their parents and teachers love to read storybooks. Since the 1990s, many Chinese scholars have tried to conduct a variety of teaching reforms with storybooks as the major focus. They found that the use of storybooks cannot only enhance young children's reading and learning interest, but also fully promote children's cognitive, language, and social and emotional development. In Hong Kong, I developed and published two sets of early Chinese literacy programs that are both based on storybooks. The first was published in 2004 and called the Story Approach to Integrated Learning (SAIL) (Li, Oxford University Press, 2004, 2007, 2013). The second was called the Story-based Project Approach (SPA) and published in 2012 (Li, Oxford University Press, 2012). This chapter will briefly introduce SPA, a fusion of SAIL and the project approach. Chapter 5 will present SAIL in detail. In SPA, every piece of project work is initiated and guided by a storybook, and the learning outcome is also a storybook produced either by a group of children or an individual child. The learning and teaching of Chinese literacy are integrated into the story-based project activities. This subsection introduces the basic ideas and measures of this approach.

The storybook as the best platform for early learning

A storybook for young children could be a simple book with pictures, storylines, themes and learning content. Some are picture books that are basically pictures, supplemented with the very simple text of a story. All of these age-appropriate storybooks are not only easy to understand, but also meet children's developmental needs and learning interests. Young children love reading storybooks, no matter whether they are picture-based or text-oriented. And a perfect children's storybook is a collection of beautiful pictures, beautiful words and stories with some touching moments. They, of course, include rich literary, aesthetic and pedagogical content. These make a storybook the best platform for literacy and visual arts education.

Normally, a good child's storybook could possess as many as eight characteristics such as lovely pictures, beautiful words, educational values, child-centered, communicative, fun, imaginative, creative. These features help to enhance children's language and cognitive development, as well as to facilitate their social and emotional development. Therefore, we believe that the storybook is the best platform for early learning.

The storybook as the best platform for teaching

A good storybook can be a combination of literature, aesthetics and education, and can cover the learning domains of language, social, mathematics, science, humanities, arts, and more. Li (2012) wrote some storybooks using the Theory of Multiple Intelligences (Gardner, 1985) to incorporate the eight multiple intelligences into a series of interesting stories. These storybooks could serve as the best teaching platform for early childhood education.

First, the teaching activities can naturally incorporate different subjects into the theme and subthemes generated from the storybooks. All the important learning domains for young children, such as language and arts, can be promoted through story-telling and story-based exploration. These story-relevant teaching activities can help promote early childhood artistic and personal growth, the social, cultural, natural environment and have lifestyle applications.

Second, an interesting illustrated storybook can provoke children's learning interest and expand child-led thematic exploration activities. Reading these interesting books is like a journey of learning, an adventure of exploration. And these well-written storybooks can provoke children's curiosity and initiate further exploration, through either theme-based learning or a story-led project. The stories can serve as a compass for children's expanded/thematic exploration. During the process, children can rewrite or further develop the story to create an unlimited space to extend their learning and exploration. In this connection, all these story-based learning or explorations can be very integrative, comprehensive and balanced, involving the three dimensions of attitudes, skills, and knowledge (ASK).

Taken together, we strongly believe that the storybook is the best platform for an integrated curriculum, project work, and a child's learning (Li, 2012). Recently, Taiwan and Hong Kong kindergartens have begun to use storybooks as the platform to build up an integrated curriculum to engage young children into interesting learning and exploration. Storybooks have been turned into referenced thematic learning, project-based work, and integrated teaching.

How to conduct a story-based project approach (SPA)

My suggested model for SPA implementation (Li, 2012) could be summarized as three stages, four steps, five common activities, six questions, and seven post-project activities.

Three stages

SPA normally goes through three major stages, with a major task at each stage. The first stage is *initiation*, when teachers use well-chosen storybooks to initiate a brand new project with their children. The storybook can be a triggering device for children's curiosity, learning interest, and project-based exploration. Teaching activities include, but are not limited to, reading aloud the story to children, questioning them about the topics and themes of the story, and provoking their interest to further explore the characters, the topics, and to solve the problems raised either by teacher or children. In this stage, the story is functioning as a provoker of learning interest, a provider of knowledge and concepts, a stimulator of learning motivation, and a call for project-based exploration.

The second stage is *development*, when students have to develop their own "research questions" and project plans, through reading, discussing, observing, interviewing, consulting, online searching, and even field studying. They have to conduct further exploration and research using some learning skills and project-relevant strategies such as reading to learn, writing to express, audio- and video-recording, questioning and interviewing skills. This stage is the critical period of SPA, when the most important learning and knowledge building activities take place. Teachers observe children's learning and exploration, monitor their progress with a focus on pace and speed, and assist them with all needed services, and so on. Parent experts can be called upon for help, especially when the topics are professionally based and complicated. This provides a good opportunity for home-school collaboration and parental involvement.

The third stage is *integration*, when teachers and students work together to conclude what they have explored and learned in the previous two stages and to present their project outcomes as a picture book, a show, a poster, or any other innovative form. SPA starts with a picture book, and ends with a picture book. From the beginning stories to the ending ones, many stories feature project-based and personalized learning and exploration. This stage functions as an assembly of learning and exploration outcomes, and a gala of knowledge building and exchange. It may come in the various forms of project exhibition, such as oral presentation, PowerPoint presentation, posters, shows and plays.

Four steps

It is suggested that SPA is delivered through steps, which are described as follows:

1   Choose a topic. A storybook could cover many topics and themes. Teachers and their young children can discuss and negotiate (in the classroom and right after the storytelling), choosing the interesting topics that have been elicited from the storybook. Each group, or even every single child, can choose the topic that interests them the most and then develop it further in project work.
2   Develop a theme web. As soon as a topic is chosen, young children (and their teachers) can brainstorm about the topic to further develop the theme web. The theme web can be presented in a variety of creative and interesting formats, such as trees, a spider's web, or a fish bone. They will help young children and their teachers to visualize all the interesting subthemes and subtopics in one complete picture. This web could function as a route map for driving in the mountains of knowledge, or a shipping line map for sailing in the seas of concepts, or a scaffold for constructing early learning and teaching. For example, on the theme of "hospital", children can

develop a set of subthemes using the theme web, such as people, facilities, and vehicles. If one group of children is interested in the subtheme of ambulances, they can dig further into this subtheme and "zoom in" to introduce the doors, windows, oxygen cylinder, and different ambulances around the world.

3   Implement the project. As soon as the theme web is done, young children (and their teachers) can start their project work. The exploration will be from the story, by the story, and beyond the story. Young children can go out to visit, observe, survey, interview, and study on the chosen topic. This step comprises a variety of activities including data/information collection, analysis, and presentation with a focus on the chosen topic and the guiding research inquiries.

4   Report the project. This is the fourth step of SPA, when young children gather to present their projects using storybooks, posters, PowerPoint presentations, shows and plays. This step is critical as the projects can demonstrate their understanding and learning of the chosen topic. They can use drawings, digital photos, videotaping, PowerPoint presentations, posters, plays, exhibitions, and other creative methods to visualize their project-based learning outcomes. Teachers can help organize a big exhibition of children's projects in class, even in the kindergarten. Some kindergartens collect and publish these projects, and parents are usually very delighted to be the readers of these publications. This is, per se, an evaluation of children's learning and exploration.

Five common activities

SPA is a story-based project approach, which commonly uses five types of activities: discussing, publishing, surveying, visiting, and showing. In the three stages and four steps, we can use these five kinds of interactive activities to guide young children's exploration. For instance, discussion can be widely used to develop the theme web, to plan the activities, to allocate the workload, and to organize the project work. A variety of posters and PowerPoint presentations can be used to reflect young children's learning and exploration and to report their progress and findings. Surveys, supplemented with some visits, allow young children to gather first-hand knowledge and experience, and facilitate their understanding of the chosen topics. Young children love to perform. Their performance could be presented to their teachers and parents, or even be videotaped or audiotaped.

Six questions

The 5W1H questioning skills should be frequently used in SPA. For example, the background information of a storybook could be gathered with these questions:

1   who? (people);
2   when? (time);
3   where? (place).

And their understanding could be examined with these questions:

4   what? (what to do);
5   why? (reason);
6   how? (what to do/what are the results).

When using the six questions in SPA delivery, teachers must pay attention to the three main points:

1   the creation of a learning atmosphere of freedom and democracy;
2   an open and major question to guide students to think, to explore, and to learn; and
3   the storybook should be interesting and attractive to young children and should have some educational value.

Using "5W1H" in discussion sessions can nurture young children's thoughts, creativity and imagination, making learning more interesting and meaningful.

Seven post-project activities

Project work is not a kind of one-off activity, and should be extended into more meaningful and interesting post-project activities. Li (2012) summarized seven types of post-project activities as follows:

1   Language activities: making simple sentences, words Solitaire, rewriting stories, reading aloud.
2   Math activities: counting, reasoning, or numeracy.
3   Natural observation: observing, recording, or participating in museum or nature visits.
4   Music activities: singing, rhythm, musical instruments and music appreciation, or singing a song about the story.
5   Art and craft: painting to express feelings and ideas.
6   Drama activities: write a play script, role play, or stage play.
7   Follow-up discussion: some follow-up discussion can be conducted to exchange ideas and thoughts, feelings and emotions, for social interaction and group building.

In this way, SPA can transform a storybook into a holistic early childhood education program that can deepen young children's learning and organize their exploration into a project. This kind of project- and story-based learning can be more advanced than passive learning with a traditional pedagogy. As we found in the implementation of SAIL and SPA, these story-based pedagogies can deepen young children's learning and understanding of the topic/theme/subject, resulting in an overall development of the eight multiple intelligences in young children. In addition, SAIL and SPA can be a catalyst for their imagination, creativity, problem-solving ability, active exploration and lifelong learning. Furthermore, with the help of information and communication technologies (ICT), SAIL and SPA can be implemented as a more ICT-based and online-based exploration and learning. Young children's project learning outcomes can also be presented in an e-version, in the Cloud, and even in multimedia. SAIL and SPA will become the best preschool Chinese literacy curriculum, and eventually become the main teaching pedagogy.

Chapter 4

The pedagogy of teaching Chinese as a second language

Teaching Chinese as L1, L2, and even L3 has not only emerged as a subject for research, but also as an educational market globally, as a consequence of the rise of China in the world economy. The ability to speak, read, and write Chinese effectively has been crucial to the success of people in academic, economic, and social realms in many East Asian communities, such as Singapore. The upward trend in the learning of Chinese will no doubt continue in the foreseeable future, due to the continuing engagement of China with the rest of the world. In North America and Europe, the learning of Chinese has been met with great passion and demand by governmental and business entities alike. Accordingly, the central government of China is trying to establish a Confucius Institute to promote Chinese language teaching and learning all over the world. However, pedagogical and curricular studies are far behind the practical needs in teaching Chinese as L2. Therefore, this chapter will fill a large gap by introducing research advancements and practical innovations in teaching Chinese as a second language.

Learning Chinese as L2 rather than L1

With the rise of China in the world economy, learning Chinese as L2 has become a topical issue in Western countries. The question of how Western learners learn to read the logographic writing of Chinese language is very challenging, as it is drastically different from their native languages in orthography. To address this question, Shen (2013) has made a comprehensive review of the existing studies focused on the core issue of Chinese literacy acquisition. To further our understanding of this topic, this section will introduce the cognitive characteristics of reading Chinese as L2, innovative strategies for teaching Chinese literacy, and the effective pedagogies used in Chinese literacy education.

Reading Chinese as L2

Chinese character has three levels of graphic structure: stroke, component (radical), and character configuration (Shen, 2013). L2 learners of Chinese need to process the information of the three-level construction to understand the grapheme of every single Chinese character. As reviewed in Chapter 1, there are three types of processing of Chinese characters: the graphic, the phonological and the semantic. All these processes have very different neurological and psychological features from those used for processing Western languages and reading Chinese is quite different from reading Western languages. It is natural to ask if there is any cross-linguistic transfer of reading skills when reading Chinese as L2. Do they share the same brain network? Are there any universal mechanisms for reading across languages?

Perfetti et al. (2013) believe that there is a universal mechanism for reading across languages, and that some common skills can be transferred. Shen (2013) reviewed the existing studies and found that English-speaking students often encode the structure of compound Chinese characters with familiar codes. Shen and Ke (2007) found that beginner L2 learners could deconstruct compound characters into radicals, and reproduce them, within only a few weeks of exposure to Chinese characters. They believed that the cognitive maturity in perceptual organization and the learning experience of the graphic structure of compound characters contributed to this. This finding implies that adult L2 learners of Chinese are cognitively ready to perceive the internal structure of compound characters, and effective instruction and practice play a key role in the rapid development of perceptual organization skills.

If there is a universal mechanism for reading across languages, it is natural to assume that the L1 and L2 learners of Chinese share the same brain network. Tao and Healy (2009) examined this unitization hypothesis by testing native English, Chinese, and Japanese native speakers who spoke Chinese and English with different levels of fluency. The subjects were asked to read passages in both English and Chinese, as well as to complete English letter and Chinese character component detection. The results suggested that the size of reading units detected increased along with their linguistic knowledge growth, but it was not related to their familiarity with the Chinese writing system. Overall, they found empirical evidence to support the hypothesis of a universal mechanism as proposed by Perfetti et al. (2013).

Zhao et al. (2012) examined the neural basis of phonological processing in Chinese L1 and L2 learners: one group comprised alphabetic language speakers who had learned Chinese as L2 for at least one year, and the control group comprised native Chinese speakers. The neuroimaging results revealed that L2 learners exhibited stronger activation than native Chinese speakers in the right occipitotemporal region (i.e. right lingual gyrus and right fusiform gyrus). Moreover, L2 learners exhibited greater activation in the ventral aspects of the left inferior parietal lobule (LIPL) and the left inferior frontal gyrus (LIFG) for irregular character reading minus regular character reading. The L1 Chinese speakers, however, exhibited more dorsal activation in the LIPL and the LIFG. They used the "accommodation/assimilation" hypothesis of L2 reading to explain these findings and suggested that L2 learners utilized an accommodation pattern for the specific requirements of the visual form of Chinese characters, and an assimilation pattern for orthography-to-phonology transformation in Chinese reading. They believe that this empirical evidence lends support to the hypothesis that there is a cross-language transfer of specific reading skills.

Very recently, Saji and Imai (2013) investigated how adult L2 learners of Chinese acquire and refine word meanings as compared to young L1 children. Learning the full meaning of a word entails learning not just the meaning of the word itself but the meaning of neighboring words and delineating the boundaries among them. The striking finding is that the adult L2 learners imposed the semantic divisions known to them from their first language and failed to appreciate the nuanced meanings understood by Chinese adults. This finding suggests that there is a cross-language influence in lexical learning at the level of the structure of semantic domains. Again, this study provides empirical evidence to support the hypothesis that there is a cross-language transfer of reading skills, especially when learning Chinese as L2.

All these findings can be explained by Language Transfer Theory, which means that learners can make use of the linguistic resources and cognitive patterns available in L1 to learn L2 (Koda, 2008). Learners' reliance on L1 learning knowledge is associated with their insufficient knowledge of L2 rules and an underdeveloped cognitive system in processing the L2. As the linguistic knowledge of Chinese characters and the ability of new cognitive structures to process characters continues to increase, the preference of using L1 experience to aid Chinese character learning gradually decreases (Shen, 2013). This leads us to believe that there might be some similarities and differences in reading Chinese as L1 and L2.

Acquiring Chinese literacy as L2

There is an increasing volume of studies into the acquisition of Chinese literacy in L2 learners. A very early study was done by Everson (1998) to understand the relationship between L2 learners' ability to name Chinese characters and their lexical knowledge. The results indicated a high correlation between capacity to pronounce the characters and the knowledge of their meanings. Further studies (Yang, 2000; Zhao, 2003) confirmed this finding in reading both single-character and multi-character words. It is very important to note that this high correlation was observed only among learners whose L1 was alphabetic and not among Asian learners whose L1 was non-alphabetic, such as Japanese and Korean (Jiang, 2003). These studies indicated that training of sound-to-script correspondence and phonological awareness might be very critical for students whose L1 is alphabetic when they are learning Chinese characters.

Shen (2013) believes that attaining intra-character sensitivity takes time, even though L2 learners can recognize the radical components at the very beginning of their learning. Gao and Meng (2000) reported that the accuracy rate for beginner learners was much lower than that of advanced learners when identifying the shape and structure of similar character substitutes in a reading text.

The beginner learners were insensitive to the subtle differences between similarly-shaped characters and were not accustomed to perceiving stroke-based writing. It has been further confirmed that the acquisition of character sensitivity takes time and improves as the character-learning experience advances (Jackson *et al.* 2003).

Intermediate L2 learners were found to be more capable of using phonetic cues than beginner learners when learning Chinese characters (Jiang and Zhao 2001). Shen and Ke (2007) found that English-speaking L2 learners of Chinese acquired semantic radical knowledge continuously, from beginner to advanced levels. Their knowledge and understanding of the semantic radicals and their roles increased significantly and steadily at each learning stage. And the skilled readers showed a slight predisposition toward semantic over phonetic decoding in lexical decisions (Williams and Bever, 2010), which could be caused by the unreliability of phonetic radicals in cuing the sound of Chinese characters. Furthermore, L2 learners must rely on the semantic decoding of characters to determine the meaning of a specific character or word, as there are so many homophones whose semantic information cannot be distinguished by sound cue alone.

The above studies suggest that L2 learners' phonological and orthographic awareness play an important role in learning to read and write Chinese characters. Compared to English, the nature and the process of developing this awareness in Chinese showed several unique cognitive constraints.

The strategies for learning Chinese as L2

Will L2 learners use different strategies to learn Chinese reading? What are they and what are the most effective strategies? Recent studies have explored these questions. Jiang and Zhao (2001) analyzed the learning strategies used by L2 Chinese beginner learners of varying language backgrounds and found they generally used six types of cognitive strategies and two types of metacognitive strategies. The six cognitive strategies included: (1) studying strokes and writing characters by following the correct stroke order; (2) paying attention to the sound and meaning of characters; (3) understanding the configuration of characters; (4) analyzing radical components; (5) reviewing the characters frequently; and (6) using the learned characters in writing. The two metacognitive strategies were: analyzing their own character-writing errors; and making a plan for character learning.

Shen (2005) studied English-speaking learners from beginner to advanced levels and produced a 59-item inventory of strategies. She found that orthographic knowledge-based strategies were commonly used by L2 learners and included the use of radical information of sound, shape, and meaning as cues to encode characters. A follow-up study (Sung and Wu, 2011) confirmed these findings and further found that gender, native language, and other experiences of learning foreign languages were associated with the preference for using certain character-learning strategies. In addition, it is very interesting to note that female students tended to use mechanical strategies more often than male students. L2 learners with no background of learning any foreign languages tended to pay more attention to the physical shape and structure of characters than the experienced foreign language learners.

Winke and Abbuhl (2007) conducted a qualitative analysis and found that L2 learners use L1 translation to encode the meaning of the character as well as using social strategies such as asking for help from people in the local Chinese community. They also adopted strategies such as flash cards, oral rehearsal, and writing pinyin and characters to facilitate both written and oral production. All these effective strategies are proven to have a positive effect on character learning – helping students identify such strategies and providing strategy training is pedagogically necessary for L2 learners (Shen, 2013).

However, the follow-up question is: are these learning strategies teachable to L2 learners? Liu (2009) found that the L2 learners who received training tended to use more strategies in Chinese literacy learning than those with no training experience. Accordingly, they could significantly reduce the amount of character-writing time during the memorization process. Shen (2011) suggested that Chinese teachers could employ many ways to help L2 learners to identify effective strategies, such as observing their learning behavior, asking them to produce a self-report, and using a questionnaire to find out which strategies students are using and whether they are effective. All these findings jointly support the conclusion that the training of effective learning strategies is useful and necessary. The following sections will further discuss the effective training programs and approaches.

Teaching Chinese as L2

There are many approaches to teaching Chinese as L2, and this section will classify them into two major domains: teaching the reading of Chinese; and teaching the writing of Chinese.

Approaches to teaching Chinese reading

There are many fundamental questions to be addressed regarding the teaching of Chinese reading to L2 learners, such as: what kind of characters should be introduced to L2 learners first for the purposes of teaching efficacy and efficiency? What is the best way to present a Chinese character to a L2 learner? Should L2 learners learn pinyin first? Can ICT be used in learning Chinese literacy? What are the difficulties encountered by L2 Chinese learners? Which teaching approach is the most effective? This section will address these five questions, one by one, in detail.

First, what kind of characters should be introduced to L2 learners first for the purposes of teaching efficacy and efficiency? Xiao (2002) found that character density had a significant effect on character learning among L2 beginning learners of Chinese. Their performance in character recognition, production, and dictation was significantly better for the characters with six strokes or fewer than for those with 12 strokes or more. This effect of stroke number has been reviewed in Chapter 1. Its pedagogical implication is that Chinese textbooks should be designed to arrange lessons on single-component characters before moving on to introducing multicomponent characters (Zhu, 2002). However, it is difficult to put into practice as, for learning purposes, the majority of current textbooks have organized lessons by topics or themes, rather than being structured according to the sequence of character complexity. This requires teachers to incorporate their knowledge of Chinese characters into lesson planning to provide opportunities for students to understand the radical components of characters (Shen, 2013).

Second, what is the best way to present a Chinese character to an L2 learner? There are three components in each character: the grapheme, the phoneme, and the meaning. Normally, in Chinese language learning, the character, its pinyin, and the English translation will be presented to L2 learners simultaneously. Chung (2002), however, found that presenting the grapheme first was better than simultaneous presentation of all three. He found that the optimal presenting order was to show a character to the students for 5 seconds and then to present the pinyin and the English translation. Later, Jin (2006) compared three highlighting conditions as follows:

1 highlighting the configuration/radical of the character only;
2 highlighting the stroke order of the character only; and
3 highlighting the pinyin of the new character only.

The results indicated that the learners demonstrated the best retention of new characters in condition 1, followed by condition 2. Chung (2008) showed that during character presentation, simultaneous provision of visual and audio pronunciation and an English translation helped beginning learners to retain the meaning of characters, and helped advanced learners to retain both pronunciation and meaning significantly better than with visual mode alone. Wu (2012) conducted an experiment over 4 weeks and found that supplying audio for online sentence reading homework significantly enhanced word recognition and recall.

Third, should L2 learners learn pinyin first? Lee and Kalyuga (2011) conducted a separate study to compare the effects of learning pinyin: an instructor either provided the sound of the new characters without presenting the pinyin, or provided the pinyin along with the new characters. The results indicated that presenting pinyin together with the new words helped learners retain these words better if they had reached the level of automatic pinyin reading, but it did not help those who had not mastered the pinyin system. This finding implies that pinyin should be introduced prior to character learning if the instructor wishes to use pinyin as an aid to character pronunciation. Shen (2011) strongly recommended learning pinyin before learning Chinese characters because:

1   it could free up cognitive resources for use;
2   students with a solid knowledge of pinyin are capable of learning new characters more quickly; and
3   a solid knowledge of pinyin would lay a good foundation for producing Chinese text using a word processor.

Fourth, can ICT be used in learning Chinese literacy? Digital vocabulary cards are widely used to help beginner learners, especially when reviewing newly learned characters. Zhu and Hong (2005) and Zhu (2010) demonstrated that learners achieved optimum memorization when reviewing digital vocabulary cards accompanied by pronunciation. McGraw et al. (2009) compared the effectiveness of three computer-manipulated vocabulary learning activities:

1   a speaking mode, in which the learner issued spoken commands to manipulate the vocabulary cards;
2   a listening mode, in which the computer gave spoken directions that learners had to follow by manipulating the cards manually with the mouse; and
3   a more traditional mode, in which the computer presented online flash cards.

The results showed that all three activities were similar in terms of vocabulary retention. However, students reported that they enjoyed the speaking mode of vocabulary activity more than the other modes.

Fifth, what are the difficulties encountered by L2 Chinese learners? Shen (2010) summarized six types of difficulties including those in tone discrimination and memorization, in finding connections between sound, meaning and shape within a radical, in discriminating between radicals with similar sounds, and in the inability to find similar sounds in their native language. Besides this, two major difficulties were reported in learning the shapes of radicals: first, discriminating and memorizing graphically similar radicals and, second, lacking the opportunities or time to practice. Shen (2010) also listed the five effective instructional methods: providing plenty of chances for repeating and reviewing Chinese characters, explaining the meaning or function of radicals, using radicals to teach characters, using play and games to teach radicals, and delivering more activities on radicals.

Last but not least, which teaching approach is the most effective? Shen (2004) compared the effectiveness of rote memorization, self-generated elaboration, and instructor-guided elaboration. Rote memorization was a shallow kind of processing, in which learners were required to repeatedly read aloud the new characters. Student self-generated elaboration was a deeper kind of processing, in which students were encouraged to think of the best way of memorizing the characters themselves. And instructor-guided elaboration was another kind of deeper processing, in which the instructor explained the etymology of the characters, analyzing the radicals and giving examples of using the characters in context. Shen (2004) found that the latter two methods resulted in significantly better performance in character retention than rote memorization. Kuo and Hooper (2004) found similar results when comparing various teaching approaches in a computer-based character instruction class. Therefore, both self-generated and instructor-guided elaboration should be encouraged in teaching Chinese as L2.

In addition, the most effective way is to use multiple sensory modalities in the character-learning process to ensure maximum sensory input and to create a rich and detailed association between the sensory modalities and characters (Chung, 2008; Li and Wu, 1996). Ren (2004) summarized a five-component approach that was more effective than the traditional approach of simple repetition. It included observation (how characters are written), visualization (picture each character), articulation (read each character aloud and explain how it is structured or formed), listening (listen to audio tapes or others saying the character sound), writing and saying (write the characters out one by one and simultaneously say the sound and the meaning of the characters). Wang and Leland (2011) found that the beginning L2 learners found three types of teaching methods particularly helpful:

1 emphasizing the study of individual characters strengthened their orthographic knowledge;
2 using characters in context supported their learning of the meaning and pronunciation of the characters; and
3 practicing the characters through cooperative learning helped create a good learning environment.

Effective ways of teaching Chinese handwriting

As indicated by the existing behavioral and neuroimaging studies, learning to read Chinese depends on writing (refer to Chapter 2 for a detailed review). But it has been hotly debated whether L2 beginning learners should take the time and effort to learn Chinese handwriting.

Those who propose this method hold the belief that learning to write characters remains important in learning Chinese reading. A recent study (Guan *et al.* 2011) found that beginning learners who practiced handwriting characters had a significant increase in the performance of character recognition and lexical decision tasks compared to those who did not. Previous behavioral studies yielded the same findings. Flores d'Arcais (1994), for example, found that practicing handwriting characters facilitated character memorization. Liu and Jiang (2003) found that using an effective way of practicing character handwriting – such as asking learners to recall the mental image of a character first before copying it – helped students to think thoroughly about the strokes, radicals, and configuration of the characters, as well as to enhance the memorization of characters. Therefore, although practicing handwriting characters is time-consuming, it is pedagogically necessary for L2 learners in learning characters. This practice strengthens orthographic knowledge, such as knowledge of radicals and character structure, and enhances character memorization and retention (Shen, 2013).

Opponents of this approach, however, argue that learning to handwrite characters might take too much time away from the practice of other linguistic skills, such as listening and speaking, and is therefore a waste of time. Software can facilitate Chinese writing and learning to handwrite Chinese characters (Allen, 2008). The prevalent input method used in typing Chinese characters is the pinyin input method. After inputting a pinyin, a list of characters with the same pronunciation pops up, from which the user can choose the intended one. In this scenario, the stroke, radical, or configuration knowledge might not be needed to type a target character or word.

In summary, teaching Chinese literacy to L2 learners should help them develop an effective cognitive system to identify the three linguistic components of the characters (sound, shape, and meaning) and to make a meaningful connection between the three (Shen, 2013). Attention should be paid to foster learners' metalinguistic awareness of syllables and characters and use multicognitive modalities to allow deeper processing of the learning materials. Moreover, learning pinyin from the beginning and continual practice of the handwriting of Chinese characters will facilitate the learning of Chinese reading. Of course, appropriate use of information and communication technologies can maximize the effectiveness of teaching Chinese.

The TPR approach to Chinese literacy

The ultimate goal of teaching Chinese literacy to L2 learners is to enable them to read and write Chinese freely. Therefore, the automatic recognition and production of Chinese characters is a prerequisite for Chinese reading and writing. But learning characters is not an easy job, and the major challenge for Chinese teachers is to develop a balanced curriculum to achieve the pedagogical goals of character learning within a limited learning period. To help Chinese teachers solve this challenging problem, we developed and published the Total Physical Response Chinese literacy program (Li and Wu, 1996), which has been widely used in Singapore and Hong Kong. This program was developed based on the theory of Total Physical Response developed by James Asher (1977).

What is Total Physical Response?

Total Physical Response (TPR) is a language teaching method developed by James Asher (1977), built around the coordination of speech and action, which draws on various language learning theories and pedagogical innovations. Asher

(1977) developed TPR in an attempt to teach language through physical motor activity, linking this to the "trace theory" of memory in psychology. This theory holds that the more often or the more intensively a memory connection (conditioning) is traced, the stronger the memory association will be and the more likely it will be recalled. Retracing can be done either verbally by rote repetition or in association with motor activity. In the 1970s, educational psychologists tended to believe that the combination of verbal rehearsal and motor activity could increase the probability of successful recall. This basic understanding of learning and memory laid the first theoretical foundation for the TPR approach.

The second theoretical foundation comes from L2 language learning. Asher (1977) regarded successful adult L2 learning as a parallel process to child first language acquisition – L2 teaching could simply follow the basic rules of L1 learning. For example, the teacher can use direct speech and commands to ask young children to respond physically and repeatedly and to establish the memory connection (retracing or conditioning). As soon as the connection is set up, children can produce their verbal responses. Asher believed that adult L2 learning should be a recapitulation of the processes of L1 children acquiring their mother tongue. Asher emphasized the development of comprehension skills before the learner was taught to speak, and that the physical movement could serve as the link between L2 language and learner's mental concepts. Accordingly, Asher made several proposals about comprehension-based language teaching:

1   comprehension abilities precede productive skills in learning a language;
2   the teaching of speaking should be delayed until comprehension skills are established;
3   skills acquired through listening are transferrable to other skills;
4   teaching should emphasize meaning rather than form; and
5   teaching should minimize learner stress.

The emphasis on comprehension and the use of physical actions to teach L2 at an introductory level has become the icon of the TPR approach.

The third foundation came from Asher's special understanding of the verb, and particularly the verb in the imperative form, as the central linguistic motif around which language use and learning are organized (1977). He classified language into abstract and non-abstract (these being most specifically represented by concrete nouns and imperative verbs). He believed that learners could acquire a "detailed cognitive map" as well as "the grammatical structure of a language" without recourse to abstractions. This verb prioritization and the associated verb-based L2 teaching are especially suitable to the learning and teaching of Chinese, which is regarded as a "verb-biased" language (Tse and Li, 2011).

The fourth foundation comes from Asher's three influential learning hypotheses:

1 everyone has a specific innate bio-program for language learning, which defines an optimal path for L1 and L2 language development;
2 the human brain has areas which account for different learning functions and collaboration of the left- and right-brain hemispheres will facilitate language learning;
3 stress (an affective filter) intervenes between the act of learning and what is to be learned, the lower the stress, the greater the learning (Richards and Rodgers, 2001).

These hypotheses might not be scientifically sound, but have been found to be very useful in teaching L2 learners.

All these strategies have been employed in our Chinese TPR program (Li and Wu, 1996). Our program is consistent with the current neuroscience theory of the acquisition of semantics proposed by Lakoff in linguistics and by Alex Martin in neuroscience ("the sensory-motor theory of meaning/semantics") (Tan, personal communication, April 29, 2008). Its central assumption is that conceptual/semantic knowledge about objects and words is organized by sensory features (e.g. form, motion, color, smell, taste) and functional properties (the motor habits related to their use, the typical location where they may be found, their social value, etc.). Object/word knowledge is organized as a distributed system in which the attributes of an object/word are stored close to the regions of the cortex that mediate perception of those attributes. Thought is embodied; that is, the structures used to put together our conceptual systems grow out of bodily experience and make sense in terms of it. Moreover, the core of our conceptual systems is directly grounded in perception, body movement, and experience of the physical and social order (Lakoff, 1987).

How to do TPR

Asher's (1977) TPR is a "natural method", which argues that L1 and L2 language learning should be viewed as parallel processes and that L2 teaching should reflect the naturalistic processes of L1 learning. The TPR movement of the body serves as a powerful mediator for the understanding, organization and storage of the macro-details of linguistic input. Language can be internalized in chunks, but alternative strategies must be developed for fine-tuning the macro-details.

Common activities

Imperative drills are the major classroom activity in TPR – teachers frequently use imperatives to elicit physical actions and activities on the part of the learners. Conversational dialogues are delayed until after about 120 hours of instruction. Asher's rationale for this is that as everyday conversations are highly abstract and disconnected, understanding them requires a rather advanced internalization of the target language (Asher, 1977). Other class activities include role-plays and slide presentations. Role-plays center on everyday situations, such as at the restaurant, supermarket, or gas station. Slide presentations are used to provide a visual center for teacher narration, which is followed by commands and questions to students such as, "Who is this?" and "Where is Dad?" Reading and writing activities may also be employed to further consolidate structures and vocabulary, and as follow-ups to oral imperative drills.

Learner roles

Learners in TPR have the primary roles of being the listener and the performer. Young children need to listen attentively and respond physically to the commands given by the teacher. They are required to respond both individually and collectively, but they have little influence over the content of their learning, which is determined by the teacher. Sometimes young learners are also expected to recognize and respond to novel combinations of the previously taught items. Novel utterances are re-combinations of constituents the teacher has used directly in training. For instance, the teacher can direct students with "Walk to the table!" and "Sit on the chair!" These are familiar to the students since they have practiced responding to them. But young children need to understand if you surprise them with an unfamiliar utterance created by recombining familiar elements (e.g. "Sit on the table!"). They are also required to produce novel combinations of their own. In this way, learners monitor and evaluate their own progress. They are encouraged to speak when they feel ready to speak – that is, when they have sufficiently internalized the language.

Teacher roles

The teacher plays an active and direct role in TPR. As Asher (1977) said, "the instructor is the director of a stage play in which the students are the actors" (p. 43). In TPR it is the teacher who decides what to teach, who models and presents the new materials, and who selects supporting materials for classroom use. The teacher is encouraged to be well-prepared and well-organized so that the lesson flows smoothly and predictably. Asher recommended detailed lesson plans, believing it is wise to write out the exact sentences that will be used, and especially the new commands, because the action is so fast-moving that there is usually no time for the teacher to create spontaneously. Classroom interaction and turn-taking is teacher, rather than learner, directed. Even when young children interact with other learners it is usually the teacher who initiates the interaction.

How to do Chinese TPR

We have developed Chinese TPR program to teach literacy to young or L2 learners (Li and Wu, 1996). This program features a five-step teaching model,

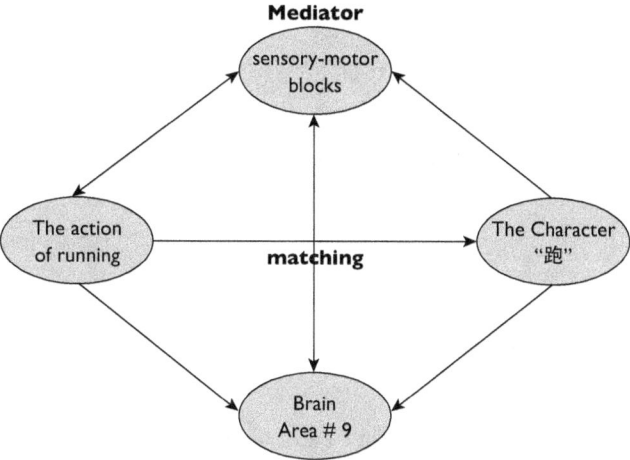

Figure 4.1 The neuropsychological mechanism of Chinese TPR

10 typical learning activities, and 90 well-planned lessons. It was widely used in Hong Kong and Singapore kindergartens in the 1990s.

The neuropsychological mechanism of Chinese TPR

As shown in Figure 1, when a teacher presents the Chinese character 跑 (which means "run'), he or she will make the action of running to indicate the meaning of the target character, and ask students to join the "running" activity. In this way, the sensory-motor activities (i.e. running) are functioning as the mediator between the associated brain areas (i.e. BA 9 in Chinese reading). The acquisition of Chinese conceptual/semantic knowledge about objects and words is organized by sensory-motor features (e.g. form, motion, color, smell, and taste) and their functional properties (the motor habits related to their use, typical location where they may be found, their social value, etc.). Chinese word knowledge is organized as a distributed system in which the attributes of an object are stored close to the regions of the cortex that mediate the perception of those attributes. TPR activities (e.g. running) play an important role in the formulation of the neural connection for the Chinese character – 跑. Whenever and wherever young learners encounter this character, they will link it with the action of running, as both are organized by the same sensory-motor features and stored in the neighboring brain areas.

The five-step teaching model of Chinese TPR

As shown in Figure 2, every Chinese TPR lesson will go through the following five typical steps:

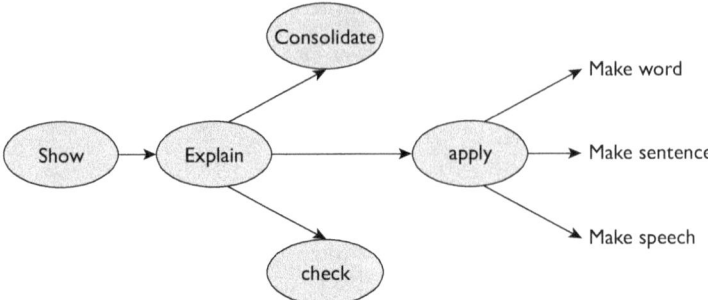

Figure 4.2 The five-step teaching of Chinese TPR

1 Show the word/character. The target Chinese character or word will be shown to the learners clearly and directly, using flash cards or PowerPoint slides. The card should be large enough to guarantee it is visible to every learner in the class.
2 Explain the word/character. The teacher will use physical or sensory-motor activities to indicate the meaning of the target character/word. Learners will have to guess and get the real meaning of the concept.
3 Consolidate the word/character. The teacher will use varying games and activities to present the target word/character to consolidate the linkage between the word and its meaning/action. Variations could be used to clearly define the real meaning of the target character/word/concept. For example, the teacher can do jumping, running, and walking to indicate to learners that only the action of running refers to 跑 in Chinese.
4 Check the learning. It is a natural follow-up of Step 3, and sometimes difficult to differentiate from it. The teacher needs to use varying games and activities to check whether learners have acquired the target character/word/concept correctly. Variations and changes will be employed to test whether the learners can differentiate the target character/word/concept from similar ones.
5 Apply the character/word/concept. The teacher will ask learners to use the target character to make a word, sentence, or speech. In this way, young learners will have opportunities to practice what they have learned. The practical use of Chinese characters and words is the final but the most critical stage of the acquisition of Chinese literacy.

Ten commonly used activities

Our Chinese TPR program has ten commonly used activities as follows:

1 body movements: many verbs or action-relevant Chinese character/word can be taught through body movements;

2 picture show: most nouns or object-related Chinese words can be taught using pictures, photos, and videos, which provide authentic information about the target object;
3 step on: learners can step on the target cards of the Chinese character/word as a response to the teacher's instruction. This is normally used to check the learning outcome;
4 toss up: the Chinese character/words are written on the six sides of a paper box and the learners have to take turns in tossing the box up and reading aloud the character/word on the top. This is frequently used in Steps 3 and 4;
5 tap and say: a group of Chinese characters/words are written on the blackboard and young learners take turns to go and tap the target ones;
6 crossword puzzle: the teacher can mix up the radicals of some Chinese characters and invite young learners to recode them into the target characters and even words;
7 rhythm and poem: write a child's rhythm or poem using the target Chinese characters and words and ask the learners to recite them to the class;
8 sing and say: to make the recitation more interesting and easier to remember, the teacher can use the melody of some children's or pop songs to sing the rhythm and the poem;
9 see and say: sometimes the teacher can use the real object to show the meaning of the target Chinese character/word; for example, a fish to show the meaning of 鱼. Young learners love to see real foods and voice out their names;
10 role play: this is the most interesting activity for young children, who are very engaged by role play in a supermarket, a restaurant, a post office, and a police station, and so on. Teachers and students can use the target Chinese characters/words in the role play, and learning is naturally taking place when playing with these cards and words.

We have tried out all of these activities in Beijing, Hong Kong and Singapore, and found that this Chinese TPR program was very well-received by young L2 learners in Singapore.

Common pedagogies shared by L1 and L2 classrooms

We have observed a common pattern in the Chinese literacy pedagogies shared by L1 and L2 teachers in Shenzhen and Singapore kindergartens (Li, 2013): whole-class direct instruction and interaction, lecturing with questioning, no play, shared reading and writing, reading aloud, language and content knowledge as the foci for instruction, preference for neutral feedback to probe children's thinking and learning, and short oral answer and sustained oral text as the dominating learning outcome. Part of these findings has already been reported by previous researchers (Li and Rao, 2000, 2005; Li, Tse, and Rao, 2012; Liu *et al.* 2005; Wu *et al.* 1999). This section will provide a comprehensive picture of actual Chinese literacy pedagogy in L1 and L2 early childhood classrooms. Understanding this pedagogy might have implications for teaching innovations and education reforms in other countries, such as the USA, where Chinese is taught as L2 by teachers directly "imported" from China.

Traditional Chinese literacy pedagogies in L1 and L2 classrooms

We have found that although Western ideas had been widely advocated and a balanced approach was well-received by Chinese practitioners, traditional direct teaching of Chinese literacy skills is still the core code (Li, 2013). This is in line with our previous findings (Li, Rao, and Tse, 2011, 2012; Li, Wang, and Wong, 2011), which have been interpreted using Bronfenbrenner's (1979) ecological system theory. At the macrosystem level, Chinese traditional culture has had a profound influence on the ideological and philosophical bases of reading pedagogy, including the views of young children, the views of learning and development, and the views of appropriate teacher-child relationships (Li, Rao, and Tse, 2012). At the microsystem level, Chinese literacy pedagogy may be influenced by the psycholinguistic features of Chinese language learning – as Chinese logographic characters denote meaning rather than phonology, rote learning and copying exercise are needed in learning the reading of Chinese (Tan *et al.* 2005). In addition, there are other constraints at the microsystem level in Shenzhen and Singapore, such as large class sizes, a teacher-centered classroom setting, untrained teachers, parental expectations, an examination-oriented system, and the competition for survival arising out of the increasing commercialization of the early childhood education system (Ang, 2008; Li, Rao, and Tse, 2012). For instance, it was reported by the teachers that most Chinese parents were very concerned about their children's academic achievement and wanted them to learn more Chinese characters to better prepare for primary school. To accommodate these highly demanding parents, all of the Chinese teachers interviewed in the present study agreed to use exams to assess students' literacy attainment. This has further promoted the overuse of rote learning and copying exercises in Chinese literacy classes.

Emerging changes in Chinese literacy pedagogy

A remarkable belief–practice divide was also found in our study: both the L1 and L2 Chinese teachers commonly reported that they believed in the balanced approach, a mixture of traditional Chinese literacy pedagogies and Western pedagogies (Li, 2013). However, although they were cognizant of the importance of child-centered learning and other Western ideas, the Chinese teachers ultimately subscribed to the importance of direct instruction for literacy learning and gave children many copying and reading exercises. This belief–practice divide has been repeatedly reported by numerous researchers into early childhood teaching in Hong Kong and mainland China (Cheng, 2001; Li, Wang, and Wong, 2011; Liu and Feng, 2005; Ng and Rao, 2008; Zhu and Zhang, 2008). Ng and Rao (2008) suggested three ways to understand this belief–practice divide in early Chinese pedagogies:

1   Chinese teachers were influenced by their cultural beliefs and their own early childhood learning experiences;
2   the teachers may be caught in a transitional period of education reform; and
3   the pressure from parents and primary schools may have a substantial influence on teachers' practices.

This means that teachers will not necessarily apply theory to practice as they are expected to (Bae-Suh, 2007) as they are strongly influenced by their teaching culture, beliefs, and parental expectations. If they want to change the teaching culture at a personal level, they have to go through the seven stages: examination, preparation, engagement, adjustment, acceptance, advocacy, and projection (Pope and O'Sullivan, 1998). According to this framework, the Chinese teachers interviewed in this study were just in the first three stages and had not achieved the level of adjustment (Stage 4) which means "fit between context and culture" (p. 223).

Nevertheless, some emerging changes and societal differences have been noted in the present study. For example, the Chinese teachers frequently used questioning and individual interactions, as well as positive and neutral feedback to encourage child-initiated learning and theme-based explorations. Some societal differences were also found in the classroom observations: pedagogies transplanted from the West, such as the project approach, a whole language approach, and the TPR approach were used in Singapore kindergartens to teach Chinese literacy. But in Shenzhen more traditionally Chinese pedagogies such as shared reading, theme-based teaching, and intuitive instructions still dominated the classrooms. These findings indicated that Singapore Chinese teachers may be more likely to adopt Western pedagogies.

Same language, different problems

Li (2013a) found that the difficulties encountered in L1 literacy classrooms included having large class sizes (too many students to teach), an absence of good literacy textbooks (the listen-and-read textbook is boring), few opportunities to teach literacy, too many individual differences to teach, and having weak/no parental involvement. These problems stemmed from the policies and regulations enacted in mainland China. For example, kindergartens are not allowed to teach literacy or use textbooks, and no subject teaching is allowed (Li and Rao, 2000; Li, Rao, and Tse, 2011). There are neither official textbooks nor guidelines in respect of these, so the published textbooks in the market are not reviewed or rated by the educational authorities. In addition, kindergarten class sizes can be large, with as many as 35 students in a 4-year-old classroom and 40 students in a 5-year-old classroom (Li, Rao, and Tse, 2011). Some parents teach children reading and writing at home, whereas others do not, leading to greater individual differences among the children. Therefore, to improve children's Chinese language learning, the L1 teachers in Shenzhen suggested including: more teaching of literacy skills; more interesting, interactive and multisensory activities and stories; and to strike a better balance between the quantity and quality of children's learning experiences. That being said, it is time for the educational authorities to rethink the policies regarding the teaching and learning of Chinese literacy to young children.

The L2 teachers in Singapore encountered a different set of problems: lack of a Chinese language environment, lack of support from demanding parents, incapable and unmotivated children from varying backgrounds, and a lack of professionalism amongst the teachers. All of these problems were caused by the bilingual education policies in Singapore. Singapore launched the compulsory bilingual education policy half a century ago and has successfully made English the first and national language for every child. Now, in other studies of this project, we found that most of the Singapore Chinese parents don't speak Chinese to their children at home, and teachers who were not responsible for a Chinese class did not speak Chinese in school. Without the language environment and support from parents, Chinese children have neither interest nor incentive to learn Chinese literacy. This helps explain why Shenzhen teachers were able to involve parents in children's literacy learning (and they want even more parental involvement), whereas very few teachers in Singapore could do so. Although Singapore parents have high expectations of their children's Chinese literacy, they do not speak Chinese at home, and the Chinese teachers have few opportunities and little time to teach their children. Therefore, to provoke and nurture children's learning interest, Singapore teachers suggested more play and better classroom settings, more daily life activities in the textbooks, more literacy learning materials included in the project approach activities, more interesting and age appropriate activities and stories, and better training (Li, 2013).

In addition to the language policies, language proficiency may also play an important role in the different problems of L1 and L2 teaching. For example, this study found some individual learning activities in L1 in Shenzhen, but nothing in L2 in Singapore. This might be related to the fact that Singapore kindergarten children are not good enough in Chinese literacy to conduct individual learning and that the teaching time for Chinese is very limited. Similarly, the other finding that the Shenzhen teachers used more positive feedback than their counterparts in Singapore did (42.6 per cent versus 19.9 per cent) might also be associated with the difference in Chinese proficiency between their students. As reported, the Singapore teachers were not satisfied with their students' learning motivation and performance, thus made fewer positive responses. All these findings imply that the educational authorities need to change the bilingual education policy as soon as possible to create a better bilingual learning environment, and should consider treating Chinese as a mother tongue language (rather than L2) for the ethnic Chinese in Singapore.

Reform leaders and policymakers need to articulate a coherent vision shared by all the stakeholders and to jointly explore the contextually appropriate way to teach Chinese as L2. Contextual appropriateness should be seriously considered when nations engage in importing Chinese teachers and their pedagogies from China. It is important to note that the best pedagogies for early Chinese literacy could be adapted from China, but could never be directly transplanted. Successful early literacy pedagogies, whether for L1 and L2 learning, should be contextually and linguistically appropriate. It is a pity that the landscape of ECE in China and Singapore has been standardized and homogenized by Western views and "universalized" in a narrow way (Tzuo, 2011). It is time for the policy makers, scholars, and practitioners in Chinese, and even Asian, countries to pay more attention to their own cultural beliefs and teaching practices and protect and pass on this "endangered educational ecology" (Tobin, 2011, p. 3) to the next generation. Nevertheless, we will discuss in detail the teaching of Chinese literacy in the early years in mainland China, Hong Kong and Singapore in Chapter 5.

Chapter 5

Teaching Chinese literacy in early childhood settings

Previous chapters have addressed the theoretical issues in early Chinese literacy education; this chapter will focus on practical matters in the field. Many sociocontextual factors are associated with the practice; namely, sociolinguistic environment, school type, program, curriculum, pedagogy, and so on. In this globalized era, early childhood education is also globalized and even "Americanized", something that refers to a trend around the world to emulate American culture and quality standards (Li and Wang, 2014). This Americanization trend has been challenged by early childhood practitioners and researchers (Li, Rao, and Tse, 2012), as many of the imported pedagogies or programs are in conflict with the indigenous cultures, beliefs, education systems and languages of the host country (Rogoff, 2003; Tobin, 2007). For example, Chinese parents with a Confucian heritage highly value discipline, self-control, working hard, early learning and academic achievement, and the Chinese language has a very demanding orthography to learn (Li *et al.* 2008; Li, Rao, and Tse, 2012). The cultural differences are so prominent that a very careful consideration of local culture and tradition is needed when incorporating Western pedagogies into Chinese classrooms. Tobin (2007) believes that cultural differences are vital in shaping the norms of teaching and learning (Tobin, 2007) as well as the trajectories of literacy development in the early years (Aram and Korat, 2010). All these new understandings urge a systematic review and empirical studies of early literacy practices in different Chinese communities. This chapter, therefore, sets out to investigate how early literacy is actually taught in three Chinese cities: monolingual mainland China, trilingual Hong Kong, and multilingual Singapore. We specifically examined the pedagogical practices of early literacy in the cities, in 1998 and 2008, to provide empirical evidence which reflected the influences of imported ideas on the practices of teaching Chinese literacy in different sociolingual contexts.

The practice of Chinese literacy teaching in mainland China

We conducted empirical studies in Beijing (the political and economic center of China) and Shenzhen (a good Chinese match for Hong Kong, with great geographical and economical similarities) during the past two decades to understand the different practices of teaching Chinese literacy in China. The two cities share the same official spoken (Putonghua) and written language (simplified Chinese characters), which have been instituted since 1956 by the central government. The Chinese characters which are taught are based on Putonghua, which originated from the Beijing dialect, and these have been used as the national standard spoken language since 1924 (Zhou, 1986). In mainland China, young children begin learning to read in Primary 1 with Roman alphabets, *Hanyu Pinyin*, rather than with Chinese characters, which might be a surprise to Western researchers (Ingulsrud and Allen, 1999).

Chinese literacy education

In 1956, the Ministry of Education of China issued the document, *Resolution of Reforming the School System*, and ruled out the teaching of both reading and writing Chinese characters from early childhood curriculum (Li, 2000). Despite repeated requests from academics and parents to review this policy, the educational authorities still follow this directive. But the parents and teachers in Beijing and Shenzhen have started the teaching of reading, and even writing, of Chinese characters in the early years (Li, 2000; Li and Rao, 2005; Li, Rao, and Tse, 2011). It is commonly observed that the school education policies of China have been influenced by those in the former Soviet Union during the 1950s and 1970s (Hayhoe, 1984) and by the USA since the 1980s (Li and Li, 2003). The early childhood curriculum is no exception. Over the three decades between 1954 and 1980, the teacher-directed and subject-based instructionism curriculum was imported from the Soviet Union and was widely used in China. As with its role model, early literacy teaching was also prohibited in China. Reminiscent of Elkind's (2001) position of "much too early", the government viewed early literacy teaching as a waste of time and was concerned that it would be counterproductive when children were not "ready" for literacy learning. Hence, it advocated the policy of waiting until children are at least 6 years old before embarking on formal literacy instruction. Now, we understand that the Chinese language has a much more difficult orthography that demands early learning and more reading and writing practice in the early years, whereas Russian has a very regular orthography that could be acquired very easily and quickly in the primary years. Language makes a difference in early literacy education policy and should be taken into consideration.

Accompanying the large-scale reforms in politics, economics and education in China, a set of reforms in the field of early childhood education commenced in the early 1980s. The reform documents promoted an integrated early childhood curriculum and criticized the subject-based curriculum (Li and Li, 2003). The *Regulations on Work in Kindergartens* issued by the China State Educational Committee in 1989 reinforced the notion of an integrated curriculum, advocated play-based learning, and denounced the explicit teaching of academic skills (China Pre-school Education Research Society, 1999). Some of the principles that underlie the approaches recommended by the *Regulations* are rooted in Western views of early pedagogy and are not consistent with traditional Chinese beliefs about early learning. For example, Chinese has emphasized rote learning and the teacher has typically been a transmitter of knowledge rather than a facilitator of learning. Early childhood educators experienced difficulties in implementing the *Regulations* because they were not accompanied by practical guidelines and because many of the regulations were inconsistent with traditional practices and beliefs about early learning (Wang and Mao, 1996). Hence, between 1990 and 2000, Chinese early childhood educators were in a transition phase and had difficulties embracing new ideas in their practice (Li and Li, 2003).

The National Curriculum Guide (NCG) issued by the China National Education Council in 1992 asserted that the teaching of Chinese characters is the duty of primary school teachers (Wu *et al.* 1999). By the end of the six years of primary education, students are expected to have mastered 3,000 characters. The literacy education policy in today's China is still rooted in the "readiness view" of literacy development. The readiness view assumes that physical and neurological maturation alone prepares the child to take advantage of instruction in reading and writing Chinese. It implies that until children reach a certain stage of maturity (i.e. about age 6 or 7, when children enter primary school), all exposure to reading and writing is a waste of time or even potentially harmful.

In 2001, the Ministry of Education issued the *Guidance for Kindergarten Education* (GOC, 2001). The document provides advice to early childhood educators in order to bridge the gap between the progressive ideas and actual practice in preschools. Detailed suggestions, accompanied by specific requirements for content in five domains of development (health, language, society, science, and art) are provided. Accordingly, many imported pedagogies and programs, such as those based on Montessori, High/Scope, and Reggio Emilia, have been promoted in China. But the early childhood educators in China were not ready for the adoption of these Western pedagogies and have encountered many challenges and difficulties (Li, Wang, and Wong, 2011).

Classroom observations in 1998 and 2008

To understand how Chinese literacy is delivered in the early years, we observed Beijing and Shenzhen kindergarten classrooms in 1998 and 2008. These observations indicated that some Beijing and Shenzhen kindergartens were using traditional pedagogies to teach Chinese literacy. The following excerpts of the written transcripts were quoted from Li and Rao (2005) and Li, Rao and Tse (2012), respectively, which reflect the different classroom contexts in Beijing (1998) and Shenzhen (2008).

K3 Class (5–6 years) observed in Beijing (1998)

Teacher A2:   Please take out your textbook, put it on your table, and look at Lesson 3.

[The children took out their colorful textbook and opened the page at Lesson 3. The textbook, *Listen and Read Approach to Chinese Literacy*, is produced and published by a commercial organization. Familiar words are repeated in different sentences to form a simple poem or story.]

Teacher A2: Now, please listen to the tape carefully. Try your best to point with your finger at each character as it is read.

[The children put their fingers on the first character of Lesson 3 and waited for the tape to start. The teacher switched on a cassette player. Only some children pointed to the correct character.]

Teacher A2: Now, please point to the correct characters and read aloud with the audiotape.

[The children listened to the audiotape, pointed to the text and read aloud. All the children repeated the correct words, even those who pointed to the wrong character. The teacher walked around the tables to help these children put their fingers on the correct character.]

We interviewed the teacher after the observation, and she claimed that this was not the teaching of Chinese reading, but a listening activity. She explained that this activity was to establish the associations between hearing, pointing and reading aloud. However, our observation indicated that this teacher was indeed teaching (pre)reading skills, using the traditional "read-aloud approach". All the children were asked to point to the characters when they read the words aloud. This approach is very traditional but was very popular in mainland China in the late 1990s, and is still widely used in kindergartens today.

K3 Class (5–6 years) observed in Shenzhen (2008)

The children sit in the chair while the teacher (T2) sits in the front, holding a big book and facing the children.

T2: Look at the cover of this book! What is the topic?
All: Birthday Balloon. [The students read aloud the title of the book]
T2: Yes! It is about birthday and balloon.
S1: Birthday present!
T2: How did you know? You didn't raise your hands. I will invite those who raised their hands. S2, Tell me whose birthday it is!
S2: The mouse's birthday!
T2: Look at this! [All: Front cover!] And this? [All: Back cover!] And this? [All: Head page!]
T2: Yes, what is the necessary information on the head page? Tell me! Hands up! S3!
S3: Birthday Balloon.
T2: You mean the title of the book. Yes, right. And more? S4!
S4: The name of the author.
T2: Very good! Yes, the author. And more? S5!
S5: The name of the company who made this book.

90 Teaching Chinese in the Early Years

T2: It is called "Publisher"! Look at here! It says "All rights reserved". It means that they own the copyright. If somebody makes an illegal copy, they must be punished. Ok, let's get to know the characters in this story. The first one is –
Ss: Kangaroo!
[The teacher then goes through the story book, page by page, with many questions and explanations. The students follow the teacher and answer all her questions, in a large group, with occasional hot discussion about some uncertain answers.]

This transcript shows that the teacher was using a big-book approach to teach reading skills. Although the teacher was successful in engaging all the children in question-and-answer interactions and the literacy learning activities, she was nevertheless using traditional Chinese pedagogy. All the activities in the above scenario were carried out in a class, with all the children answering the same questions and being involved in the same activity directed by the teacher. In this manner, the teacher was transmitting literacy knowledge to the whole class through direct instruction and questioning.

Coincidentally, the two observations (with a ten-year interval), jointly indicated that Chinese kindergarten teachers tended to use traditional Chinese pedagogies to teach early literacy. Direct instruction, whole class teaching, and some teacher-student interactions through questioning, might be the major pedagogical features of early Chinese literacy classrooms in China.

The practice of Chinese literacy teaching in Hong Kong

Hong Kong is a typical biliterate and trilingual community (Li and Rao, 2000). Chinese and English are the official languages and Cantonese is spoken by over 90 per cent of the population. The importance of Putonghua has markedly increased during this decade, with the handover of the sovereignty from the United Kingdom (UK) to the PRC in 1997. A child growing up in Hong Kong will primarily speak Cantonese at home and with friends and will have to learn to read and write complex Chinese characters and English alphabets upon entering the nursery class of a kindergarten at age 3. In most of the kindergartens, children will also have to learn Putonghua either in an immersion curriculum or in a separate class.

Chinese literacy education in Hong Kong

The *Manual of Kindergarten Practice* issued by the Hong Kong government (Education Department, 1984) provided guidelines on general curriculum aims, teaching principles, program planning, organization and content, as well as recommendations for the schedule, organization of space, basic furniture and teaching resources. The first edition of *Guide to the Pre-primary Curriculum* was published by the Hong Kong Government in 1996 (Education Department, 1996). This is a common curriculum guide for both kindergartens and child care centers, which recognizes that "education" and "care" cannot be separated in the provision of services for young children (Rao et al. 2003). The Guide promotes a child-centered approach and stresses the all-round development of children. It espouses contemporary views on effective early teaching and learning and provides suggestions for facilitating intellectual, communication, personal, physical, and aesthetic development.

But Hong Kong parents desired early literacy acquisition and English learning. Kindergartens understood that English is required in primary school, and therefore taught it in the early years as a form of preparation (Wong and Rao, 2004). This emphasis on the early beginnings of literacy acquisition has resulted in the use of teaching practices suited to school children or adults, but unsuitable for preschoolers. Such practices include extensive whole-group instruction and intensive drilling and rote memorization of isolated skills for groups or individuals (Ho and Bryant, 1997b; Law, 1999; Opper, 1992). Without sufficient education and professional training, most of the teachers did not have adequate knowledge and skills regarding language development and literacy teaching to enable them to help all children become successful readers. In response to this, the educational authorities in Hong Kong expressed concern that some kindergartens had gone too far in using a formal academic curriculum, using inappropriate teaching methods for children below the age of 6 (Rao, 2002).

Hence in 1999, the Education Department published a list of "Dos and Don'ts" for kindergartens (Education Department, 1999). The list of "Dos" includes: having a curriculum that covers moral, cognitive, physical, social, and aesthetic aspects of development by organizing activities that promote all-round development; organizing various child-centered learning activities; using the mother-tongue as the language of instruction; and respecting individual differences. The vast majority of the Hong Kong population speaks Cantonese as their first language, but parents also want their children to learn English. A common practice in Hong Kong is to learn Cantonese and English simultaneously, but this has so far resulted in poor standards in both languages. Against this background, the list of "Dos and Don'ts" points out that focusing on separate language development can help to improve the situation. The list suggests that parents and teachers should not teach the writing of Chinese characters before children are aged 4 and that, if teaching the writing to the children of 4 years or older, do not do mechanical copying exercises, do not do one-way lecturing, and do not design a difficult curriculum which focuses on academic achievement.

In 2000, the Education Commission put forward proposals to enhance the professional competence of early childhood educators, improve quality assurance, reform the monitoring mechanism, enhance the links between early childhood and primary education, and promote home–kindergarten co-operation (Education Commission, 2000). However, these education reform documents did not go further with the early childhood curriculum.

Consequently, the second edition of the *Guide to the Preprimary Curriculum* (GPC) was issued to further regulate the early childhood curriculum in Hong Kong kindergartens (Curriculum Development Council, 2006). It noted that children in Hong Kong were exposed to both Chinese and English at the preschool level and considered the early years a time to promote the mother tongue (i.e. Chinese) and the second language (i.e. English). Therefore, for the first time, the official document made some mention of teaching English and Putonghua in kindergartens. This is a good response to the reality that almost all kindergartens in Hong Kong do have English lessons. As English is highly valued by parents as a route for advancement in the education system and society, this GPC gives the green light to the learning and teaching of English in kindergartens. In addition, it suggests some approaches, strategies and activities for the early language curriculum such as the whole language approach, emergent literacy, reading aloud, story-telling, and play activities. It advises that the principles of teaching the mother-tongue language are applicable to both the mother-tongue and the second language (including English and Putonghua).

Classroom observation in 1998 and 2008

We conducted classroom observations in some Hong Kong kindergartens in 1998 and 2008 to collect authentic data on early literacy practice in the city. The observations were reported in Li and Rao (2005) and Li, Rao, and Tse (2012), respectively. The following excerpts from the written transcripts are quoted from the two reports to provide an illustration of what we observed.

K3 Class (5–6 years) observed in Hong Kong (1998)

Teacher B3: Please put your hands on your knees and keep quiet. Look at the whiteboard.
[The children became quiet and turned to the whiteboard. Some boys in the rear of the classroom were still chatting, and the teacher paused for several seconds to wait for them. They stopped talking and looked at the teacher.]
Teacher B3: Look at this character, what is it? It is "faa1[1] (flower)"
[The teacher read this new character and showed how to write it and directed the children's attention to the placement and order of the strokes. The teacher told a story about this character to make it memorable.]
Teacher B3: Follow me, read it aloud, "faa1 (flower)! faa1 (flower)! faa1 (flower)!"
[The students read it repeatedly, whole-class reading alternating with individual turns. The reading was followed by a 15-minute period for writing the new characters they had just learned in the group session.]

We observed that this teacher used the traditional teacher-directed instruction to teach Chinese characters, which had been used in China for thousands of years. The teacher focused on the three major components of the Chinese character:

the shape, the sound, and the meaning. In our follow-up observation of a typical teaching session in a Hong Kong kindergarten, drill-and-practice was found to predominate in the teaching of Chinese characters. The teacher read some new characters, showed the students how to write them, and directed the students' attention to the placement and order of the strokes. The teacher told stories about some characters to make them memorable, but most of the characters were taught using mnemonics instead of by highlighting structurally significant features. The students read the new characters repeatedly, so that whole-class reading alternated with individual turns. After the teaching was a 15-minute practice of writing the new characters they had learned in group sessions (Li and Rao, 2005).

K3 Class (5–6 years) observed in Hong Kong (2008)

The children sit in the chair while the teacher (T2) stands beside the screen. The PowerPoint of the story, *The Lion's Hair*, is shown on the screen.
T2: Hello, children! Today I will read a very interesting story to you.
[The cover page of the story is shown on the screen. The teacher points at the title using the pointer, and reads the story aloud, slide by slide.]
T2: [after completing the reading] Could you tell me the name of this story?
All: The Lion's Hair!
T2: What is it talking about? S3, could you tell us?
S3: The lion had thick hair before. But one day his hair was burned so he has no hair.
T2: What happened next? S5, could you help us?
S5: Later, the crocodile helped the lion with his tears.
T2: What was the result?
All: Lion's hair has grown long.
T2: Great! Now could we read aloud the whole story? [All: Yes!] Do you have confidence? [All: Yes!]
[The students read aloud the story on the screen.]
T2: Very good! Which animal in the story is your most favorite? Now let's do a vote!
[The teaching assistant sticks a chart on the blackboard, which presents the Chinese names of all the animals in the story. The children take a sticker as the vote and come up to the blackboard one by one to choose their favorite character. The teacher and teaching assistant count the votes.]
T2: Let's look at it! The election result is: our most favorite animal is –
All: Crocodile!
T2: Yes! How many votes has he got?
All: 11 votes!
T2: Kids! This story tells us, although he looks very ugly, the Crocodile likes very much to help others. Without his tears, the Lion could not get his hair back. If you are willing to help others, you will be welcome. Right?

We (Li, Rao, and Tse, 2012) found that the teacher used the Story Approach to Integrated Learning (SAIL) learning package to teach Chinese literacy. SAIL is a Hong Kong style narrative curriculum and pedagogy widely used in kindergartens (Li, 2007b). Basically, every theme starts with a special story that provides a meaningful learning context and an interesting storyline to help integrate the various learning content and activities into a story journey. Each story provides an open framework to maximize teacher and children engagement in the theme-based exploration. A later section of this chapter will explore SAIL in greater detail. The abovementioned case indicates that the young children had some naïve but sensible value judgments about the characters, and that the teacher respected the children's decisions, although the activity is still teacher-directed. Nevertheless, the above excerpt shows a scenario of whole-class teaching, direct instruction, content-based learning and teacher-directed activities, which is still a good example of traditional Chinese pedagogy.

Comparing the two classrooms in Hong Kong could help us understand the changes and progress in early Chinese literacy education in Hong Kong. In the 1990s, Hong Kong kindergarten teachers tended to use very traditional Chinese pedagogies to teach, whereas in the 2008 observation, some kindergarten teachers employed the Story Approach to Integrated Learning (SAIL) approach to teach Chinese literacy.

The practice of Chinese literacy teaching in Singapore

Singapore is a well-known multiethnic and multicultural community, which has four official languages: English, Chinese (Putonghua as the spoken language and simplified Chinese characters as the written form), Tamil, and Malay. These languages enjoy equal status, reflecting the government's policy of "pragmatic multilingualism" (Kuo and Jernudd, 1993). The bilingual education policy was established in 1956, and the compulsory learning of two languages was instituted just after its independence in 1966 (Cheah and Lim, 1996). This policy has led to English being used as the first language either at home or in schools, with the mother tongue of every child being learned as a second language. The Chinese children in Singapore are no exception – they learn to read and write in English first, and then in Chinese.

Chinese literacy education in Singapore

In Singapore, Chinese is the second language (L2) for Chinese children as they learn English (L1) first and speak it at home and in school (Li and Rao, 2000; Li and Rao, 2005). For half a century the educational authorities of Singapore did not issue any official guidelines on preschool Chinese curriculum and, consequently, the Chinese curriculum was left to kindergarten proprietors. All the kindergartens were privately owned and operated in a highly competitive environment. Therefore, the early childhood curriculum focused on language, literacy, numeracy, arts, music, and computing skills, and the direct teaching of Chinese literacy was very popular in Singapore kindergartens. Without enough qualified Chinese teachers in town, however, Singapore kindergartens had to "import" a large number of Chinese teachers from mainland China. These imported teachers were trained in China as L1 teachers and brought Chinese traditional pedagogies with them, such as the direct teaching of Chinese literacy.

In 2005, the Singapore government launched guidelines on preschool English and Chinese curricula, establishing the six "iTeach" principles for early childhood education:

1 integrated learning;
2 teachers as supporters of learning;
3 engaging children in learning through play;
4 ample opportunities for interaction;
5 children as active learners; and
6 holistic development (Li, Rao, and Tse, 2012).

Singapore kindergartens put "iTeach" into practice and tried out some new ideas and practices such as inquiry-based learning, child-centeredness, developmentally appropriate practice (DAP), emergent literacy and whole language, the project approach, and so on.

Class observations in 1998 and 2008

We conducted classroom observations in some Singapore kindergartens in 1998 and 2008 to collect authentic data on early literacy practice in the city. The observations were reported in Li and Rao (2005) and Li, Rao and Tse (2012), respectively. The following excerpts are quoted from the two reports to provide an illustration of what we observed in Singapore.

K3 Class (5–6 years) observed in Singapore (1998)

Teacher C1: Listen to me carefully; this is "ji1" (chicken), "ji1"! "ji1"! What is the difference between "ji1" (chicken) and "ya1" (duck)? Note the left radical, "ji1" is "you4" (又). "ya1" is "jia3" (甲), they are different. But they share the same radical "niao3" (鸟) (bird) on the right.

[The students gazed at their teacher curiously and silently, trying to grasp the major points and identify the two characters. Some children did not focus their attention on the task and were playing with their classmates.]

Teacher C1: Now, please use your index finger to write the two characters in the air, follow me …

[The teacher wrote the characters on the whiteboard, rehearsed the order of strokes, and analyzed the structure again. Children had to read the new characters repeatedly, whole-class reading alternating with individual turns.]

Teacher C1:   Okay, take out your exercise book and write the two characters 10 times each.
[During the following 15 minutes, the children copied the characters in their exercise books. Some children had difficulty with the task and the teacher walked around the class helping children as appropriate.]

We (Li and Rao, 2005) analyzed this scenario and concluded that this was a typical and traditional Chinese teaching approach. Typically, the teaching of Chinese literacy goes from single characters to compound ones, from high frequency to low frequency ones, and from regular to irregular characters. This Singapore teacher was teaching Chinese reading and writing in this way, and this was also followed by Hong Kong teachers. The typical routine for teaching a character in Hong Kong and Singapore was to pronounce it, discriminate it from other characters, write it "in the air", rehearse the order of the strokes, analyze the structure, and then explain the meaning. Children had to read the new characters repeatedly, alternating between whole-class reading and individual turns. Like their counterparts in Hong Kong, the Singapore children also had to practice writing the new characters they had learned in group sessions.

K3 Class (5–6 years) observed in Singapore (2008)

The children sit in rows on the floor. The teacher (T5) sits beside the whiteboard, facing the children.
T5:   Today we will talk about the story of "seeds". There are many kinds of seeds. Most of the fruits we eat have seeds. You can eat them, plant them, and even cook them. For example, some beans are food. There are many stories about seeds. So, our project today is to make your own storybook about seeds. You can work individually or in pairs to work out a storybook. First, you need to discuss with your group mate to conceive your story of seeds. Second, you need to draw the story on the paper. Third, I will come to help you write down the Chinese words for the storybook. All right? Please come to pick up white papers. No more than two kids in one group, please.
[The children come up to take the papers and pencils and go to work in groups. The teacher walks around to help the children work on their projects. Most of the children are talking about their stories. Two boys go to toilet.]
T5:   [20 minutes later, the teacher starts to work with a girl who has completed her storybook.] S11, please tell me your story and let me write it down for you. Hmm, let's start from this picture.
S11:   I am an apple seed. My home is in a garden.
T5:   I am an apple seed. My home is in an Australian garden.
S11:   My home is in an Australian garden.
T5:   And then? [The teacher writes the Chinese words for the girl.]

[During the following 11 minutes, the teacher helps the girl to write and reorganize her own story about an apple seed. The teacher reads aloud the entire story to the girl, who seems very happy with the work co-authored by her Chinese teacher.]

We (Li, Rao, and Tse, 2012) found that the Chinese teacher was using a project approach to conduct emergent literacy activities, in a teacher-directed way. Although time-consuming, the children worked on their own storybooks with the teacher's assistance. However, the teacher was soon tired, as she had to help 18 children to complete 10 storybooks within an hour. It is important to note that this project was initiated, planned, implemented, and completed by the Chinese teacher. This is not in line with the Katz and Chard's (1989) definition: a project is an in-depth investigation of a topic which is posed either by the children, the teacher, or the teacher working with the children. The key feature of a project is that it is a research effort deliberately focused on finding answers to questions about a topic and is undertaken by a group of children within a class. No student research efforts could be found in this teacher-directed, content-based, product-oriented and whole-class involved learning activity. Instead, a fusion of Western pedagogy (the project approach) and traditional Chinese pedagogy (all children being involved in the same activity, directed by the teacher) is found in this scenario.

Comparing the 1998 and 2008 Chinese literacy classrooms, we could find some pedagogical innovations in the Singapore kindergartens. This finding implies that some Singapore kindergartens are very open to new ideas and approaches. In brief, we (Li, Rao, and Tse, 2012) found that Hong Kong and Singapore teachers used SAIL, the story approach, and the project approach, whereas Shenzhen teachers were very comfortably still conducting their direct teaching. Although some innovations were observed in their teaching, a common pattern was also found in the qualitative analyses: whole-class teaching, teacher-directed activities, product-oriented learning, and more didactic teaching. This indicated that traditional Chinese pedagogy was still evident in their classrooms, which will be further discussed in the following sections.

Three gaps observed in China, Hong Kong and Singapore

We have conducted many comparative studies into early literacy teaching and learning in China, Hong Kong, and Singapore over the past two decades. Both quantitative and qualitative analyses have confirmed the common pattern of Chinese literacy pedagogy in these Chinese communities: although some Western pedagogies were observed, whole-class teacher-directed instruction was still the mainstream activity. In addition, we found three gaps in the practice of early childhood teaching of Chinese literacy. This section will introduce the common pattern and the three gaps.

The common pattern of teaching Chinese literacy

The common pattern we (Li, Rao, and Tse, 2012) found in the Chinese communities was whole-class, theme-based, and teacher-directed teaching, with some storytelling and questioning. In a typical early Chinese classroom, the teacher's talk centered on curriculum content, using themes and students' progress as guidelines for instruction. Children were well disciplined and the learning was really effective. The teachers reported their priorities in their teaching practice to us: first was the early teaching of Chinese reading and writing, followed by the use of direct instruction, the regular setting of copying exercises, and the high incidence of choral reading aloud. The teachers adhered to specific teaching approaches and lesson plans, and they assigned homework that would involve parents. All these could be labeled as traditional Chinese pedagogy. Although progressive ideas and a balanced approach have been advocated and were known to the Chinese practitioners, the fact remains that, in all the three locations, the teachers implemented, to varying degrees, traditional teaching methods.

This phenomenon could be explained in the light of Bronfenbrenner's (1979) ecological systems theory. First, at the macrosystem level, Confucianism is the cornerstone of Chinese culture and this is influential on the thinking, learning and teaching journey of Chinese people. Confucianism emphasizes imparting to young children a sense of conformity, discipline, self-control, a passion for effort, and academic achievement (Rao *et al.* 2010). This is why Chinese parents traditionally have high expectations of children's early learning and their academic achievement (Li and Rao, 2000). The influence of Confucian heritage culture (CHC) has been noted in many previous studies, such as Ng and Rao (2008) and Pearson and Rao (2006), and was apparent in our studies (Li, Rao, and Tse, 2011; Li, Rao, and Tse, 2012). Although the teachers said they had accepted the ideological and philosophical bases of Western reading pedagogy, these are overridden by the deep-seated CHC inculcated into them by society itself (Hu, 2002; Wang and Spodek, 2000; Zhu and Wang, 2005).

Second, at the microsystem level, the psycholinguistic features of the Chinese language have limited the teaching of Chinese literacy. The writing system of Chinese features logographic characters that denote meaning rather than phonology, and its teaching calls for a different pedagogy. For instance, Tan *et al.* (2005) claim that Chinese reading development depends, to a large extent, on writing skills training. They suggest two interacting mechanisms to explain the central role of logograph writing – the first being orthographic awareness, which facilitates the development of coherent, effective links between visual symbols, phonology, and semantics, the second involving the establishment of motor programs that lead to the formation of long-term motor memory images of individual Chinese characters. These two mechanisms both require large amounts of rote learning and copying exercises. The need for such intensive practice helps explain why the kindergarten teachers were reluctant to abandon direct instruction, rote learning, copying exercises, and homework. Teacher-directed activities, as such, are considered to be crucial for the successful learning of Chinese reading, but it is important to note that they can still be accommodated within teaching methods that are child-initiated and can offer students opportunities for a certain degree of self-directed learning (Li, Rao, and Tse, 2012).

Third, the dominance of such a traditional Chinese pedagogy in Chinese communities reflects a sense within teachers that there are few realistic alternatives available given the existing social climate and teaching situation: class sizes are large; pre-determined classroom layouts place the teacher in front of the children; there is an examination-oriented system; and parental expectations and demands are very high (Hu, 2002; Li *et al.* 2008; Tang and Maxwell, 2007). As a consequence, Chinese teachers were aware of the importance of child-initiated learning and enlightened approaches, yet they found it impossible to introduce these pedagogies to replace the traditional methods (Li, Rao, and Tse, 2012). Furthermore, such traditionalism does not offend parental expectations and is comfortably housed in the Chinese exam-oriented education system (Lee and Tseng, 2008; Li and Rao, 2000, 2005; Rao *et al.* 2009; Tang and Maxwell, 2007).

Nevertheless, the present study did identify some changes in Chinese classrooms, reflecting that some Western ideas or even pedagogies have been put into practice in the three localities. Teachers in all three locations raised more open-ended questions to engage more children in question-and-answer interactions, and children were encouraged to offer their own views and to vote for their favorite story characters. Attention was given to the ways individual students were progressing, and positive feedback was given to show the teacher's respect and appreciation. Although the pace of change is slow, and possibly cautious, there are signs that Chinese literacy teaching in Hong Kong and Singapore has progressed over the last decade (Li and Rao, 2005). The qualitative evidence has indicated that, in addition to theme-based direct teaching, there is evidence of Western pedagogical practice, such as the project approach in Hong Kong and Singapore. For example, we (Li, Rao, and Tse, 2012) found that some Singapore teachers were doing a project to conduct some emergent literacy activities, although it was transformed into a teacher-directed learning activity.

However, the adaptation of Western pedagogies was uneven across Shenzhen, Hong Kong and Singapore. For instance, some child-initiated activities, theme-based explorations, and tailor-made school curricula were evident in classrooms in Hong Kong and Singapore. Strategic questioning of children in groups was frequently observed in Hong Kong. Individual interactions and feedback were also preferred. The project and whole language approaches were employed in Singapore. This supports the contention that societal differences in Chinese communities influence the degree of openness to foreign educational practices. And, this finding reflects the central tenet that teaching and learning differ across sociocultural contexts.

This is in line with the sociocultural perspectives that observe teaching activities taking place in cultural contexts and being mediated by language and values – teaching activities can be best understood when they are investigated in their cultural-historical contexts (John-Steiner and Mahn, 1996). Classrooms are part of a wider community (of school and beyond), which has cultural practices and social norms, where teaching activities are socially embedded and culturally shaped. The custom of using direct instruction might be seen as part of the cultural practice of traditional Chinese teaching. The wider cultures in which schools are situated impinge on classrooms in ways often unnoticed by participants who are too familiar with the culture (John-Steiner and Mahn, 1996). It is, thus, understandable that reformist leaders tend to overlook cultural conflicts when proposing the transplantation of Western pedagogies into their cultures, and this makes our studies very critical in understanding the socio-cultural differences in early childhood classrooms.

The curriculum reform in China kindergartens is a de facto revolution of teaching ideas, which included "respecting children", "active learning", and "play-based teaching and learning" (Liu and Feng, 2005). Our study (Li, Rao, and Tse, 2012), however, found that most of these ideas were accepted by the teachers in their self-reported beliefs, but had not been put into their teaching practice. The remarkable results of this reform might be the belief–practice, policy–practice (Li, Wang, and Wong, 2011), and preschool–primary gaps (Li, Rao, and Tse, 2011) found in our studies. In the following sections, we will thoroughly discuss why the three gaps exist in these Chinese communities.

The belief–practice gap

Our study (Li, Wang, and Wong, 2011) found a remarkable gap between the teacher-reported beliefs and practices. Although half the teachers reported that they preferred a child-initiated approach and believed in a balanced approach of teacher-directed and child-initiated learning, their common pattern of teaching is mostly whole class-based, teacher-directed, and theme-based direct instruction. The teachers in the interviews reflected that their priorities in teaching practice were the early teaching of Chinese reading and writing, the use of direct instruction, the regular setting of Chinese character exercises, and a high incidence of choral reading aloud. They retained some specific, Chinese teaching approaches; such as, sticking to pre-set lesson plans and assigning homework that would involve parents in training children's literacy skills. There was a remarkable belief–practice gap, especially when many Chinese teachers believed in progressive ideas and a balanced approach but implemented traditional teaching methods, to varying degrees. This belief–practice gap has been repeatedly reported by Cheng (2001, 2006), Liu and Feng (2005), Ng and Rao (2008), Zhu and Zhang (2008) and us (Li, Wang, and Wong, 2011).

Again, we employed Bronfenbrenner's (1979) ecological systems theory to understand this gap. First, conformity, discipline, self-control, hard work, and academic achievement are highly valued and intentionally cultivated in Chinese culture (Rao *et al.* 2010). Chinese parents are very concerned and proactively involved in children's early learning and academic achievement (Li and Rao, 2000). Second, Chinese language features a difficult orthography which demands a large amount of rote memorization and practice. This need could be met through direct instruction, rote learning, copying exercises, and homework. Third, there are some constraints imposed by the reality of Chinese classrooms: large class sizes, pre-determined classroom layouts, limited resources, an examination-oriented system, and high parental expectations and demands (Hu, 2002; Li *et al.* 2008; Tang and Maxwell, 2007). Last but not least, the teacher training programs in Chinese communities need to be improved to equip Chinese teachers with modern literacy teaching techniques, as most of the Chinese teachers we observed were not confident in teaching early literacy. This suggests that early childhood teacher education and in-service training might be very important elements of education reform.

A policy–practice gap

We also found remarkable discrepancies between the classroom practice and the objectives of the curriculum reform (Li, Wang, and Wong, 2011). Play was highly promoted by the educational authorities but was seldom used in classroom instruction. Instead, the early teaching of Chinese literacy skills, rote learning, copying exercises, and testing were frequently observed. Although prohibited for decades, the copying and reciting practices were still used in Chinese kindergartens. This policy–practice gap is repeatedly observed in our previous studies (Li, Wang, and Wong, 2011; Li, Rao, and Tse, 2011).

Liu and Feng (2005) attributed this gap to the top-down nature of China's curriculum reform. They and the Chinese policymakers subscribed to Western progressive ideas and curriculum models without much consideration of the cultural and societal contexts of China, as we discussed earlier. Unfortunately, these imported ideas are not culturally appropriate (Li, Rao, and Tse, 2012), clashing with Chinese tradition and social values. For example, the educational authorities in China banned the early teaching of literacy skills, but Chinese parents were desperate for it. In effect, Chinese teachers struggled to satisfy the state on the one hand and parents' demands on the other – Chinese teachers had to confront and cope with different sets of expectations and demands. In addition, the six factors were also influencing the success of curriculum reform in China: class size, teacher quality, resources, parental expectation, the exam-oriented education system, and the socio-cultural environment (Li, 2002). Without careful and systematic articulation of these decisive variables, any curriculum reform will not be successful.

Furthermore, curriculum reform in China has been challenged by Tobin (2007) within a critical theoretical framework, which cautions against transplanting the beliefs and practices from another culture and is skeptical of obtaining meaningful evaluation of such practices using criteria from a different culture. The DAP beliefs, practices, and standards presented by NAEYC may work well in their countries of origin, but this does not mean that they can be transplanted easily to other communities and cultures. The policy–practice divide found in this study is a challenge to the assumption that American standards are universal and culture-free (Tobin, 2007). Cultural values, teacher and parent expectations, and the established educational system should be considered when seeking to change literacy practices in the early years. Cultural tradition and social values are both resources and limits, and such awareness is important for improving pedagogy in the age of globalization (Tobin, 2007). We can learn from and influence each other, but we should not take for granted that there is a universal and culture-free standard in the world.

Preschool–primary gap

We also found a remarkable preschool–primary gap in our 2011 study (Li, Rao, and Tse, 2011). Normally, there should be a kind of pedagogical continuity between preschool and primary school, what is called "vertical continuity" and which refers to the transition from one level to the next. Alongside this there is a kind of horizontal continuity that is concerned with the influence on ongoing transitions of the home, school and community. Young children may experience vertical and horizontal transitions simultaneously, and these may present significant challenges (Kagan and Neuman, 1998; Neuman, 2002). Vertical discontinuity occurs when early childhood programs use developmentally appropriate play-based learning approaches, and traditional primary schools use more structure and teacher direction. This vertical discontinuity is a challenge to young children, as they cannot change learning styles over the six-week holiday between finishing early childhood education and starting formal school (Walker, 2007). There is, therefore, a strong rationale for promoting pedagogical continuity in the early years, with a more gradual introduction to structured learning (Bogard and Takanishi, 2005; Fabian, 2002; Kauerz, 2006).

Three approaches are normally used to promote pedagogical continuity in the early years, and three distinctive consequences can be detected in related studies (Petriwskyj *et al.* 2005). The first is the holistic approach, in which all the stakeholders (parents, educators and policymakers) make a joint effort to articulate the settings, curricula and pedagogies of preschools and schools to promote structural consistency and pedagogical continuity in the transition. This approach is applied in Scandinavian countries and parts of Italy, where early childhood education is of relatively high quality and formal education commences relatively late. Pedagogical continuity is a well-publicized concept among homes, preschools, schools, and communities, so the transitions are very smooth and comfortable. The second is the top-down model which posits that changes should primarily be made in early childhood settings to achieve vertical alignment between two educational levels, thus pre-primary curricula and pedagogies have to become more difficult and formalized. In Greece, for example, the new national curriculum is centrally planned, aiming at an equal integration of preschool education into the unified design of primary and secondary education (Sofou and Tsafos, 2009). This approach could reinforce the schoolification of early childhood education. The third is the child-centered (bottom-up) approach applied in some areas of Europe, where curriculum integration is very flexible and deliberately incorporates school pedagogy that is child-initiated and play-oriented, and the early years curriculum (aged 3–8) is dedicated almost wholly to responding to the children's individual needs.

All the three of these approaches have, to a certain extent, been applied in Chinese contexts. However, the outcomes of published studies are somewhat inconsistent in terms of rigor, purpose and focus (Chan et al. 1999; Chow, 1993; Education Department, 1993; Li and Rao, 2000; Li and Rao, 2005; Wong, 2003). In Hong Kong, for instance, the educational authorities have experimented with a child-centered approach by introducing the activity approach and integrated learning into primary schools, and through advocating "learning through play" in the pre-primary sector (Rao, 2002; Wong, 2003). Chow (1993) found that the top-down approach had been readily adopted by early childhood educators to shape pre-primary learning and to better prepare young children for primary school learning. Chan et al. (1999) and Wong (2003) found that pedagogical discontinuity remained a stumbling block for the learning and attainment of children in Primary 1. Wu et al. (1999) also report marked discontinuity in terms of pedagogy and learning styles across school sectors in China. For instance, young children experience learning by heart at home, through play in the preschool, and through didactic teaching in the primary school (Li, Rao, and Tse, 2011).

To promote pedagogical continuity in the early years, the educational authorities in Hong Kong and China have, since 2000, launched large-scale curriculum reforms (Li, Rao, and Tse, 2011). Whereas the Hong Kong educational authorities recommend a holistic approach and systematic pedagogical continuity across educational levels, mainland Chinese reform leaders have subscribed to a largely child-centered approach. They have sought to transform the widespread teacher-directed learning in traditional primary schools into child-initiated, integrated, and interactive learning (Hu, 2002; Lee and Tseng, 2008). "Innovative" concepts and approaches such as the project approach, integrated learning across subjects, the activity approach, and "learning through doing", have been forcefully and directly transplanted into Chinese schools (Li, 2005; Zhu and Zhang, 2008).

These radical reforms have been widely criticized by Chinese researchers and teachers, and their effectiveness has been questioned (Li, 2002; Li and Li, 2003; Zhu and Zhang, 2008). For example, it has been found that young children in Hong Kong experience greater pedagogical continuity in terms of formal literacy teaching at home, in preschools and in primary schools than is the case for their counterparts in mainland China (Li and Rao, 2000, 2005). And Hong Kong children have better literacy attainment than their Beijing counterparts from preschool years to Primary 3 (Li *et al.* 2008). Nevertheless, the complicated relationship between pedagogical continuity and literacy attainment has not been systematically explored in the various Chinese contexts, and many studies used evidence from ad hoc attainment surveys and teachers' own descriptions of their classroom practice. There has been no rigorous observational study of authentic practice in actual primary classrooms, nor has longitudinal data been gathered to permit an examination of the impact of pedagogical continuity on children's Chinese literacy development over time.

Therefore, we compared the two patterns of promoting pedagogical continuity in Chinese early years contexts with the authentic observational data of large scale samples in Shenzhen and Hong Kong (Li, Rao, and Tse, 2011). In Hong Kong, pedagogical continuity was promoted using a holistic approach and curriculum objectives, subject syllabi, and pedagogies across educational stages were articulated by the education authorities. The approaches used in kindergartens anticipated those used in the first year of primary school, where students could expect to encounter the activity approach, integrated learning, and the story approach, as well as formal literacy activities. In Shenzhen, although a child-centered approach was, in theory, promoted by the education authorities, a top-down model prevailed in early years classrooms. Shenzhen Primary 1 teachers used no child-centered initiatives whatsoever and, instead, they turned to teacher-directed practice and pedagogy. They considered that their task was to lay a solid educational foundation that could be built upon in the Primary 1 curriculum. The kindergarten teachers felt obliged to adopt an attainment-focused curriculum, their duty being to subject the young children in their care to whole class teaching and formal methods of teaching the Chinese characters and pinyin (Li, Rao, and Tse, 2011).

At the micro-system level, there are real-life considerations that teachers in Shenzhen confront every day. These include large class sizes, teacher-centered classroom layouts, the competition for survival arising out of commercialization, and Chinese parents' persistence on providing their children with knowledge-based learning and formal instruction (Hu, 2002; Li *et al.* 2008; Tang and Maxwell, 2007). The large average class size in Shenzhen Primary 1 classrooms limits teachers' choices and encourages the adoption of top-down strategies that are easier to manage. One can imagine that, in a typical class of 40–60 students who are crammed in a small classroom with a class teacher, the only way to accommodate the students is to have them sit side-by-side in long rows, to design a timetable that strictly segregates learning into subjects, and to have sequences of lessons with pencil and paper assignments. Within such an environment, a child-centered, interactive and integrated mode of learning is not easy to implement. This suggests that education reform in mainland China needs to give more attention to the realities of the Chinese early years context when planning and making blanket proposals (Li, Rao, and Tse, 2011). Commendable and well-intended as the curriculum reforms in China may be, their rapid adoption is really not feasible.

Significant societal differences in Chinese literacy attainment at all levels were found in this comparison. Location was a significant contributor to the prediction of variance in Time 1, Time 2 scores and the gain scores. Our study (Li, Rao, and Tse, 2011) found that Hong Kong students outperformed their Shenzhen counterparts in Chinese literacy attainment, both at preschool and primary levels, concurrently and longitudinally. This finding is consistent with that of Li and Rao (2000; 2005) and Li et al. (2008) and suggests that Hong Kong Chinese literacy pedagogy might be significantly more effective than that in Shenzhen. Further analyses of gain scores show that although both groups make gains at similar rates in Primary 1, the Shenzhen children are still way behind their Hong Kong counterparts at the end of their first school year.

This significant "city effect" in Chinese literacy attainment might be caused by the different approaches employed to promote pedagogical continuity in the early years context. In addition to being steered by clear curriculum and syllabus guidelines, the Hong Kong teachers reported that they had purposefully considered the challenges and problems relating to school transition and accordingly made adjustments to their teaching. The teaching observed in Hong Kong kindergartens did a lot to prepare students independently to reflect, predict, question and hypothesize about Chinese writing and other aspects of literacy, an ability that is ideal for preparing students for the complexities of today's technology-based schooling (Bowman et al. 2001). And we found that the reform blueprint for the Hong Kong education system in the twenty-first century (Education Commission, 2000) appeared to be well implemented and that curricular and pedagogical continuity were apparent. Shenzhen, by contrast, was encountering problems in all the areas of school transition identified by Petriwskyj et al. (2005). The problems included communication linkages, coherence of experiences, and system coherence. The primary teachers in Shenzhen were critical of the prevalence of whole-class and formal coverage of aspects of literacy teaching in the kindergarten years. They preferred not to have the key literacy skills taught in kindergarten or, at least, to have them taught effectively so that all new students were on the same starting line on entry to primary school. It is common to find in continuity studies that teachers find fault with what has and what has not been taught in the preceding stage, and that this problem can be minimized through effective "communication linkages" (Petriwskyj et al. 2005). Accordingly, more preschool-school communication and closer collaboration and exchanges of ideas should be done to facilitate mutual understanding.

This helps explain why the Shenzhen kindergarten teachers favored a top-down approach, instead of the child-centered approach proposed by the authorities. They were convinced that a formal and strictly controlled syllabus would best boost the early acquisition of reading and writing skills. This finding implies that an amalgamation of Confucian and Western cultures might help overcome some of the present shortcomings in system cohesion in contemporary Chinese communities (Rao, Ng and Pearson, 2009). Certainly, policy makers should take cultural traditions into account when considering new measures.

The Story Approach to Integrated Learning (SAIL)

The concept of developmentally appropriate practice (DAP) has been widely accepted and supported by early childhood educators all over the world. This framework, however, has been challenged by many scholars for being ethnocentric and ignoring the range of life contexts and knowledge experienced by children from diverse cultural, ethnic, linguistic and value contexts (Canella *et al.* 2007; Kessler and Swadener, 1992). These concerns have been addressed by different approaches; for example, the narrative curriculum is widely regarded an ideal platform. This chapter will introduce a new narrative curriculum, the Story Approach to Integrated Learning (SAIL) (Li, 2004; 2007; 2013), which has been widely used in Hong Kong kindergartens.

What is SAIL?

Learning is central to all early childhood education matters. Understanding how learning occurs and develops in the early years has been the mission of developmental and educational psychologists for decades. Although there are many different theories and approaches to understanding the phenomenon of learning, most of them could be classified into four main categories: behaviorism, cognitivist, social construction of knowledge, and postmodernism. SAIL is developed based on the postmodernist perspective of learning and development.

From the postmodernist view, knowledge is:

1 tentative, fragmented, multifaceted and not necessarily rational;
2 socially constructed and takes form in the eyes of the knower;
3 contextual rather than being "out there" waiting to be discovered; and
4 can shift as quickly as the context shifts, the perspective of the learner shifts, or as events overtake us (Kilgore, 2001).

Knowledge is contextualized and therefore individuals can hold two completely incongruent views of one subject at the same time. The postmodern approach to learning is founded upon the assumption that there is not one kind of learner, nor one particular goal for learning, nor one way in which learning takes place, and nor is there one particular environment where learning occurs (Kilgore, 2001).

Another important feature of postmodernism is its emphasis on the diversity of the world and its objection to the core emphasis of modernism on unity and universality. Postmodernism welcomes uncertainties, complexities, subjectivities, and diversities, because there are multiple realities, multiple perspectives, and multiple learners in the world. Accordingly, Li (2007a) summarized postmodernist perspectives on early childhood learning as follows:

1 children pay close attention to the immediate reality wholeheartedly;
2 children exert effort to make sense of the world;

3   children create theories by filling in the blanks in their understanding of the world;
4   children's learning varies and depends on contexts;
5   children learn about the world via personal stories and narrative enquiries;
6   children prioritize the wholeness of everything;
7   children believe in the magic power of words, which are the fountain of early thinking.

In Hong Kong, there are different approaches to early childhood teaching and learning – for instance, the Project Approach, High Scope and Reggio Emilia – and each of these is based on different theoretical orientations. However, since many of these approaches are based on Western educational research, their applicability to the context of Hong Kong kindergartens is questionable. Li (2008) analyzed the feasibility of implementing these mainstream curriculum models in Hong Kong kindergartens, and arrived at the conclusion that the Project Approach, High Scope and Reggio Emilia are not implementable whereas the narrative curriculum is culturally appropriate.

Apart from the difficulties in implementing Western approaches in the Chinese context, Hong Kong kindergartens are facing challenges posed by the highly pluralistic and diversified postmodern world that is characterized by an influx of knowledge and multiple realities. In order to meet the new challenges, it is vital for kindergartens in Hong Kong to adopt a culturally, contextually and child-individually appropriate practice (3CAPs) (Li, 2007) in teaching and learning. Reflection on the curriculum theories indicates that the postmodernism autobiography theory and Story Approach might be the best model for Hong Kong kindergartens to develop an integrated curriculum (Li, 2008). Story could be both a cognitive and an affective means to deliver knowledge, it is very easy to remember and it is capable of being expanded into an integrated curriculum. To implement the story approach in Hong Kong kindergartens, Li developed and published the learning package called SAIL (Story Approach to Integrated Learning) with Oxford University Press in 2004, the second version (SAIL2.0) in 2007, and the third (SAIL3.0) in 2013.

SAIL is a transdisciplinary teaching approach using stories as the framework to construct an integrated curriculum and to bring out themes and learning activities. The third version of SAIL was published to embrace the diversity and freedom of children, which are core values of postmodernism. Apart from incorporating new theories, the SAIL3.0 package also followed the *Guide to the Pre-primary Curriculum* (Curriculum Development Council, 2006) by emphasizing the importance of life education in order to foster children's interest in scientific and aesthetic areas. Teachers can use stories as a platform to develop a series of project activities – for instance, art, creation of new stories and drama performance – so as to enhance teacher–child interaction and support children's engagement and decision-making in their own learning. With these amendments, SAIL3.0 is now an effective tool to smooth children's transition to primary school by embracing the importance of reading, and to enhance children's language development with emergent literacy and a whole language approach.

How to do SAIL

Learning with SAIL is a journey of story and exploration, which aims at developing children's multiple intelligences through hands-on experience and active exploration of materials through multiple senses and human interaction. With SAIL, teachers are able to follow the storyline and develop explorative learning activities to enhance children's language, mathematical, interpersonal, intrapersonal, music, arts, and spatial intelligences. The stories in SAIL provide children with a complete learning context so that their life experiences can be easily linked to the learning activities, and these activities thus become more meaningful to them. To assess children's development in different areas, it is suggested that teachers use a learning portfolio to document daily teaching and learning activities.

SAIL can be done in four steps: storytelling, theme exploration, extension activities, and portfolio assessment.

1   Story-telling. Before telling stories to the class, teachers should mentally rehearse the content and scenario of the stories so that they become ready for their storytelling performance. When telling stories, teachers should pay attention to their eye contact, gesture and intonation. More importantly, teachers should link the new story with children's past experience so that the story becomes more meaningful to them.

    In addition, children can also tell stories. When being asked to tell stories, children may feel worried, excited or shy. However, as teachers, it is important to encourage children by:

    (1) providing a suitable theme which is based on children's life experience;
    (2) allowing children to think and organize their thoughts before telling the story;
    (3) dividing children into groups so that they can be inspired by listening to others, and can rehearse the story among their peers before telling the class; and
    (4) playing music which is related to the story so as to facilitate children's imagination.

After the storytelling, it is essential to have feedback immediately so as to consolidate children's understanding toward the story. Different post-story activities – such as direct repetition of the story, question-and-answer sessions, counting the number of characters, role play, creation of artwork and peer interviews – are good ways to help children remember the story. During feedback sessions, teachers should guide children's attention to the main points of the story through proper questioning skills, for example, by asking "When?" "Where?" "Who?" "What?" "Why?" and "How?" (the "5W1H" questions), so that children can analyze and conclude the story in a more systematic way.

2   Theme exploration. As a series of integrated activities, theme exploration aims to deepen and widen children's understanding about different subject matter developed from the story. To achieve this goal, teachers may develop story theme webs with the children. A story theme web is basically a kind of visual thinking framework that helps children to find out the links between different subjects and themes in a story, and to provide children with a starting point for their project, investigation or creation of new stories.

   Daily news sharing is another way to aid children's exploration of a story theme. Children love news sharing and are highly engaged in this kind of activity (Li, 2007). News sharing could link the story with children's daily experience and encourage them to pay more attention to what happens around them every day. They can also gain a more concrete picture of how to apply what they have learnt in a story to real life. Music, physical, and art activities are the necessary tools to support a story because all of these activities provide children with a meaningful and complete scenario for learning. A good scenario provides children with room for imagination. For example, after telling the children a story about animals, teachers may play a song with different animals as characters during their music period. With the aid of appropriate musical instruments, children can start imagining themselves as the animal characters and acting out the stories accordingly.

   After children have familiarized themselves with the original story, teachers can guide them to develop or write a new story. Although using the same story as the prototype, young children can create different, new stories as they have different family backgrounds, life experiences, abilities and interests. Children are encouraged to develop their new stories in the following ways:

   1   rewriting the beginning of the story by creating a biography for the characters;
   2   rewriting the ending of the story by creating an ideal ending for the characters;
   3   creating songs or poems based on the content of the original story, and so on.

Drama, an alternative way of storytelling, can also be used to explore the theme. Drama performance provides children with room to imagine, explore, perform, communicate and express their opinions and feelings towards a story. During drama performance, children are engaged in the learning activity physically, emotionally, intuitively and intellectually. By role-playing different characters, children have a chance to feel what others feel, and this helps them to develop their perspective-taking and introspective ability.

3   Extension activities. After developing various activities around the story theme, children might have found one or two interesting areas. To further understand the particular phenomenon or concept, children might need to do some projects. Doing projects in Hong Kong kindergartens is different from the project approach advocated by Katz and Chard (2000), as the choice of theme and progress of investigation are monitored and guided by the teachers. With the teacher's guidance, children choose the topic that interests them most for investigation. Through solving authentic problems with project work, children become the principal investigators who are responsible for their own learning and living, and the new knowledge they build up in the project will have more personal meaning and longer retention than those they learn from listening.

The project investigation can be done in three steps:

1   children find out the interesting areas for further investigation from the story;
2   children collect evidence by doing observations or experiments, or by searching different sources such as the internet, books, photos, news and interviews;
3   children consolidate and present their findings through various media, such as short written report, drawings, PowerPoint and storytelling.

Teachers can act as the observer, supporter, co-operator, guide and helper when children do project investigation. To these ends, teachers should acknowledge the importance of hands-on experience and direct manipulation in the investigation process and limit their intervention as far as possible. When children get stuck at any critical point, their interest in the theme may dramatically reduce, or they may immediately ask teachers for a correct answer to the problem. At this point, rather than directly providing children with answers, teachers should scaffold children's learning by guiding them to observe their peers, or help them link their past experience and learnt knowledge with the new problem.

4   Assessment portfolio. Assessment plays an important role in early childhood education because it allows teachers and parents to understand children's development in different aspects. Assessment also provides information for teachers to adjust their teaching style and curriculum to fit the learning style of the children.

In the past, parents in Hong Kong placed high value on traditional assessment methods, for instance, dictation, copying and paper-and-pencil tests. However, rather than helping teachers and parents to understand children as a whole person, these methods can only test children's factual knowledge and rote memorization skills. To assess children's learning in all developmental aspects, a learning portfolio would be a more appropriate choice. After observing children's daily activities and collecting their work, teachers should systematically store and analyze these data so that the portfolio becomes the evidence of children's learning and an indicator of their teaching effectiveness.

In sum, appropriate assessment should be a continual and dynamic process that is done in a variety of phases. It is suggested that teachers should use various methods in collecting data, and should engage children in the assessment process. Children's personal diaries, weekly journals, peer and self-evaluation should also be collected to establish a triangulation to validate the results obtained from teacher observation. With such a triangulation of assessment sources/methods, it is possible for teachers to obtain a complete picture of children's development in different areas.

An example of SAIL

The appendix to this chapter is a five-day teaching plan that shows how SAIL was actually carried out in a local Hong Kong kindergarten. The theme was "food", and all the learning activities were developed based on one of the SAIL stories, *The Princess's Birthday Party* (Li, 2007). Other teaching materials, including supplementary stories, videos, food and money, were used to help children link the story with their life experiences.

The learning activities naturally covered the three key elements (knowledge, skill, and attitude) and six learning areas suggested by the *Guide to the Preprimary Curriculum* (Curriculum Development Council, 2006). A balance of the six learning areas was proposed in the teaching plan. Mathematical and scientific explorations could be done as whole class or group/free choice activities. Emergent literacies could be facilitated through group discussion and presentation. Music, arts and physical education could also be delivered to the children.

All the learning activities stemmed from the core story, and were interlinked tightly with each other, forming a complete and meaningful learning context for the children. For instance, before conducting a field study in a supermarket, all the common foods that could be found in local supermarket were first introduced to the children through the core story, and then the concepts of money and how it is used were introduced for later application in the visit. These activities also showed how mathematics could be closely linked with stories as well as with children's daily experiences. Apart from the whole class activities and the group/free choice activities, music and physical activities were also a necessary piece to complete the whole puzzle of learning with SAIL. After learning the song *Min-nong* (*Pity on Farmers*), teachers made use of the lyrics and pictures in the storybook to carry out life education, asking children to cherish food and appreciate the farmers' hard work.

The four steps to doing SAIL were shown in the lesson plan, except for the step of the assessment portfolio. The teachers started each school day with storytelling and immediate feedback. Although there was no explicit news sharing in the teaching plan, the teachers did deliberately link current issues with the story and other learning activities; for example, the ways of preventing avian flu and the concept of "bring your own bag". A visit to supermarket was conducted as an extension activity. Although a field study is not a complete project in itself, its nature is a kind of project investigation, containing the process of "plan, do and review". For instance, before going to the supermarket, the children had to plan what they were going to buy with the limited money they had. The children then had to immediately check the feasibility of their plan in the supermarket and even had to change their shopping plan accordingly. In this case, the children actively applied what they had learnt about money to solve their real-life problems. At the end, after the children had presented their difficulties to the class, the teachers sorted out the common difficulties and systematically consolidated and analyzed the children's presentations. As the children could test their hypotheses through trial-and-error, and reach their own conclusions with teachers' guidance, this activity enhanced the children's problem-solving abilities.

The core values of postmodernism were shown in various story-based learning activities. For instance, the art activities allowed children to learn necessary skills while fostering their creativity and individuality. Open-ended questions were used to guide group discussion and presentations so that children were encouraged to use their imagination to think of possible outcomes. Different answers and various outcomes were really welcomed by the teachers, with respect for diversity in child development. The extension activities of the "healthy menu" and the supermarket visit broke the boundaries between home, school and community. The enhanced collaboration and increased understanding between different parties in turn facilitated the young children's daily and life-long learning.

SAIL is an example of a postmodernist curriculum with 3CAPs, because the stories not only provide an open framework and the flexibility for individualized learning, but also reflect the cultural, contextual and individual differences of the children (Li, 2007). Through school-based and even class-based tailoring, early childhood educators can present their young learners with a culturally, contextually and individually appropriate school-based curriculum. And through the co-construction of these stories by teachers and students, learning activities with SAIL can become children's personal stories, living stories, and ultimately, their autobiographies. In this connection, we agree with the claim that the early childhood curriculum should be young children's autobiographies (Li, 2007) – the authentic curriculum delivered by SAIL can provide children with a meaningful context to foster the development of the necessary abilities that will allow them to survive in this ever-changing, postmodern world.

Note

1 Cantonese is a toned language, the numerals after Romanized forms represent the tone (highest = 1, lowest = 6) of each word; 1 = high level, 2 = high rising, 3 = mid-level, 4 = low falling, 5 = low rising, 6 = low level.

APPENDIX TO CHAPTER 5

SAIL Example: Five-Day Learning Activities

Day 1:

A. Whole class activities

1. Read aloud the SAIL storybook *The Princess's Birthday Party* (pp. 4–11) with the aid of PowerPoint, and introduce to children the types of food presented in the story.
2. Cover some food with a piece of black cloth: the food may have some unique shapes, texture and order such as ginger, dried mushrooms, a hairy gourd, garlic, cheese, and so on. First, ask the children to guess what they are by touching them. Second, remove the cover and ask the children to observe the food closely. The teacher may ask the children to taste some of the food (e.g. the cheese) if possible. Then, the teacher may ask the children to share their observations and perception of these foods, using Chinese words to describe their characteristics (shape, texture, order and color).
3. Encourage the children to use a sentence pattern "I like eating _____ food" to make sentences orally.

B. Group/free choice activities

1. Explorative game: "Hard versus soft bread" (introducing the concepts of "hard" and "soft")

    - use the big book of *The Princess's Birthday Party* (p. 24) to tell the children the process of making bread;
    - put a baguette into a paper bag. Ask the children to touch and guess what is inside;
    - put soft butter bread into a zipper bag. Let the children touch the bread and help them to tell the difference between the baguette and soft butter bread;
    - introduce to children the concept of hard and soft.

2. Creative game: "Tasty noodles" (Artwork: cut 15cm long straight lines)

    - cut string/knitting wool into 15cm-long straight lines (use ruler to measure);
    - decorate the plate with color and paste the string/wool onto the plate;
    - use colored paper or any other materials to add extra toppings on the noodles.

3. Writing activities. Ask the children to write the two Chinese characters: 硬 (hard); 软 (soft).
4. Free choice activities: language/science/music/art/library/family corners

C. Follow-up activities

Ask the children to design a "healthy menu" with their parents. The children may either take some photos or draw some pictures of the procedure for making the dish so that they can present it easily to their classmates the next day. They need to write the menu in Chinese.

Day 2:

A. Whole class activities

1. Review yesterday's story by reminding the children the types of food that have been introduced. Introduce "fruit" and "vegetable" and then show the children a (picture of a) carrot.
2. Tell the story *Carrot's Journey* using the CD provided by SAIL.
3. After the storytelling, the teachers may ask the children the following questions:

    - What made carrot itchy?
    - Where did carrot stay in this journey?
    - What did carrot virtually become? Where did carrot finally go?
    - What should you do after going to the toilet? (Big book p. 18)

4. Elaborate on the content of pp. 18–19 in the big book of *The Princess's Birthday Party*. Tell the children about the relationship between food, nutrition and growth, e.g. dietary fiber, which can be found in fruit and vegetables, can enhance peristalsis and prevent constipation, etc.
5. Show the children the food pyramid (where should different types of food be placed in the pyramid) and remind them of the importance of a balanced diet.

B. Group/free choice activities

1. Social game: "Healthy menu"

    - ask the children to take turn to share the "healthy menu" they have designed with their parents;
    - during the presentation, encourage the children to make sentences using the pattern of "I love eating ____ and ____" according to the content of their menu;
    - form the children into groups of 6–7. Ask them to discuss which student's menu in their group is the healthiest, and then ask the children to present their discussion result to the class with good reasons. We can encourage them to apply the knowledge that they have just learnt about the food pyramid during the discussion/reasoning process.

2. Manipulative game: "Clipping candies" (the ability to use chopsticks and add within 10)

- There are 3 equations on a plate. Calculate the correct answers and use chopsticks to pick the answers (CPM number granule) out.
3. Writing Chinese characters: 健康菜单 (healthy menu).
4. Free choice activities: language/science/music/art/library/family corners.

C. Follow-up activities

Teach a new song to the children – Min-Nong (Pity on Farmers) – which is a Chinese classic poem.

Day 3:

A. Whole class activities

1. Ask the children to guess what type of food (fish) the teacher is going to introduce today. Use a riddle to provide the hints.
2. Review the story of *The Princess's Birthday Party*. Point out to the children the fact that most of the fish we eat nowadays are from fish ponds because over-fishing in open sea greatly reduces the number of fish habitats. Since natural resources are always limited, we should treasure them.
3. The teacher may continue, saying, "Now Little Princess knows the source of fish. How about meat and rice?" Use the pictures from the big book to illustrate these facts.
4. When talking about the sequence of rice cultivation, apart from showing the children pictures, the teachers may use the lyrics of Min-Nong (Pity on Farmers) that they have learnt yesterday to illustrate the hard work of farmers, so they can build up of appreciation of the hard work of farmers.
5. Show the children the video clip (government advertisement) "Don't touch living poultry" to point out the ways to prevent Bird Flu.

B. Group/free choice activities

1. Creative game: "Fruit basket" (Artwork: tear and paste)
    - show the children the pictures of fruits and a basket;
    - use colored pencils to outline a fruit basket on white drawing paper;
    - tear color paper into small pieces and stick onto the fruit basket.
2. Language game: "Delicious puzzle" (sentence making and spatial concept)
    - finish the puzzle first, and then write the correct answer (according to what is on the puzzle) to complete the sentence;
    - read the sentence aloud.
3. Writing Chinese characters: 鱼 (fish), 水果 (fruit), 肉 (meat), 米 (rice).
4. Free choice activities: language/science/music/art/library/family corners

C. Follow-up activities

Introduce the game – "Smart little scarecrow". Train the skills of scoot turning and balancing.

Day 4:

A. Whole class activities

1. Review the story *The Princess's Birthday Party* and guide the children in thinking of the common ways of getting food. Guide the children to think of the answer "supermarket" to provoke the children's interest of paying a visit to a supermarket in the following day.
2. Tell the story *Little Worm, Large Discovery* on the SAIL CD and show them the photos of a supermarket. Ask the children to observe the appearance of the supermarket, the goods to be sold, the ways of classifying goods into different categories, etc.
3. Use puppets to "role play" different behaviors in the supermarket (e.g. bringing our own bags, running in the supermarket, putting goods in the wrong place, etc.). Ask the children to differentiate the proper behaviors from the improper ones, and discuss in small groups the reason why these behaviors are considered as proper/improper.
4. Ask the children, "To buy food from supermarket, what do we need?" so as to introduce the children to the values of notes and coins in Hong Kong.
5. Let the children see a supermarket product (e.g. a can of soft drink) with the price tag on it. Ask the children to observe and find out how much they have to pay for it.
6. Use the story *The story of money* to tell the children the origin and history of money. Then, imagine how our lives would change if there was no money (e.g. we would have to trade by bartering). Ask the children to discuss this in small groups and then present their thoughts to the class.

B. Group/free choice activities

1. CPM teaching aids: "Milk series box 9–11" (knowledge of money)
2. Maths game: "Happy shopping" (money usage)
   - put the correct coins into the boxes according to the prize stated on the cardboard.
3. Writing Chinese characters: 超市 (supermarket), 钱 (money), 购物 (shopping).
4. Free choice activities: language/science/music/art/library/family corners

C. Follow-up activities

Ask the children to bring along with them $10 and a shopping bag for the supermarket visit activity the next day.

Day 5:

A. Whole class activities

Pre-visit preparation:

1. Group the children into three or four teams.
2. Ask each team to write down a shopping list.
3. Introduce the "Dos and Don'ts" (proper and improper behaviors that were discussed yesterday) of visiting the supermarket.

During the visit:

1. First guide the children to walk around the supermarket and introduce the goods.
2. Let the children go shopping with their team members. Each team will be guided by a teacher, who is supposed to observe and help the children to complete their shopping.
3. Remind the children to check whether they have enough money and to use the shopping bags that they have brought.

After the visit:

1. Ask each team to check whether they have successfully purchased all the items on their shopping list.
2. Ask the children to share their shopping experiences, difficulties and stories within their teams.
3. Each team sends a representative to tell their shopping stories to the class.

B. Follow-up activities

Ask each child to write up or draw something about today's supermarket visit.

Chapter 6

Assessing Chinese literacy attainment in the early years

Assessing Chinese literacy attainment in the early years has been a desire, as well as a challenge, for Chinese teachers, parents, and researchers, who wish to ensure that young children have all the fundamental skills necessary for school success. Assessment is desirable because it provides information about children's performance and abilities and affords a better understanding of individual learning needs, as well as how to best differentiate instruction. Through this, teaching Chinese literacy could be differentiated, so that all children could benefit from their preferred modalities. In addition, a professional Chinese literacy assessment could help identify learning difficulties and disabilities in young children and suggest early intervention. However, Chinese literacy assessment is not a thoroughly researched area – some fundamental and controversial issues have not been resolved. This chapter will first address the important debate about Chinese literacy assessment, and introduce two useful Chinese literacy scales that could be widely used in the early years.

Summative versus formative assessment

In early childhood programs, assessment data are widely used to understand and improve young children's learning. Nowadays, many scholars are promoting formative assessment, which is a kind of ongoing and authentic evaluation of young children's learning progress. But most Chinese parents are still in favor of one-off examinations (summative assessment) to let them know how smart their children are. This summative versus formative assessment controversy is observable in Hong Kong, mainland China and Singapore and will be addressed in this section.

Chinese literacy assessment: Why and how?

Why should we assess Chinese literacy? And how should we do it? Snow and her colleagues (Snow and Van Hemel, 2008; Snow and Oh, 2011) have asked similar questions about literacy assessment: "Why are we assessing? What are we assessing? How do we conduct the assessments? Who is being assessed?" The answers to these questions enable teachers to make an appropriate match between the assessment instrument and the learner characteristics. For example, assessment decisions will vary if children are L2 versus L1 Chinese learners or if children are at 2 years of age rather than at 12 years of age.

First, why are we assessing Chinese literacy? Assessment information could be used to support children's Chinese learning and be collected through a variety of methods, including observations, checklists, literacy scales, and tests (formal assessments). Teaching and learning Chinese are reciprocal processes, with each influencing the other. Only through assessment is a Chinese teacher able to understand how children are learning and, in turn, how to improve their teaching. Chinese literacy assessments should be age-appropriate in both content and the method of data collection. More important is that these assessments should be linguistically appropriate, fitting into the features of Chinese literacy. They should be easy to administer and the data collection techniques should not be difficult for Chinese teachers to use. There should be detailed guidelines about the appropriate assessment practices to ensure accurate and reliable data collection, given the fact that not all Chinese teachers are trained in assessment. It is hoped that the assessment results could help teachers better plan their lessons and organize their classrooms to provide rich learning environments for young children.

Second, how to do it? This is the core problem to be addressed in this chapter. The most difficult task for Chinese teachers, perhaps, is to clearly understand the assessment purposes and to select the appropriate instrument. Chinese assessment results could provide information about the progress of children's learning, as well as the effectiveness of Chinese teaching – the findings are really dependent on the selection of the assessment tools. A comprehensive Chinese literacy assessment system should involve a multi-source approach, such as (1) ongoing observations of children using checklists and anecdotal records, (2) their work samples and learning portfolios, and (3) some formal assessment measures that may be part of the literacy program. Authentic observations to record children's Chinese learning could be conducted continuously and repeatedly during daily life in school or at home. This kind of authentic and observational assessment is needed as young children are rapidly changing and growing. Daily observations can provide immediate feedback about Chinese literacy progress which can then inform the Chinese teachers of how they can adapt their teaching to meet learning needs. Children's work samples can also provide ongoing evidence of Chinese learning progress and development. Chinese teachers can collect samples of children's writing and other works which are dated and place them in a folder; hence, a learning portfolio. Their Chinese learning growth will be evident when the collected materials are reviewed by teachers and parents. Observation data and work samples are typical of formative assessment, and this will be elaborated in the next subsection.

Formative assessment

Formative assessment is an ongoing process which involves repeatedly and continuously gathering information from several sources, organizing and then finally interpreting the evidence. Teachers can document children's individual growth and development by compiling a learning portfolio, which is interactive and cyclical by nature and can be used to inform instruction and monitor children's progress (Wright, 2009). Formative assessment can be, and should be, part of the Chinese instructional process. For instance, when incorporated into classroom practice, it can provide the information needed to adjust Chinese teaching and learning while they are taking place. Formative assessment can provide authentic and genuine evidence of children's learning progress, and thus could help Chinese teachers decide the next steps during the teaching and learning process.

Here, the question is how can formative assessment be carried out to evaluate young children's Chinese literacy learning? Teachers can consider using classroom observation, children's work, self-evaluation and other approaches and strategies. But, first of all, teachers need to set up clear criteria and goals so that young children can understand teachers' clear expectations. We can use children's work, classroom exercise, or exemplars of what is expected to help children understand where they are, where they need to be, and what effective process they must undergo to get there. This can make the assessment itself a kind of Chinese literacy learning.

Classroom observations

Classroom observations are more than walking around the room to see if the students are on task or they need clarification. Observations can assist teachers in gathering more evidence of young children's Chinese learning to inform lesson planning. This evidence can also be recorded and used as feedback for children about their learning or, as anecdotal data, shared with them during individual feedback and parent-teacher meetings. Besides this, questioning strategies should be embedded in Chinese lesson planning. Asking better questions can open up many opportunities for deeper thinking and can provide Chinese teachers with significant insights into children's learning and understanding.

Peer or self-evaluation

Young children can also use self and peer assessment to reflect on their Chinese learning and progress. Teachers can pair up or even group young children to get them engaged in learning assessment. Peer evaluation can provide young children with more insights and reflections on their learning interests and learning outcomes.

Learning portfolio

All the educational authorities are promoting learning portfolios for young children. Maintaining a learning portfolio could help young children better understand their own learning as evidenced by their classroom work. And it could also provide "authentic evidence" about young children's learning to both teachers and parents. This process of children keeping ongoing records of their work will not only engage them, but also help them to see where they started and the progress they are making toward the learning goal. However, maintaining a learning portfolio for every child in a certain class (of large size) could be quite time- and resource-consuming; therefore, more teachers and more time are needed. This good practice is indeed quite demanding in terms of time and money.

Five-stage literacy document cycle

All the above mentioned strategies can be integrated into the formative assessment process, which can, in turn, inform Chinese teaching. Jones (2003) proposes a five-stage literacy documentation cycle with each step describing a process of collecting and examining data. Chinese teachers could follow the cycle of data collection to continually monitor children's learning.

1. Identify goals. Every learning activity has its goals, and so does the assessment. Chinese teachers could clarify the purpose of the assessment, determine which goals are being targeted, and identify the evidence of learning.
2. Collect data. This step includes planning and collecting multiple sources of data such as observations, checklists, digital audio and video tapes, portfolios, records of children's conversations and drawings, as well as other informal techniques.
3. Examine data. Every week, or at least every month, Chinese teachers could conduct a reflective examination of the data to determine the strengths and challenges of each child and to determine whether the identified learning goals have been achieved.
4. Revise teaching. Chinese teachers need to modify their teaching to better fit the young children's learning and developmental needs, based on the findings from the data.
5. Evaluate the new teaching plan. Chinese teachers could evaluate whether the modification has resulted in learning success, and, if not, whether any other modifications need to be made.

The cycle can be conducted for a single child or for a group of children – this cycle can be used to monitor children's progress toward meeting a particular goal. This kind of progress monitoring can vary in frequency and duration depending on the learning growth of individual children.

Summative assessment

Summative assessment refers to those formal assessments that are administered periodically to understand, at a particular point in time, what learners know and do not know. It is normally conducted once or twice a year to provide a snapshot of what a learner knows and is able to do. The major objective of summative assessment is to gauge young children's learning relative to certain standards or requirements. Being administered after teaching across a semester, summative assessments can help evaluate the effectiveness of Chinese programs and curricula. We believe that both types of assessments, formative and summative, are necessary to provide teachers, principals, and families with the evidence needed to determine if children are making appropriate progress in Chinese literacy learning.

Both formative and summative assessments could provide information about a child's learning progress and achievement, and the two types of assessments can support the findings of each other. Whereas formative assessments can provide feedback to the curriculum and instruction, summative assessments can help to determine whether the children have achieved the learning targets. Chinese literacy assessment should be a balanced fusion of both summative and formative ways of information gathering – we should not depend too much on one or the other. Instead, we should purposively and flexibly conduct both summative and formative classroom assessment practices to gather information about children's Chinese literacy learning.

Two types of summative assessment are commonly used in Chinese literacy assessment.

1 Criterion-referenced. Some Chinese term tests could be used to assess learners' mastery with particular learning content or against a pre-set benchmark. This is very popular in Chinese primary schools and there is a test for every unit, which is developed based on the learning content of the target unit.
2 Norm-referenced. Some Chinese literacy scales are designed to compare one group of students against another and are administered, scored, and interpreted in a standard manner (standardized). This type of early literacy scale typically consists of multiple-choice items, arranged in subscales, which normally include vocabulary knowledge, visual and auditory discrimination, letter recognition, and letter-sound correspondence (Genishi, 1993). In the following sections, we will introduce two Chinese literacy scales, both of which are norm-referenced.

Preschool and Primary Chinese Literacy Scale (PPCLS)

Any test should be reliable, valid, practical, culturally sensitive and congruent with the curriculum it is intended to assess (Nurss, 1992). So does the Chinese literacy test. To evaluate early Chinese literacy attainment in Beijing, Hong Kong, and Singapore, we developed and validated the Preschool and Primary Chinese Literacy Scale (PPCLS) (aged 3 to 10) (Li, 1999). In our previous studies (Lau, Li and Rao, 2011; Li and Rao, 2000; Li and Rao 2005), the PPCLS was found to be a reliable and valid measure of Chinese literacy attainment. Test-retest reliability, with a sample of 480 children in Beijing, Hong Kong and Singapore, was 0.82 (Li and Rao, 2000). The internal consistency of the scale was 0.85 as measured by coefficient alpha and it normally took 10 to 15 minutes for a trained tester to complete the test with one child. This section will introduce the development and validation of the PPCLS, and the full version is included in Appendix I.

Instrument development

Zhu (1991), the pioneer of Chinese language assessment, proposed three approaches to Chinese literacy scale development:

1 the whole-pool testing approach is to test with all the items in the whole pool;
2 the random-sampling approach is to randomly choose a set of testing items from the whole pool; and
3 the stratified sampling approach is to divide the whole pool into different strata (according to degree of difficulty) and then randomly select the final testing items proportionally from the different strata.

Zhu noted that the whole-pool testing approach might be very time-consuming, whereas the random-sampling approach might not reflect the desired degree of difficulty. We tend to believe that the stratified sampling approach could achieve a balance between reliability and workability and is the best approach to developing the PPCLS.

To make the PPCLS culturally sensitive and congruent with the curriculum, we chose the 2,600 Chinese characters commonly listed in the Primary Chinese Syllabuses in China, Hong Kong and Singapore. The 2,600 items made up the whole pool of the PPCLS testing. Then, we took the stratified sampling approach to classify the 2,600 items into 10 strata according to their degree of difficulty and randomly selected 20 items from each stratum. A total of 200 testing items has been sampled, and the ratio to the pool is $200/2600 = 1/13$. This makes the PPCLS simpler and easier to administer than simply testing all 2600 items.

The same 200 testing items were developed into two versions of the PPCLS: one spoken in Putonghua and written in simplified Chinese characters to be used in Beijing and Singapore; the other in Cantonese and traditional characters for the Hong Kong sample. The different sociolinguistic contexts of Beijing, Hong Kong and Singapore have to be considered in order to make the PPCLS culturally sensitive and linguistically appropriate. A Chinese painter in Beijing created the artwork for the PPCLS to ensure that each item is culturally appropriate to Chinese communities. Zhu (1991) suggested that a primary Chinese literacy test should normally have four subscales: listen-and-point, recognize-and-read, dictation, and write from memory. The PPCLS is targeted at preschools and primary school children, so it has to be easy for children of this age. Its final version consists of four subscales: character-picture matching (grapheme-semantic association), listen-and-point (visual and auditory discrimination), recognize-and-read (character recognition), read-and-say (character utilization).

The development of the PPCLS has gone through three stages. First, an expert panel of educators, linguists and psychologists from Beijing, Hong Kong and Singapore was asked to assess the appropriateness of the testing items and comment on its content validity. The results from these reviewing activities were taken into account when the first version of the PPCLS was developed.

Next, a pilot study using the PPCLS was conducted in Beijing and Singapore. Twenty preschoolers were sampled from each community. Each child was administered the PPCLS by the researcher, in individual sessions. A significant correlation was found between the PPCLS total score and the years of literacy education for the children, $r = 0.63$, $p < 0.001$. The results of this pilot study were used to modify the instrument.

Third, several other decisions were made based on observation notes and discussions with local teachers. For example, the Subscale E "Handwriting Skill" was originally designed for children above the age of 4 and was not appropriate for the younger children who participated in the present study. It is therefore not included in the final version of the PPCLS, which consists of 200 items addressing four competencies (see Appendix I).

Instrument validation

Altogether 480 Chinese children were randomly sampled from Beijing, Hong Kong and Singapore, with 20 boys and 20 girls from each age group in each city. Four age groups were sampled: 2.5 years (+ 2 months), 3.5 years (+ 2 months), 4.5 years (+ 2 months), and 5.5 years (+ 2 months). Each child took about 15 to 30 minutes to complete the test, in individual sessions. Among them, 80 preschoolers in Beijing and Singapore were re-administered the test after 2 weeks to index test-retest reliability. The following psychometric properties were examined.

Means and standard deviations were calculated for the total PPCLS score and for each of the four subscales. This was done separately for the four age groups and for the three city samples. Alpha coefficients were calculated for the PPCLS total score and for the subscale scores. All these data are presented in Li and Rao (2000). The coefficients of the full scale for each group were all high (range 0.79 to 0.82), indicating that the testing items within each subscale converge on a common construct. Regarding the subscales, all but 2 of 12 coefficients exceeded 0.7. They were considered adequate evidence of internal consistency reliability and scale unidimensionality.

The Pearson correlations among each of the four subscales and the total PPCLS score were calculated separately for the three samples. All the subscale scores were significantly related to each other and to the total score; the values for the coefficients ranged from 0.36 to 0.94, $p < 0.001$. The test-retest reliability

Table 6.1 Test-retest reliability for PPCLS subscales and total score

Subscale	Beijing (n = 40)	Singapore (n = 40)
Grapheme/semantic association	0.82	0.81
Visual/auditory discrimination	0.80	0.77
Character recognition	0.81	0.80
Character utilization	0.84	0.82
Total score	0.82	0.80

Table 6.2 Analysis of variance for PPCLS scores with the age of child as the independent variable

Subscale	df	Beijing	Hong Kong	Singapore
Grapheme/semantic association	3	12.01***	52.48***	10.94***
Visual/auditory discrimination	3	11.73***	76.53***	18.18***
Character recognition	3	14.57***	55.27***	37.20***
Character utilization	3	1.97*	10.99***	4.46**
Total score	3	15.99***	79.64***	28.42***

Note: *p < 0.05; **p < 0.01; ***p < 0.001.

was assessed using Pearson correlation analyses. The results are presented in Table 6.1. These analyses revealed high test-retest reliability for the Beijing (r = 0.82, p < 0.001) and Singapore samples (r = 0.8, p < 0.001). The test-retest reliability parameters for the 4 subscales exceeded 0.8, with the exception of the VAD in Singapore sample (r = 0.77). These indicate that the PPCLS has adequate test-retest reliability in these communities.

A set of one-way analyses of variance for PPCLS scores, with the age of the child as the independent variable, was conducted for the children in Beijing, Hong Kong and Singapore, respectively. The results are shown in Table 6.2, which indicates significant group differences on all subscales and the total scores in Beijing, Hong Kong and Singapore.

Discussion

The PPCLS appears to have adequate reliability and validity for use with young children in Beijing, Hong Kong and Singapore.

The coherence of the PPCLS and its subscales is suggested by the high internal consistency of the subscales. The only exception was the Singapore sample, which had modest internal consistency in the three samples. This may be due to the fact that the sample in Singapore varied greatly in sociolinguistic and socioeconomic conditions, and the diminished alpha coefficient for the Singapore sample may reflect varying samples rather than structural inadequacy (please refer to previous chapters for more information about Singapore). Our follow-up studies (Li *et al.* 2008; Li, Rao and Tse, 2012) in Singapore young children found that the internal consistency of the PPCLS was acceptable in Singapore.

The PPCLS and its subscales also demonstrated satisfactory test-retest reliability, excepting the VAD test in Singapore. The VAD assesses the ability of visual and auditory discrimination by presenting one target character and three distracters chosen for graphic, phonetic or semantic similarities. Our previous studies (Li and Rao, 2000) indicated that the children in Singapore, immersed in a multilingual environment, tended to do less well with VAD than their counterparts in Beijing and Hong Kong.

Several indexes also demonstrated the high validity of the PPCLS. If the PPCLS has the properties of a developmental scale, easier items would precede more difficult items. Hence, with increasing age, children would pass more test items and we would expect a significant positive correlation between age and the PPCLS scores for children in the three communities. The present study indicated that the PPCLS scores correlated significantly with the age of the children across, and within, the three communities. The results of ANOVA showed that the children differed significantly in the 4 age groups on the PPCLS, and the older children outperformed the younger children on the subscales and total scores. These confirmed the suitability, and supported the use, of the PPCLS as a developmental instrument in Chinese communities.

In summary, the PPCLS appears to have adequate reliability and validity for use with preschool and primary school children in Beijing, Hong Kong and Singapore. It assesses a broad range of indicators of Chinese literacy proficiency in the different Chinese communities.

Primary Chinese Reading Literacy Scale (PCRLS)

The *Primary Chinese Reading Literacy Scale* is a brand-new scale developed for the summative assessment of Chinese reading literacy for Primary 1–6 students. Reading is a multilevel processing of cognition, understanding, absorption and application of written materials (the text), an important way for readers to engage in learning and getting information. As a developing and dynamic interaction between reader and text, reading itself is also developing in the primary school years. The PCRLS is designed to assess the reading literacy of L1 Chinese learners in China.

What is reading literacy?

In the Programme for International Student Assessment (PISA) study reading literacy is defined as the capability for understanding, using, and reflecting on written texts, in order to achieve one's goals, to develop one's knowledge and potential, and to participate in society. This is a conventional definition of reading literacy. Nowadays, we tend to believe that reading is a set of mental activities involving the psycholinguistic and socio-historic-cultural processing of written texts, a kind of dialogue and exchange between the text and the reader. Postmodernism views reading as a kind of creative activity, seeking understanding and self-understanding in order to build a "new me". It is not easy to evaluate children's Chinese reading literacy as reading itself involves the text, the reader's own knowledge and experience, life experiences, cultural background, mentalities, and so on. Reading itself is a subjective understanding of the Chinese text, the author's intention, emotions, moods, views, etc. Therefore, reading literacy is highly related to the reader's background, knowledge, experience and insights into the meaning of the text and could be viewed as the self-realization of the reader.

In China, Chinese reading literacy refers to the knowledge, ability and experience of children to read Chinese. The ultimate goal of Chinese reading instruction is to develop young children's Chinese reading skills, which include comprehension, memorization, and speed reading. Conventionally, the Chinese reading abilities are made up of information processing skills, reading comprehension ability, exploratory reading ability, automated reading skills, reading aloud and silent reading abilities, browse and search capabilities, the ability to access books, excerpts, the ability to make the reading cards, to write an executive summary, and so on. In 2001, the Ministry of Education in China issued *Full-time compulsory language curriculum standards* (trial version) (hereinafter referred to as the New Standard), which set three learning outcomes for Chinese reading instruction:

1   developing independent reading skills;
2   focusing on the emotional experience; and
3   forming a good sense of language.

Five components were proposed for Chinese reading literacy in the New Standard:

1   Text-decoding ability. This is the ability to decode Chinese characters and sentences to make rapid and accurate processing of written texts, which involves orthographic, graphical, phonological, and semantic processing activities. This is the first and most important component of Chinese reading literacy.
2   Reading comprehension. This refers to the understanding of materials based on text decoding, existing knowledge and experience. It involves a series of mental activities, such as association, analysis and synthesis, induction and generalization, judgment and reasoning, and other thinking activities. Reading comprehension is the core element of Chinese reading literacy.
3   Reading retention. This refers to the ability to store, recall or recognize what has been read and is highly associated with memory. This ability is very critical in Chinese reading as it helps children to search for information and facilitates them in understanding the texts based on the integration of reading experiences.

4 The pragmatics of reading. This refers to the ability to apply what has been learnt from the reading materials into learning and daily life, including a new point of view, a good word/sentence, a good deed, etc.
5 Appreciation and evaluation. This refers to the abilities to appreciate and evaluate the ideological content of the reading materials, forms, and other aspects. This is the highest level of component of Chinese reading literacy.

Current tests of reading literacy

To date, several international evaluation projects have been involved in testing the reading literacy of Chinese children. All these international tests are designed and conducted in order to compare students' reading ability worldwide.

PIRLS

The Progress in International Reading Literacy Study (PIRLS) is a large, international comparative study of the reading literacy of fourth grade students (9–10 years old). This is jointly led by the International Research Centre (ISC) and the International Association for Evaluation of Educational Achievement (IEA), involving 35 countries/areas including Hong Kong. The PIRLS study was designed to investigate the factors which affect students' ability to read and their attitudes to reading, with the aim of providing empirical evidence for the improvement of education policy. The assessment focuses on three main areas of literacy; namely, the process of comprehension, the purposes for reading, and reading behaviors and attitudes. Two purposes for reading are examined: reading for literary experience, and reading to acquire and use information. Reading comprehension covers four areas:

1 conduct and articulate an information search;
2 draw direct conclusions;
3 explain and integrate ideas and information;
4 inspect and evaluate article content, language and textual elements.

Reading behavior and attitudes are evaluated through surveying the students, parents, teachers and principals with questionnaires.

PISA

The Programme for International Student Assessment (PISA) is a project run by the Organization for Economic Cooperation and Development (OECD). It gauges and compares the skills and knowledge of 15-year-old students worldwide. The assessment focuses on students' achievement in three main domains: Science, Reading, and Mathematics. The concept of literacy underpinning PISA is a functionalistic one; that is, 15-year-old students should apply competences they have learned at school in the context of authentic tasks that are part of their daily lives. In the light of this functional concept, PISA examines the degree to which adolescents are able to understand and integrate texts they are confronted with in their everyday lives. It assesses students in their ability to retrieve texts and access them, to interpret and integrate texts, and to reflect and evaluate texts. Aspects such as reading speed are not prioritized.

Chinese reading tests

Recently, many Chinese scholars have developed Chinese reading tests to evaluate students' reading ability. The test developed by South China Normal University defines reading ability in terms of language decoding, organizing, pattern identifying, screening and storing, understanding and transferring skills. The test is administered with assignments at three levels, corresponding to the lower, middle, and high primary grades.

Ni (2003) suggests that Chinese reading tests should follow four principles:

1   they should be conducted in multiple ways including dictation, reading in silence, reading aloud, oral and communication;
2   they should be a combination of open as well as closed book tests;
3   they should contain more than just multiple choice questions and should include many types of question; and
4   they should be a fusion of formative and summative assessments.

A new Chinese reading test has recently been developed and validated by Shu and her team (2013) at Beijing Normal University.

The common problems and new directions of Chinese reading tests

The tests are very boring

Most of the Chinese reading tests are administered as termly examinations, which are either boring or too serious, or both. The instructions are often very abstract and narrow; for instance, "read the essay, complete the questions that follow", "explain the word", "draw a line in the text of the sentence that means . . ." and so on. Questions are also in relatively simple formats; such as, multiple-choice and cloze procedure. These types of tests indicate that these are examination tasks and may make younger students more anxious and depressed.

The questions are irrelevant to students' daily life

Many items in the reading proficiency tests are isolated concepts and skills, and are irrelevant to children's daily life. For example, many reading materials are biographies of great people or heroes and young children are not familiar with them. Their reading interests and preferences have not been accounted for in the item development. Neither their practical use nor their communication needs are carefully considered in the test development.

The test objectives are very simple

Traditional Chinese reading tests focus on the dimensions of knowledge and skills, neglecting other important dimensions such as attitudes and values. For example, the test of reading comprehension is always asking students to summarize the central idea of a paper, and rarely asks students to consider their feelings or evaluations of the paper. This reflects an ignorance of the emotional dimension of the students concerned.

China has launched a millennium reform of basic education with a focus on curriculum structure and content. A set of new objectives has been set up for the learning and teaching of Chinese reading. The general objectives of primary school Chinese reading are that students can:

1   enjoy reading;
2   read aloud correctly and fluently in Mandarin;
3   read at a speed of more than 300 words per minute;
4   comprehend Chinese texts appropriately;
5   understand fairy tales, fables, narratives, poetry, etc.;
6   acquire skimming and scanning skills to capture the required information;
7   be familiar with the use of the punctuation such as comma, periods, question marks, exclamation points, colons, quotation marks, comma, and semicolon;
8   recite 160 Chinese poems;
9   establish the habit of reading newspapers and use libraries and the internet to get information.

The new primary Chinese reading syllabus highlights respect for students' autonomy and independence in reading, the variation of reading materials and methods, and the accumulation of language materials. It has also laid out clear requirements for a Chinese reading test:

1   it should be a comprehensive and inclusive test of students' reading experience, comprehension and feelings, including reading interests, skills, habits and personal preferences;
2   it should evaluate both reading aloud and reading in silence;
3   it should include intensive reading and focus on experiential reading and creative reading comprehension;
4   it should also test skimming and scanning abilities to see whether students can capture important information;
5   it should test the appreciation and evaluation of literary works;
6   it should also test students' ability in reading ancient poetry, with a focus on testing their understanding and accumulation of knowledge.

This new syllabus has indicated several new trends in Chinese reading tests. More specifically, the syllabus:

1. emphasizes students' reading experiences, feelings, and values;
2. underscores the importance of students' overall perception and understanding; and
3. takes into consideration students' reading interest and habits.

The structure and content of the PCRLS

The PCRLS is developed for Chinese students with reference to the new Chinese language syllabus issued by the Chinese educational authorities. Chinese reading ability is defined, in the new syllabus, as a complex set of competences in literacy, comprehension, application, accumulation and evaluation. PCRLS requires a reading test to cover the three dimensions of Chinese reading, namely, knowledge and skills, processes and methods, attitudes and values.

The 3-D structure of the Chinese reading test

Table 6.1 shows the matrix of PCRLS including the three-dimensional structure and five-ability of the content. The testing forms are also listed to match with the content and structure. This table outlines the scope, structure, content and method of PCRLS, indicating the weighting of knowledge, abilities, attitudes and the degree of importance assigned to the testing topics and scores.

The development of the testing materials

Primary students have varying reading abilities at different grades. Students at the first stage (Grades 1–2) are at the initiation stage of reading. The testing materials suitable for this stage are simple fairy tales, fables, songs, etc. At the second stage (Grades 3–4), students can conduct reading activities smoothly with familiar reading materials. At the third stage (Grades 5–6), students can read to learn and to think. They can read more abstract, longer, and more complex sentences. They should be more concerned about reading the whole article than just sentences or paragraphs. In short, the testing materials should

Table 6.3 The structure of the *Primary Chinese Reading Literacy Scale*

Ability	Dimension	Method	Weighting (%)
Literacy	Knowledge and skills	Multiple choice	20
Comprehension	Knowledge and skills	Multiple choice	20
Application	Processes and methods	Short answer	20
Accumulation	Processes and methods	Cloze	20
Evaluation	Attitudes and values	Long answer	20

be familiar to the students and very close to their daily lives, and so we wrote all the testing materials based on Chinese children's reading interests, concerns and daily experiences.

Types of testing question

Question types are very critical in the evaluation of reading ability. Multiple choice, cloze, quiz, short and long questions are used to test the varied abilities of Primary 1–6 students in the PCRLS and to reflect the relevant purpose and content. All of the questions are designed to evaluate students' acquisition of the information contained in the article, as well as their understanding of the article. The questions can be divided into two major categories:

1. objective questions that are very simple and easy to mark. Although these objective questions are time-saving, they are able to tap into students' thinking skills and exclude the possibility of students' guessing the answers;
2. subjective questions requiring short and open answers, arguments, and conclusions, which are subjective and personal, but which can reflect students' thinking and presenting skills, imagination and comprehension, values and feelings, and so on. However, the responses to these subjective questions are not easy to evaluate against the scoring criteria – marking subjective questions can become subjective and arbitrary. To make the PCRLS easier to administer and mark, we developed "objective" questions and tried to make them more challenging in terms of the demand on students' reasoning and thinking skills. In this connection, the PCRLS is testing primary students' reading ability with objective questions requiring more subjective answers. For the text of the PCRLS, please refer to Appendix 2.

In addition to the abovementioned PPCLS and PCRLS, there are many informal ways of assessing young children's Chinese literacy. Chinese teachers, in their teaching practices, have developed many useful games and play situations to casually and formatively assess young children's literacy attainment. Nevertheless, they are still using traditional assessments such as dictation, writing from memory, copying, reading comprehension tests, and essay tests. As always, we are advocating a combination of formal and informal ways, a fusion of formative and summative assessments, and a mix of traditional and innovative approaches to evaluating young children's learning of Chinese literacy in varying contexts. Assessment itself, however, should also be culturally appropriate, contextually appropriate, and child appropriate (3CAPs) – the best assessments (if there are any) should follow this principle. Only in this way will Chinese literacy tests be the most appropriate.

Appendix 1

Preschool and Primary Chinese Literacy Scale (PPCLS)

Appendix IA

学前及初小儿童中文识字量表指导手册

Preschool and Primary Chinese Literacy Scale Manual

1998试用版©

版权归香港大学教育系李辉所有。未经著作人书面许可，任何人不得以任何形式或方式复制、转印或散发本手册及相关材料。本手册内容属保密级别，请严格遵守基本保密规则。

本量表在制作过程中得到啬色园教育研究基金 (Sik Sik Yuen Educational Research Fund) 鼎力资助，在此谨致谢忱。北京工业大学奚其炎先生在百忙中亲自为本量表画图，特此鸣谢！

1 简介

本手册是专为《学前及初小儿童中文识字量表(试用版)》(Preschool & Primary Chinese Literacy Scale) 施测人员提供详细技术说明而编写的。为行文方便，以下将使用中文简称"量表"和英文简称"PPCLS"来指称本《学前及初小儿童中文识字量表(试用版)》。特别需要提请注意的是：请勿将本量表外传给非施测人员，以确保本量表的保密性与可靠性。

1.1 目的、用途与局限

本量表是一种专门测量学前及小学低年级儿童中文识字量的工具，不适用于小学三年级及其以上的儿童。在现有研究水平下，它为教师、家长和学校提供了相对科学而准确的测查手段，以便了解儿童实际识字水平和识字教学效果。

本量表可以用来考察新入学(园)儿童的实际识字量，以便教师因材施教；也可以在学期中间或结束时用来检测幼儿园、小学的识字教学效果；更可以作为识字教学改革实验的测量工具，以协助探索最佳教学方法。

本量表只能测定儿童语言能力中的识字能力，如果想全面了解语言能力发展的情况，请用其他相关测量工具。必须强调指出的是，本量表所测量的只是被测儿童实际认识汉字数量的估计值(误差是±13个字)，并不能测查儿童的智力或其他方面的发展水平。虽然识字量对于儿童早期认知发展有非常重要的促进作用，但识字量的多少并不能代表儿童智力或天资的高低。我们不希望各位儿童因为在本量表中成绩的高低不同而受到家长或教师的"区别对待"。

1.2 特点

本量表是在参考借鉴国内外有关儿童识字量表的基础上，结合学前及初小儿童年龄特点、认知特点而研制的。在北京、香港和新加坡等地的预试验结果表明，本量表具有一定的信度和效度，测试形式容易被学前及初小儿童接受。主试(即施测人员)不用做事前准备，施测过程简单明了，能够相对客观、准确和快速地测出儿童的实际识字水平。

1.3 主试资格

本量表主试一般不需要特别参加培训课程，只须将本手册认真阅读一遍并确保已经熟练掌握每个细节即可。也即，主试要在正式测验之前熟悉本量表所有测验工具并熟悉测验的每一个环节。

2 量表与施测

以下介绍本量表所用的测试材料及其施测要求。

2.1 量表清单

本《学前及初小儿童中文识字量表》包括以下几种材料：

2.1.1 指导手册

即本指导手册。它详细介绍了本量表的目的、内容、使用方法及注意事项。

2.1.2 测验A：字图匹配

要求儿童从每页的四幅图中找出一幅能够准确表达测试汉字意义的图片。主要考察儿童对汉字字义的掌握（即形义匹配能力），不需要口语表达或任何语音活动。

2.1.3 测验B：听音指字

要求儿童从每页的四个汉字中找出主试所念出的那个测试汉字来，主要考察儿童对汉字字音的掌握（即音形匹配能力）。

2.1.4 测验C：指字认字

要求儿童依次指认每个汉字并相对准确地读出字音来，主要考察儿童对汉字的再认能力。

2.1.5 测验D：认字说话

要求儿童依次指认每个汉字，并用每个字组一个词或是造句或是说一句话，主要考察儿童对汉字音形义的掌握及其中文语用能力。

2.1.6 测验记录纸

用来详细记录被试基本信息及其在测验中各项目的具体表现。所有用过的测验记录纸均属保密资料，除主试和研究人员以外，任何人不得接触这些记录纸。

2.2 施测要求

本量表属个体测验性质，需要主试和被测试儿童一对一单独进行，因此对时间和空间安排均有一定要求，详见下述。

2.2.1 空间安排

本量表需要主试和儿童单独在一个安静的房间里进行测试。房间里要有一张高度适中的桌子，主试和被试儿童必须各有一把适合自己高度的椅子。房间里的灯光和温度都要适中，并保证测试进行过程中不受任何外在因素的干扰。主试不可配带BP机、手机，测度进行中不可停下来打电话或四处走动。

2.2.2 座位安排

较为理想的座位安排应该如图一所示那样：主试和被试并排而坐，主试如果是右利手，则可让被试儿童坐在自己的左侧；少数左利手主试则可安排儿童坐在自己的右侧。

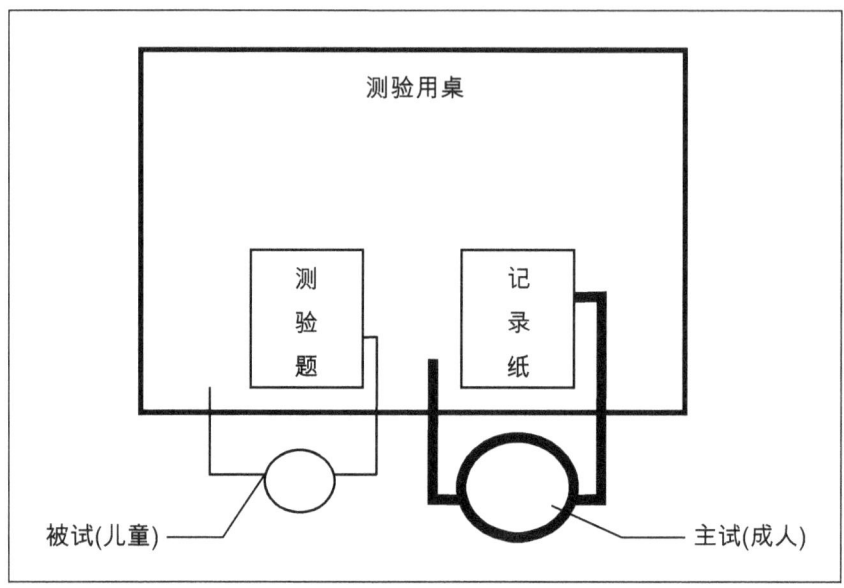

图一：《学前及初小儿童中文识字量表》施测时座位安排

2.2.3 时间安排

原则上每个被试都可以在30分钟内完成本量表测试，最多不得超过60分钟，否则就必须自动停止测试，以充分保证儿童的身心健康。全部完成一个儿童的测试后，方可安排下一个被试进入房间测试。不可为节省时间而安排儿童在房间里预先等候。

3 施测要求

本量表与其他测验量表一样，是以假定所有被试在测试中都会表现出他们的最高能力水平为基本前提的。因此，主试人员应当非常准确细致地记录下被试儿童在测验中的反应，这对于正确评价某个儿童的能力是至关重要的。如果主试不能够准确客观地记录儿童的回答，这个测验就是无效的，或者说至少结果会是错误的。请各位主试在测验时务必记住这一点。

3.1 建立友好合作气氛

对于学前及初小儿童来讲，情绪和气氛均会极大影响他们的能力表现和外在反应。因此，主试应当从一开始就和被试儿童建立起友好合作关系，让他们感到轻松自在而不是紧张拘束。如何做到这一点？这并没有固定的模式，而主要取决于主试的个人经验。一般来讲，如果主试和被试儿童互不熟识的话，就需要在正式测试之前闲聊几句，以便舒缓儿童的紧张情绪，拉近同被试之间的心理距离，让他/她感到亲切。另外，在测验过程中也需要多用言语鼓励儿童的参与和回答。

3.2 熟悉测验记录纸

测验记录纸是记录本量表施测结果的唯一载体，<u>不可随意摆放或未经许可就向第三者公开。否则，会被追究法律后果</u>。请不要忽视这一点，切切！

记录纸第一部分内容是关于被试的基本信息，务必详细准确地记录。不要有任何误差，以免影响对测验结果的准确解释。

第一项"<u>被试姓名</u>"，请认真填写被试儿童的中文名字。我们将在处理数据时自动用数字代码覆盖，以保障每名被试儿童的隐私权；第二项"<u>现就读于</u>"，请填写被试儿童所在的幼稚园/幼儿园/学校的名称；第三项"<u>班级</u>"，请填写被试测验时所就读的班级；第四项"<u>教师姓名</u>"，请填写该班负责教师的名字；第五项"<u>主试姓名</u>"，请填写您自己的名字。

第六项"<u>测验得分</u>"是指被试儿童在本次测验中的最后得分，请在所有测验均完毕以后再计算出被试的总得分，并请填入本栏；第七项"<u>测验日期</u>"，请填写施测当天的日期；第八项"<u>出生日期</u>"请填写被试儿童的出生日期；第九项"<u>实足年龄</u>"，请根据第七项、第八项计算出儿童的实足年龄。必须指出的是，<u>实足年龄只精确到月</u>，如果被试的实足年龄是"5岁3个月零22天"，则其实足年龄应该填写为"5岁3个月"，而不是"5岁4个月"，切记。

以后各部分是用来分别记录测验A、测验B、测验C、测验D的测查结果的。详见后面说明，此略。

4 施测指导语

本章将详细介绍如何运用本量表对儿童识字能力进行测试。注意：以下所有用""引起来的部分，都是主试要在测验中对儿童所说的话。香港地区的主试在用粤语进行测试时，可根据当地语言表述习惯略作改动，但要保证语意相同。<u>北京和新加坡的测试不可随意改动下面""内所列语句</u>。

4.1 介绍测验内容和目的

主试在正式测验之前，需要向被试儿童简单介绍一下测试内容及其目的，打消儿童的神秘感和紧张情绪，并尝试建立轻松友好的合作气氛。在此之前，如果时间允许的话，主试可以和被试闲聊几分钟。以下是主试需要对儿童说的话：

"你好！小朋友！请告诉我，你叫什么名字？"

"你今年几岁？你知不知道自己的生日是哪一天？"如果儿童不能准确说出自己的生日，就不用再追问下去，以免影响其情绪和自信心。

"好！现在老师要和你玩一些识字游戏，看看你到底能认识多少个汉字，好不好？"

"准备好了没有？那我们就开始了！"

4.2 测验A：字图匹配

将测验A打开放在儿童的眼前，指着项目1对儿童说："现在我们先玩一个看字找图的游戏。你看，这里有个汉字，上面有四张图片，请你告诉老师，哪张图片画的才是这个汉字的意思呢？用手指给我看，好吗？"

如果儿童第一遍答错了，主试可以说："嗯，想想，应该是哪张图呢？"每个题目只可以有两次机会。无论第二遍儿童回答得正确与否，主试均应微笑着说"谢谢！真好！"不能对儿童表现出消极或不喜欢的情绪，不能通过声音、语气或身体姿势来暗示儿童，更不能否定儿童的答案。

每个项目留给儿童回答的时间不多。如果主试问完问题后，儿童马上摇头表示不知道答案，就可以说"嗯，这个题目难了点，我们看下一个吧"；如果儿童在想了一分钟后，仍然说不出明确答案，可以这样对他说"看看到底哪个更像一些，指给我看就行了"；如果这样以后儿童还是答不出来，就跟他说"看来这个题目也很难。我们不管它，再看下一个吧。"

当儿童确切指中某张图片后，无论其对与错，请将其答案写在记录纸的相应位置。请注意，只是将其指中的图片的编号(1, 2, 3, 4)写进记录纸中"被试儿童的答案"一栏里。不要判断其对错，这个任务留待全部测验结束后再做。

4.3 测验B：听音指字

将测验B打开放在儿童的眼前，指着项目1对儿童说：

"现在我们再玩一个听音指字的游戏。你看，这上面有4个汉字，待会我会说出一个汉字，请你猜猜我说的是哪个字，用手指出来给我看，好吗？"

如果儿童第一遍答错了，主试可以说："嗯，想想，应该是哪个字呢？"每个题目只可以有两次机会。无论第二遍儿童回答得正确与否，主试均应微笑着说："嗯！谢谢！真好！"应尽量鼓励儿童来参与测试，而不是打击或否定他/她。

<u>主试在念出测验用字的时候，要采用"以词代字"的办法，比如"身"字，就要说"请你告诉我身体的'身'是哪个字？"不要只念单字，否则会因同音字太多导致儿童无法准确判断。</u>

以下是各项目可以用来"以词代字"的词语：
项目1：今天的"今"；
项目2：出去的"出"；进出的"出"；
项目3：左右的"左"；左手右手的"左"；
项目4：阳光的"光"；光线的"光"；灯光的"光"；
项目5：坐下来的"坐"；坐在地上的"坐"；
项目6：身体的"身"；
项目7：姐姐的"姐"；
项目8：前后的"后"；后来的"后"；
项目9：红色的"红"；红绿灯的"红"；
项目10：夏天的"夏"；
项目11：一 两 的" "；一 小鸟的" "；
项目12：得到的"得"；
项目13：喜欢的"喜"；
项目14：回答问题的"答"；答案的"答"；
项目15：黄色的"黄"；红灯黄灯的"黄"；
项目16：对不起的"对"；一对两对的"对"；
项目17：样子的"样"；榜样的"样"；
项目18：做操的"操"；操场的"操"；
项目19：自己的"己"；
项目20：出汗的"汗"；汗水的"汗"；

儿童用手指出某个字后，无论其对与错，请将其答案写在记录纸的相应位置。请注意，只是将其指中的字的编号(1，2，3，4)写进"<u>被试儿童的答案</u>"一栏里。不要判断其对与错，更不要流露出任何表情来。如果儿童<u>没听清楚</u>，可以适当再说一遍给他听。至于重复次数，一般不超过三次，这由主试根据个别儿童的个别情况来决定。

4.4 测验C：指字认字

将测验C打开放在儿童的眼前，指着项目1对儿童说：

"现在我们再玩一个指字认字的游戏。你看，这里有很多汉字，请你用手指着字，一个一个地读给我听，好吗？"

如果儿童读错了某个字，你就可以说"嗯！想想，应该是什么呢？"每个字只可以有两次机会。无论第二遍儿童回答正确与否，你都应该微笑着说："谢谢你！真好！接下来是什么字啊？"不能对儿童表现出消极或不喜欢的情绪。如果儿童问你"老师，对不对？"或者用一种寻求证实的眼光来看着你时，你就应该说"嗯，答得不错，继续努力！"或者用一种鼓励的眼光看看他，但不能给他/她任何提示或暗示。也就是说，主试不能采取任何方式告诉儿童其答案正确与否。

4.5 测验D：认字说话

将测验D打开放在儿童的眼前，指着项目1对儿童说：

"现在我们再玩一个认字说话的游戏。你看，这里有很多汉字，请你用手指着字，一个一个地读给我听，每读一个字，都要用这个字说一句话，或者组一个词语，好吗？"

如果儿童读错了某个字或组错了词(句)，你就可以说"嗯，想想，应该是什么样子呢？"每个字只可以有两次尝试机会。无论第二遍儿童回答得正确与否，主试均应微笑着说："(嗯！)谢谢！真好！接下来是什么字啊？怎么说啊？"如果儿童不经思索就快速说出答案，可以请他"慢慢来，想一想，再告诉我好吗？"

4.6 测验结束

全部测验结束后，应向儿童致谢，并对他/她说："你做得真好，谢谢你。非常高兴和你在一起做这些识字游戏。再见。"然后将儿童带出测验房间，并请下一位被试儿童进入测试房间，重复上述测试过程。

而对于量表测试结果的解释和说明，则需要由相关专业人员根据专业程序来进行。主试或其他一般人员均不宜对测试结果置评甚至公开测试结果。

Appendix 1B

Preschool and Primary Chinese Literacy Scale – Test A

学前及初小中文识字量表

（简体字版）

测验A：字图匹配

本量表在制作过程中得到啬色园教育基金鼎力资助，在此谨致谢忱。
Special acknowledgments go to the **Sik Sik Yuen Education Research Fund** for its financial support.

1

2

3

4

1

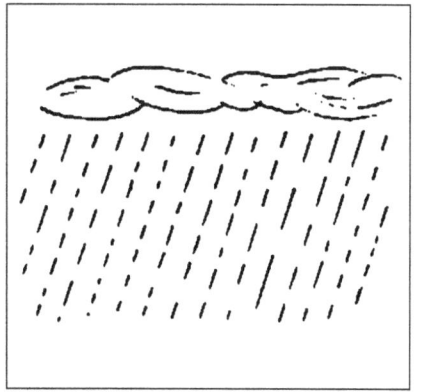
2

3

4

146 Appendix 1

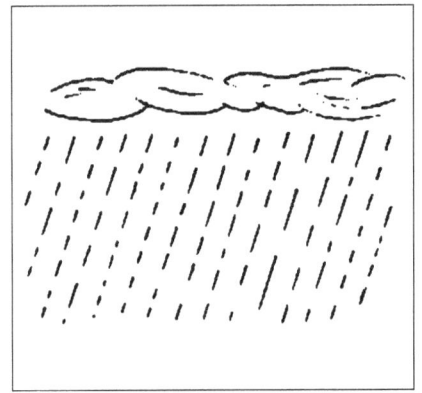

1

2

3

4

1

2

3

4

叶

148 Appendix I

1

2

3

4

树

1

2

3

4

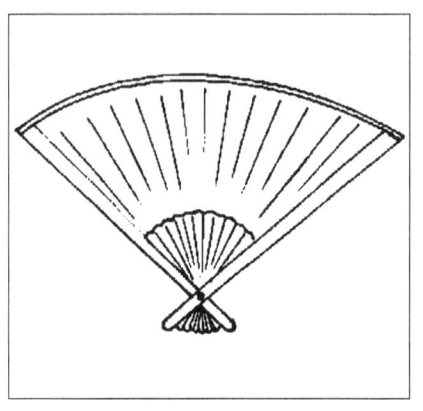

1

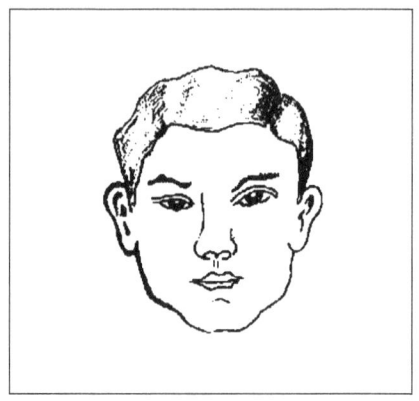

2

3

4

扇

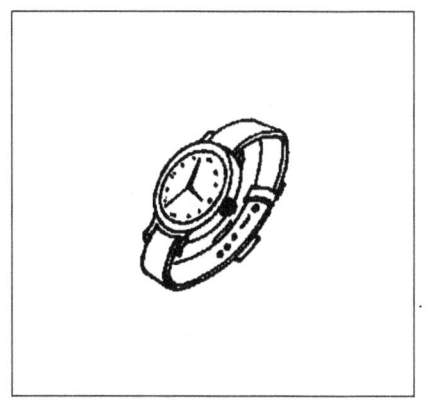

1

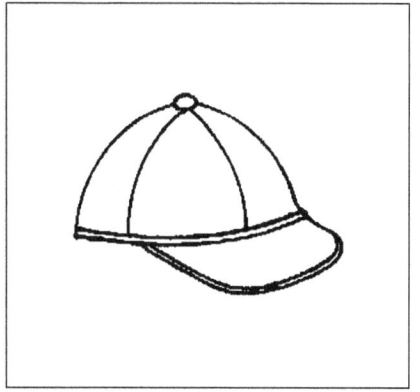

2

3

4

帽

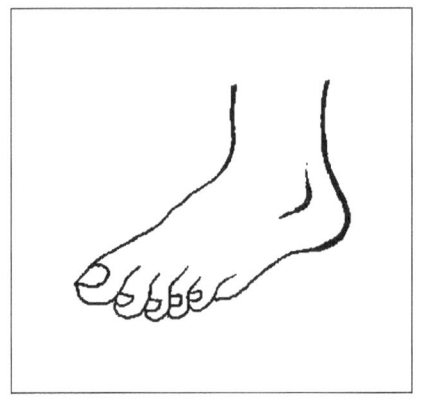

1

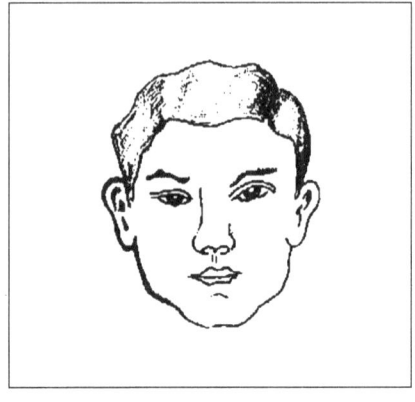

2

3

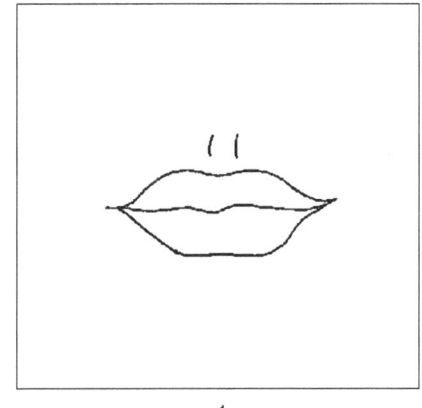

4

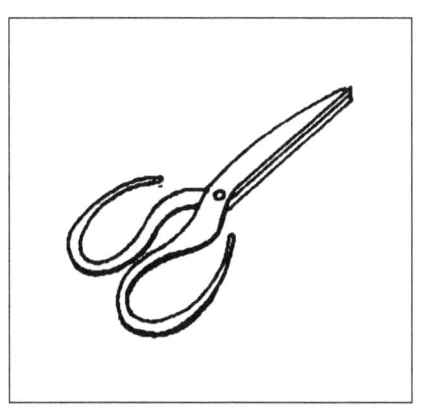

1

2

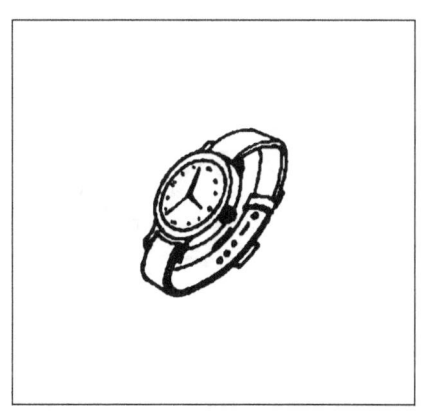

3

4

表

154 Appendix 1

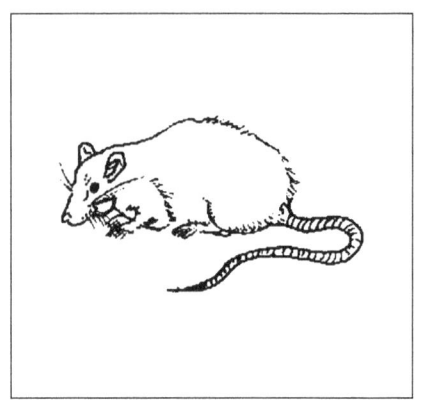

1

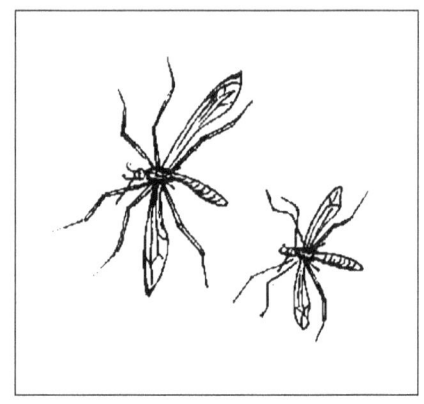

2

3

4

蚊

1

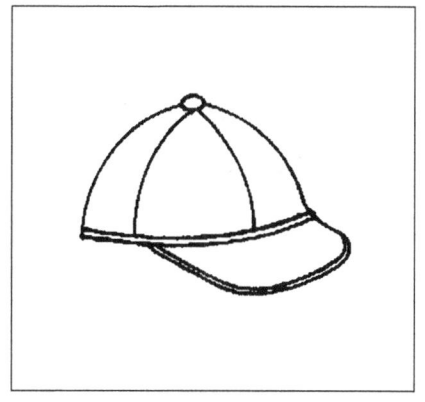

2

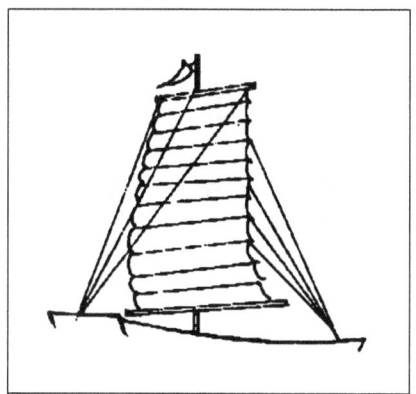

3

4

1

2

3

4

窝

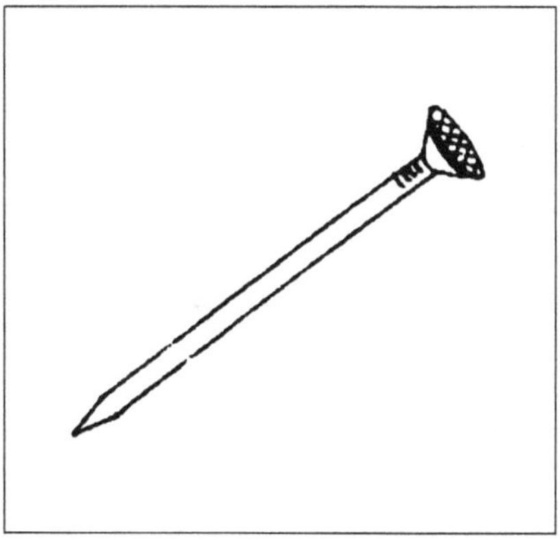

1

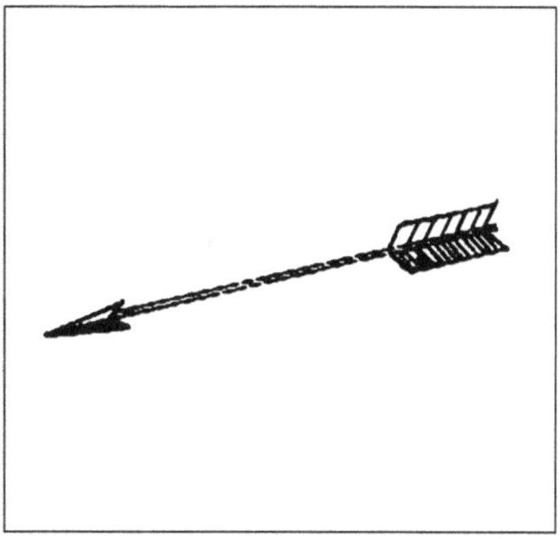

2

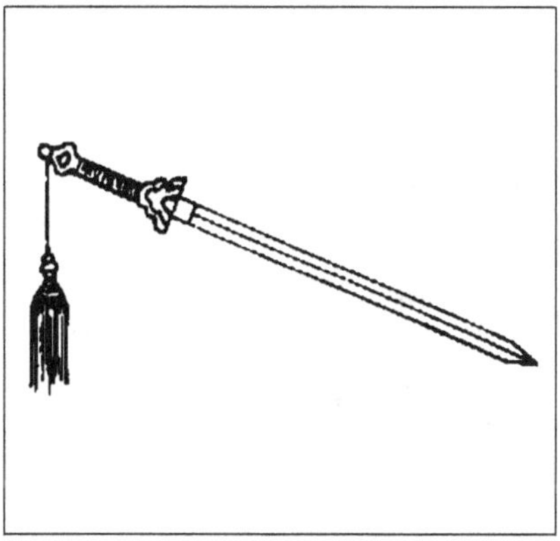

3

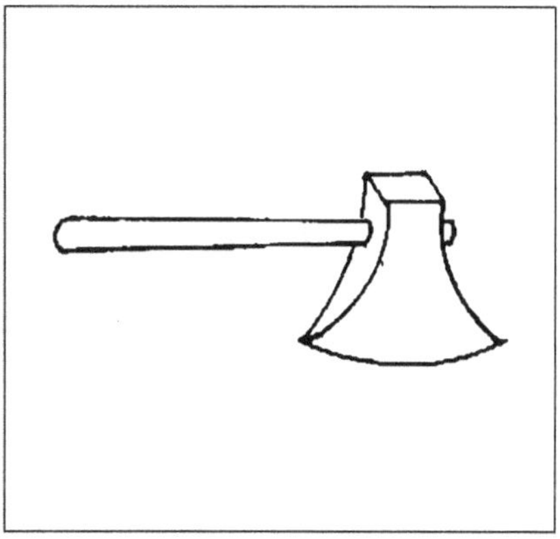

4

钉

1

2

3

4

湖

PPCLS – Test A 159

1

2

3

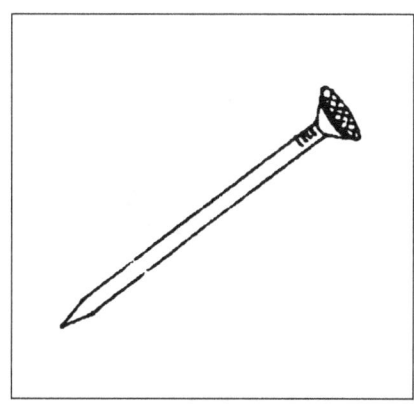

4

剪

160 Appendix 1

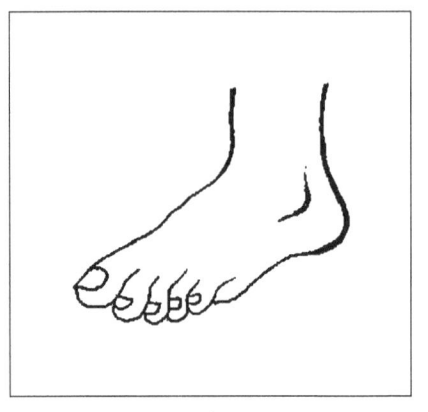

1

2

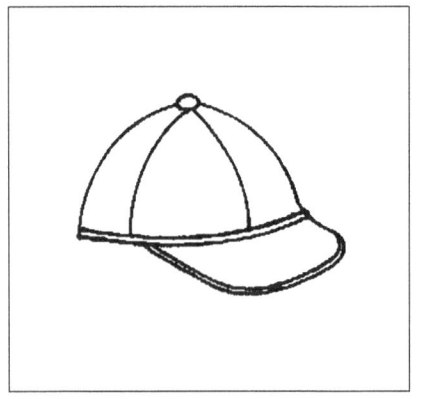

3

4

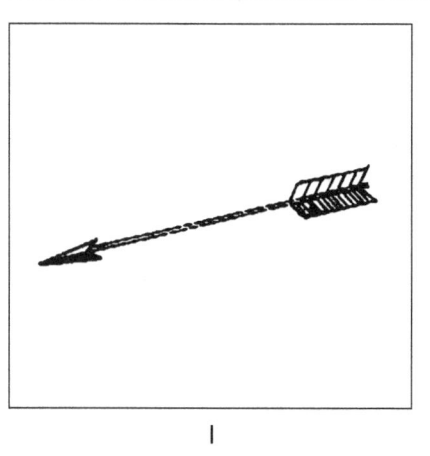

1

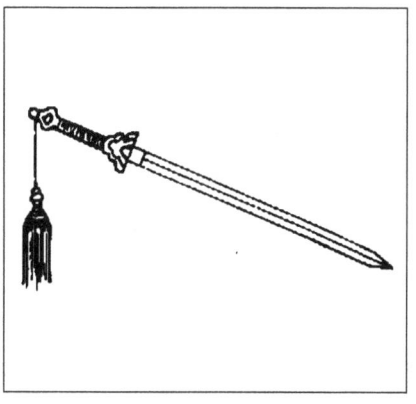

2

3

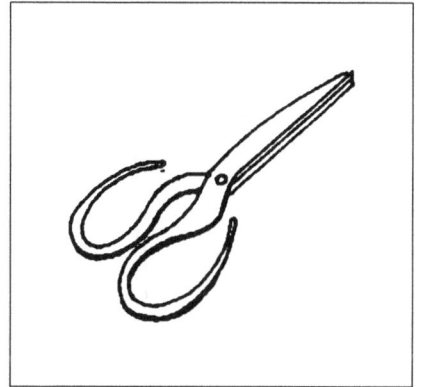

4

162   Appendix 1

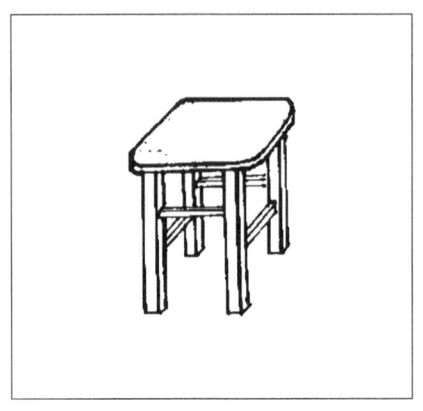
1

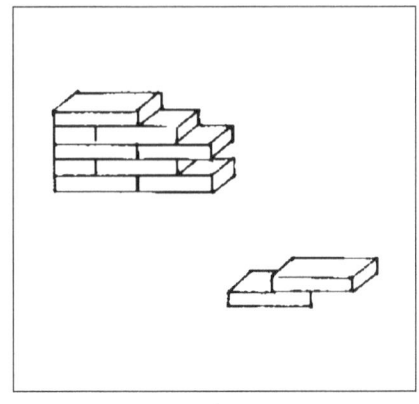
2

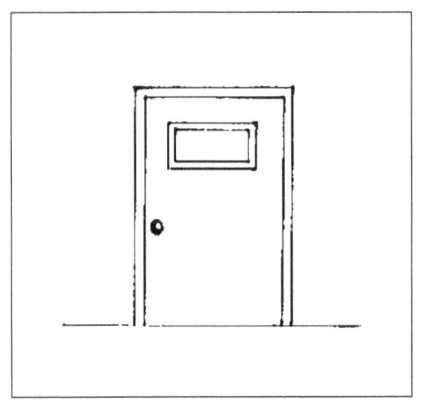
3

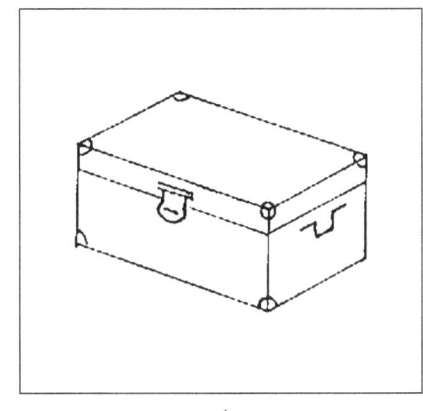
4

箱

1

2

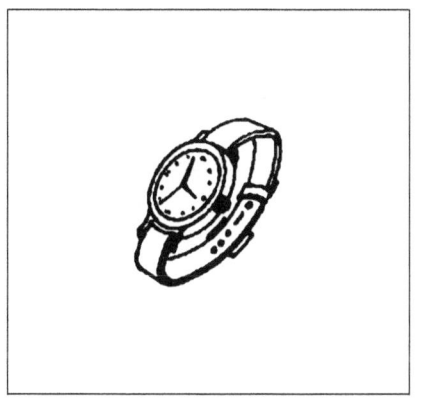

3

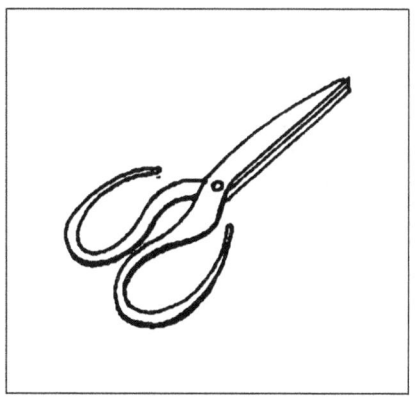

4

锁

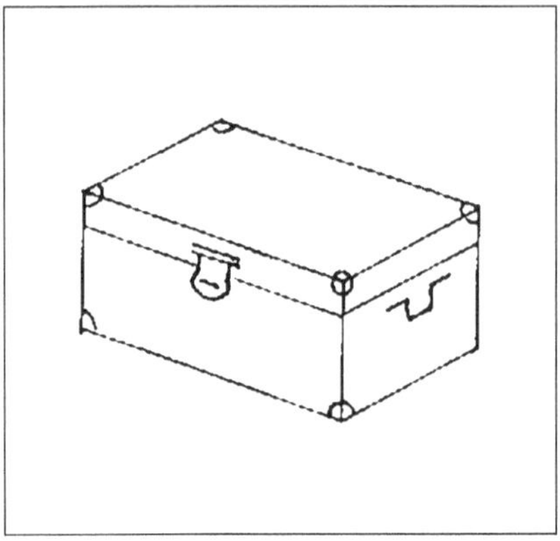

164 Appendix 1

| 1 | 2 |
| 3 | 4 |

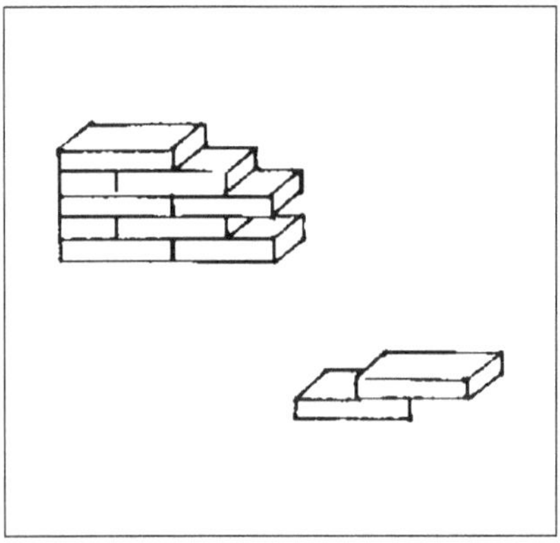

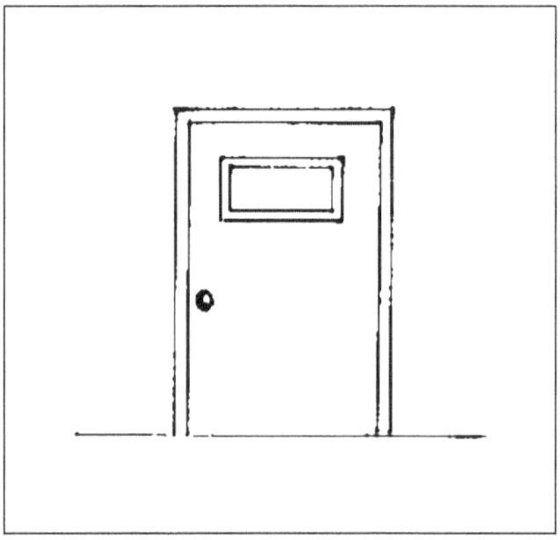

砖

PPCLS – Test A   165

1

2

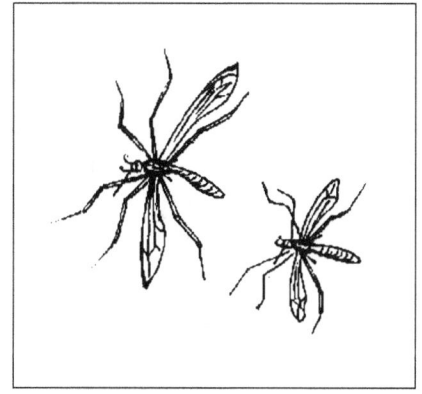
3

4

166 Appendix 1

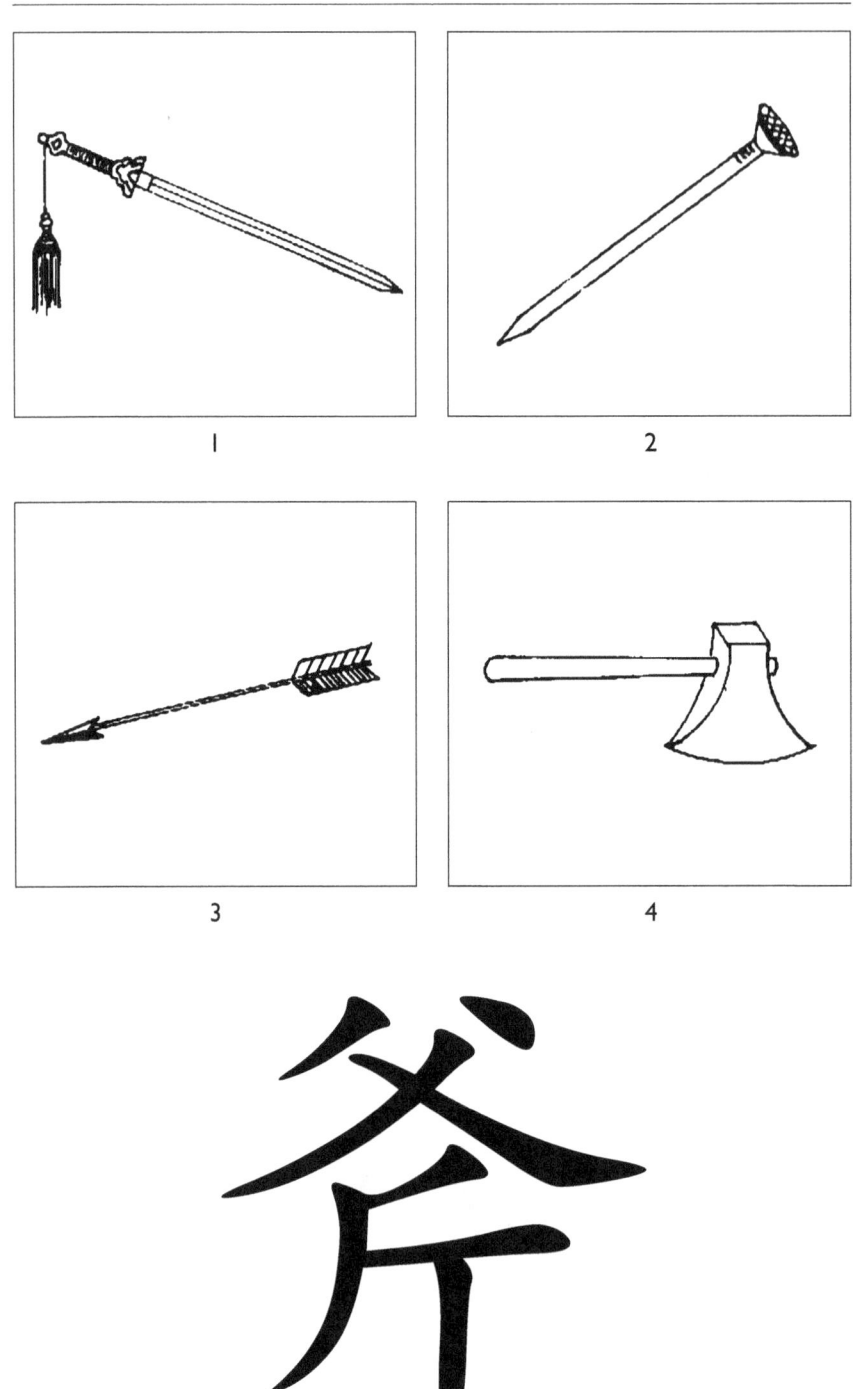

1

2

3

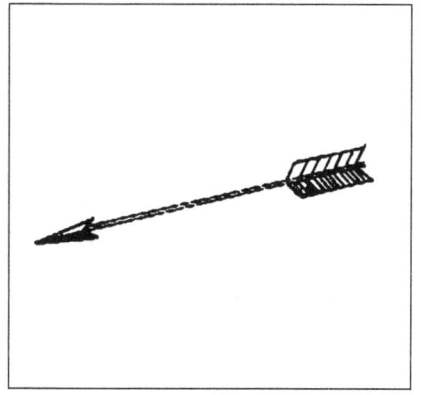

4

168 Appendix 1

1

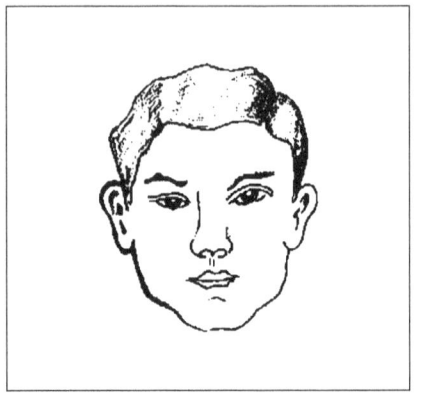

2

3

4

须

Appendix 1C

Preschool and Primary Chinese Literacy Scale – Test B

学前及初小中文识字量表

(简体字版)

测验B：听音指字

本量表在制作过程中得到啬色园教育基金鼎力资助，在此谨致谢忱。
Special acknowledgments go to the **Sik Sik Yuen Education Research Fund** for its financial support.

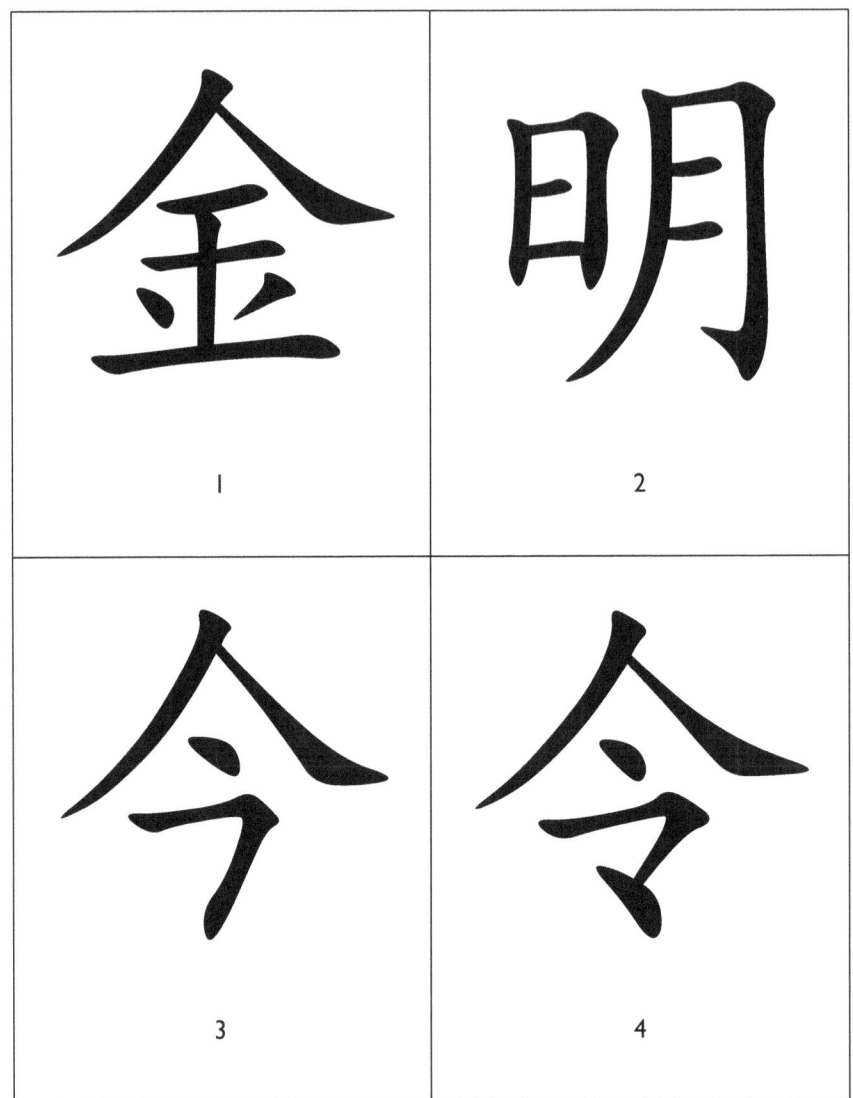

测验B：听音指字，项目1

测验B：听音指字，项目2

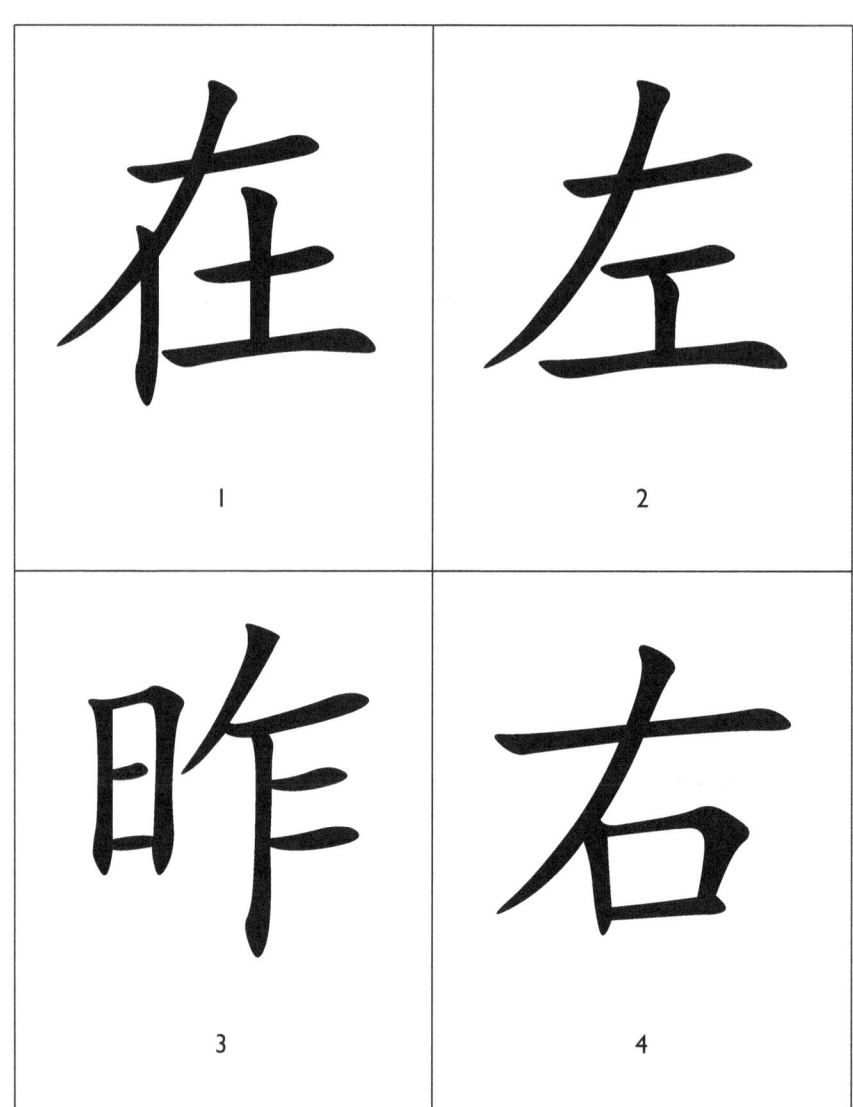

测验B：听音指字，项目3

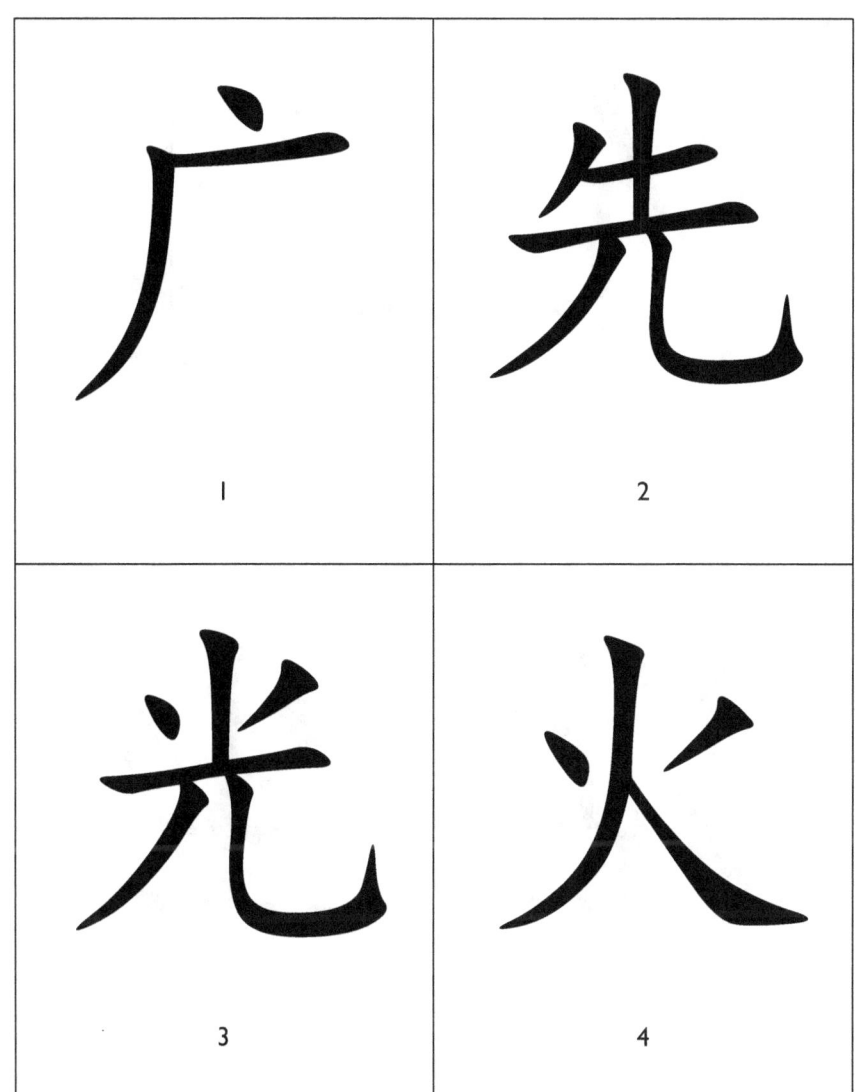

测验B：听音指字，项目4

测验B：听音指字，项目5

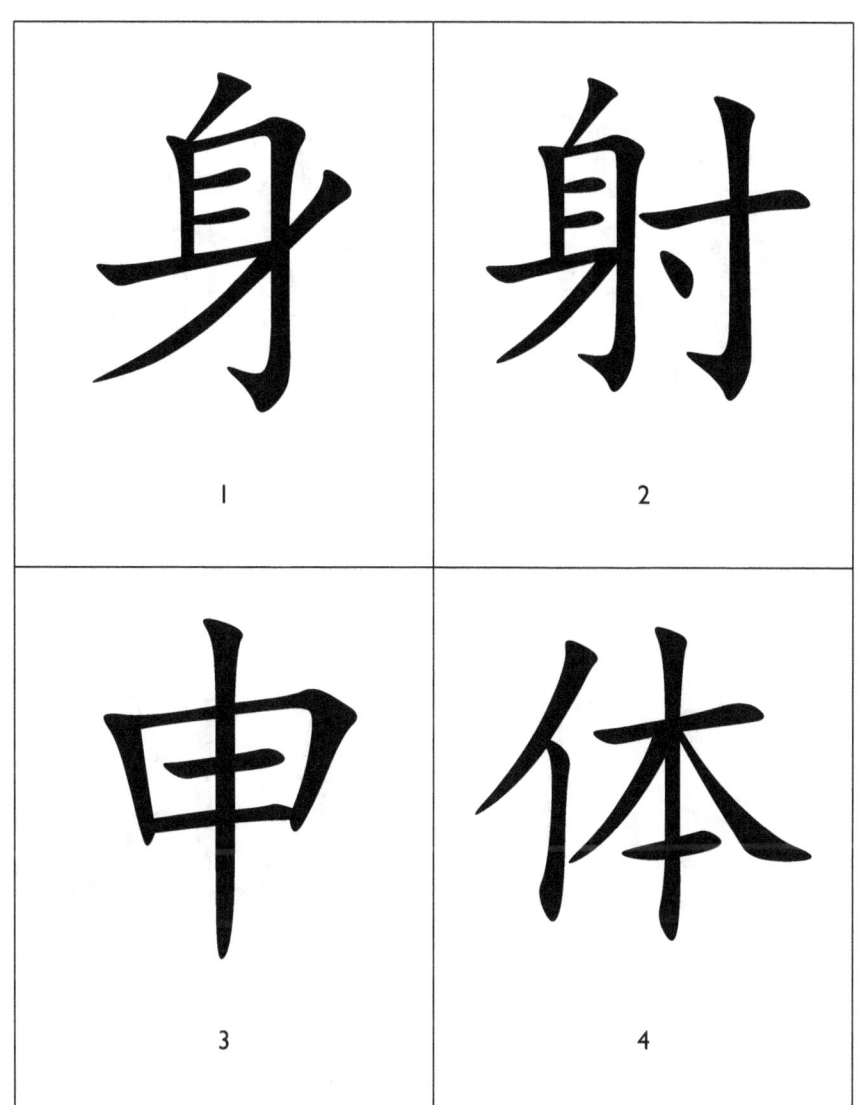

测验B：听音指字，项目6

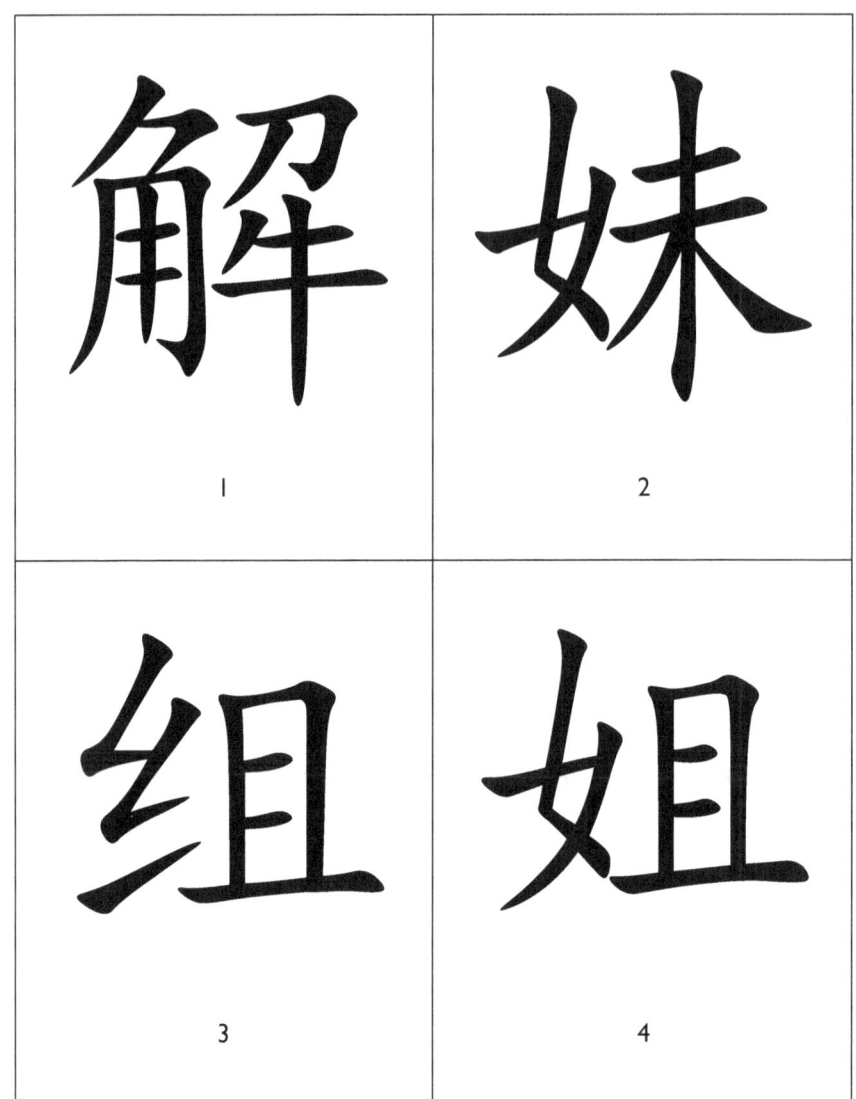

测验B：听音指字，项目7

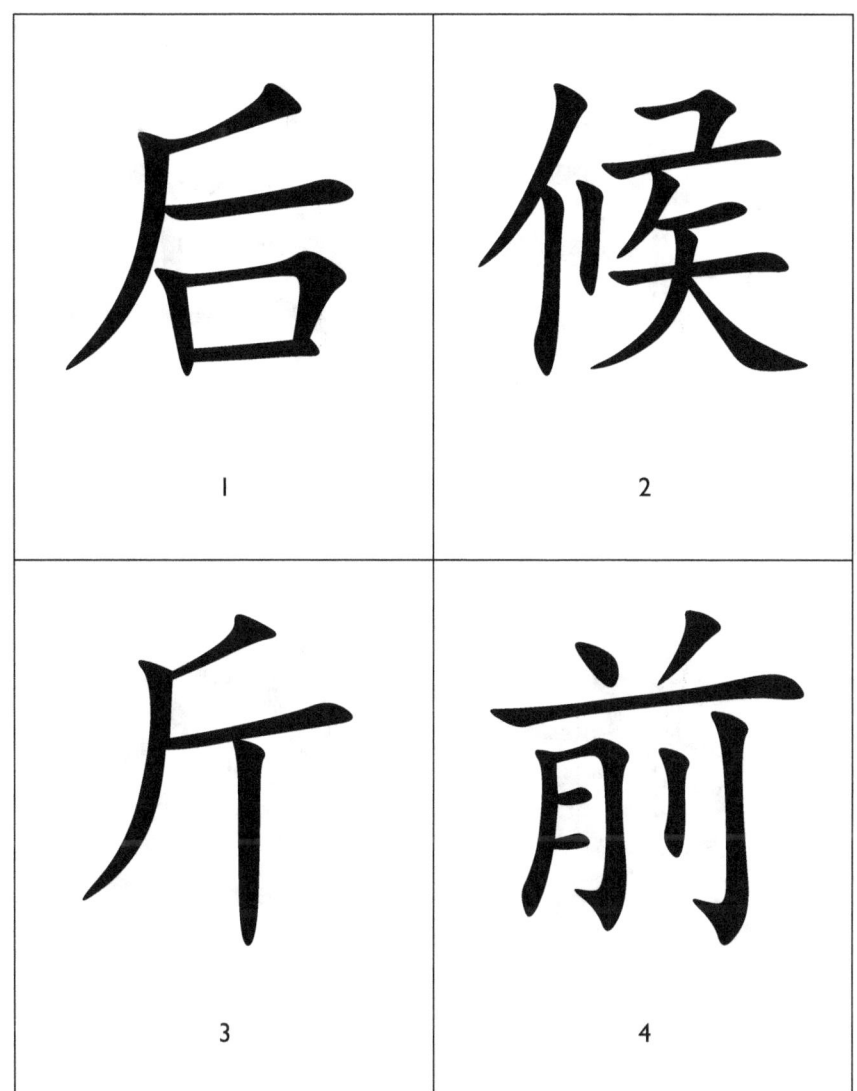

测验B：听音指字，项目8

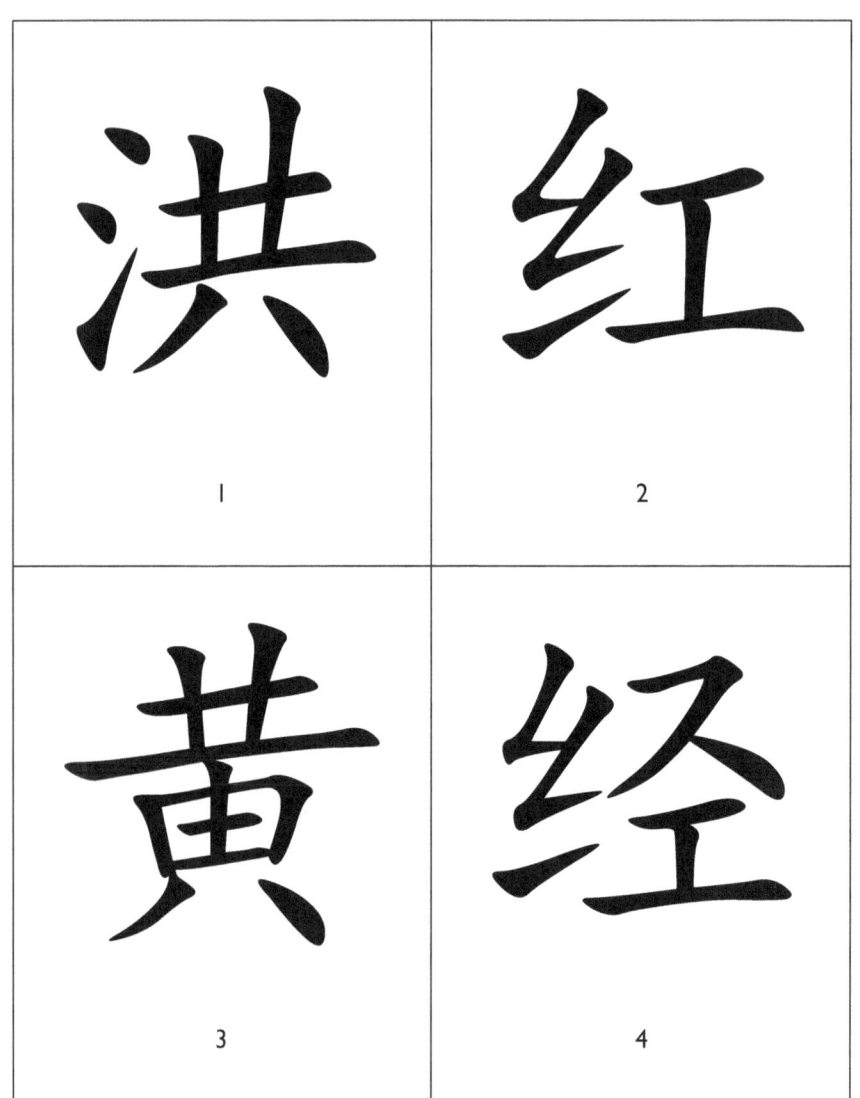

测验B：听音指字，项目9

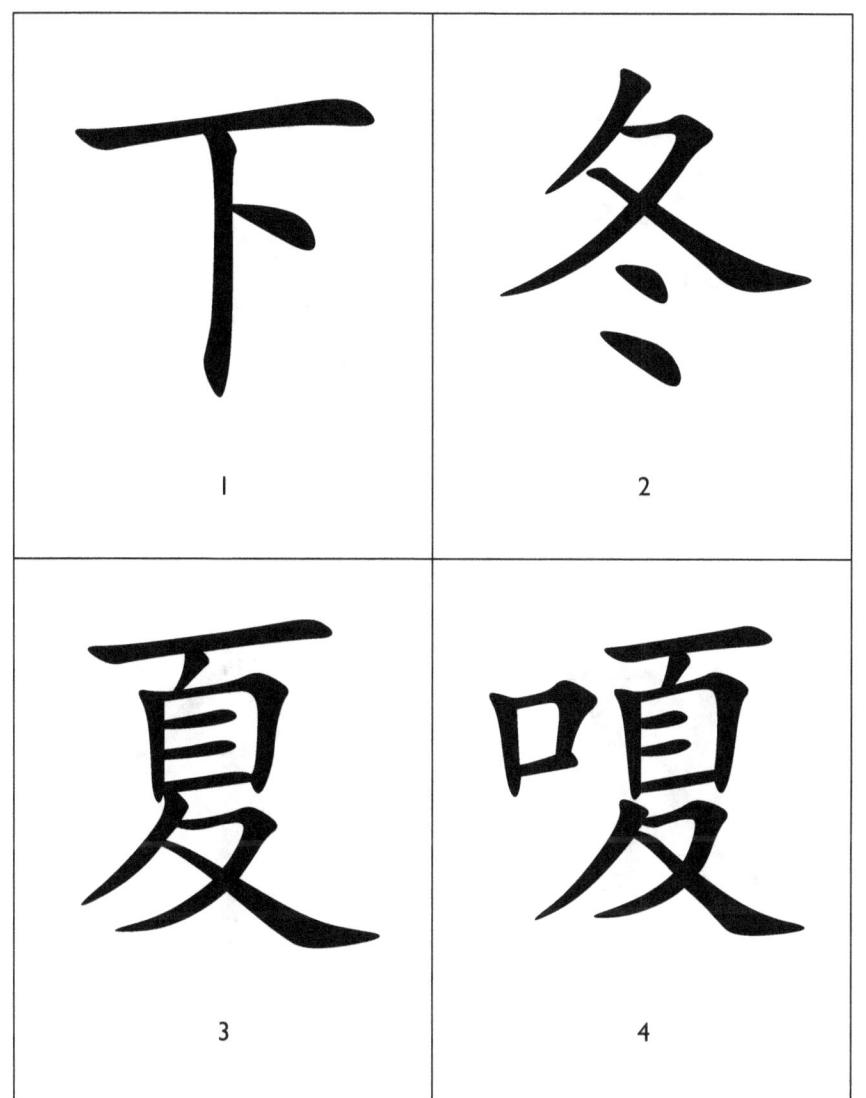

测验B：听音指字，项目10

测验B：听音指字，项目11

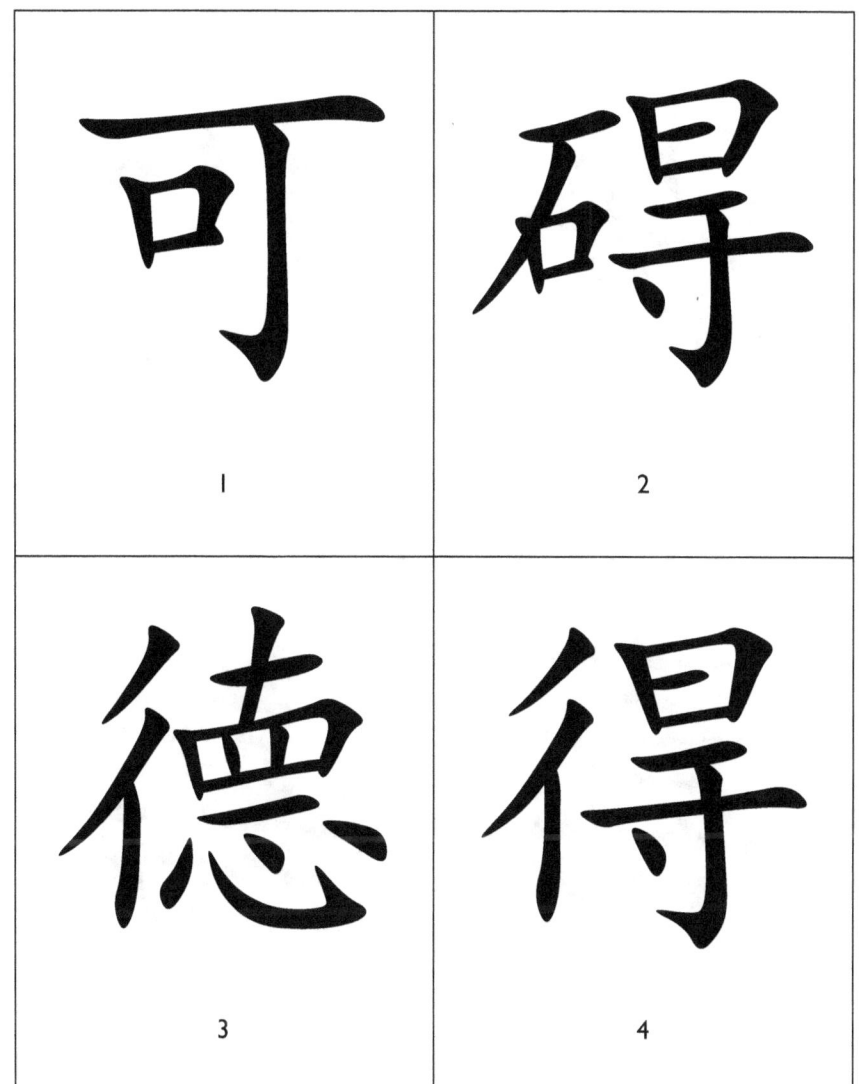

测验B：听音指字，项目12

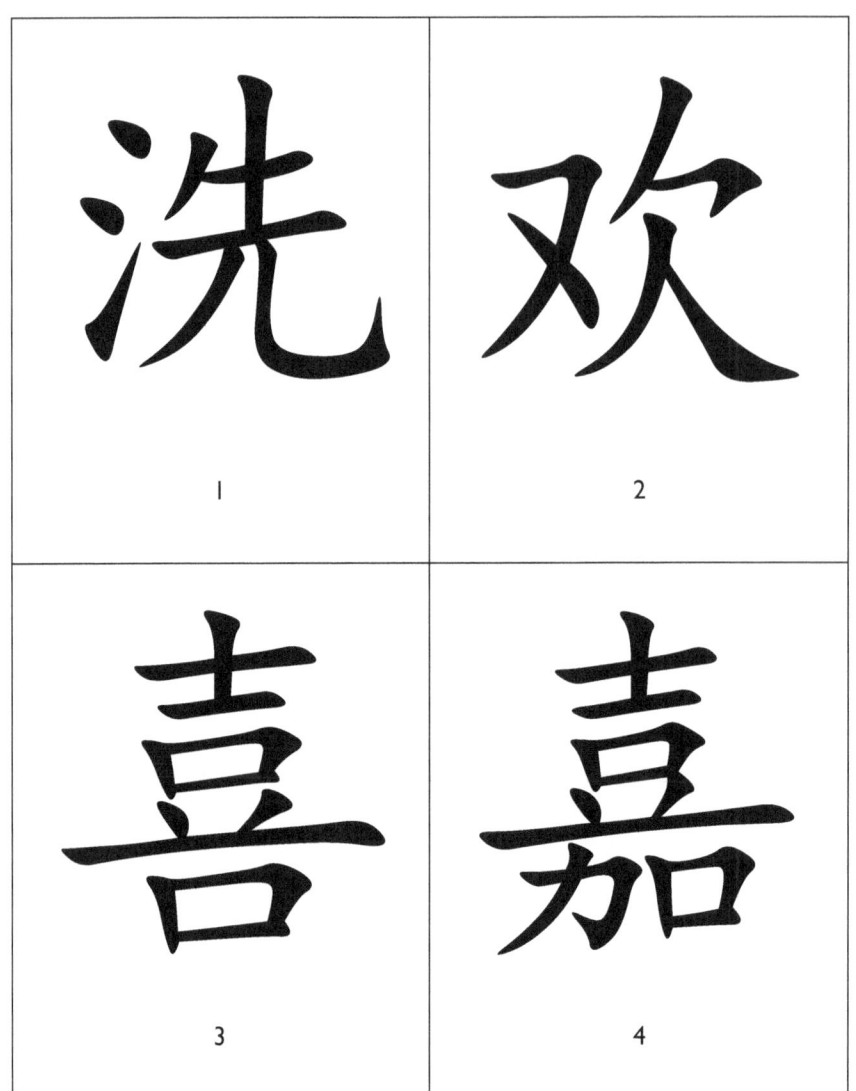

测验B：听音指字，项目13

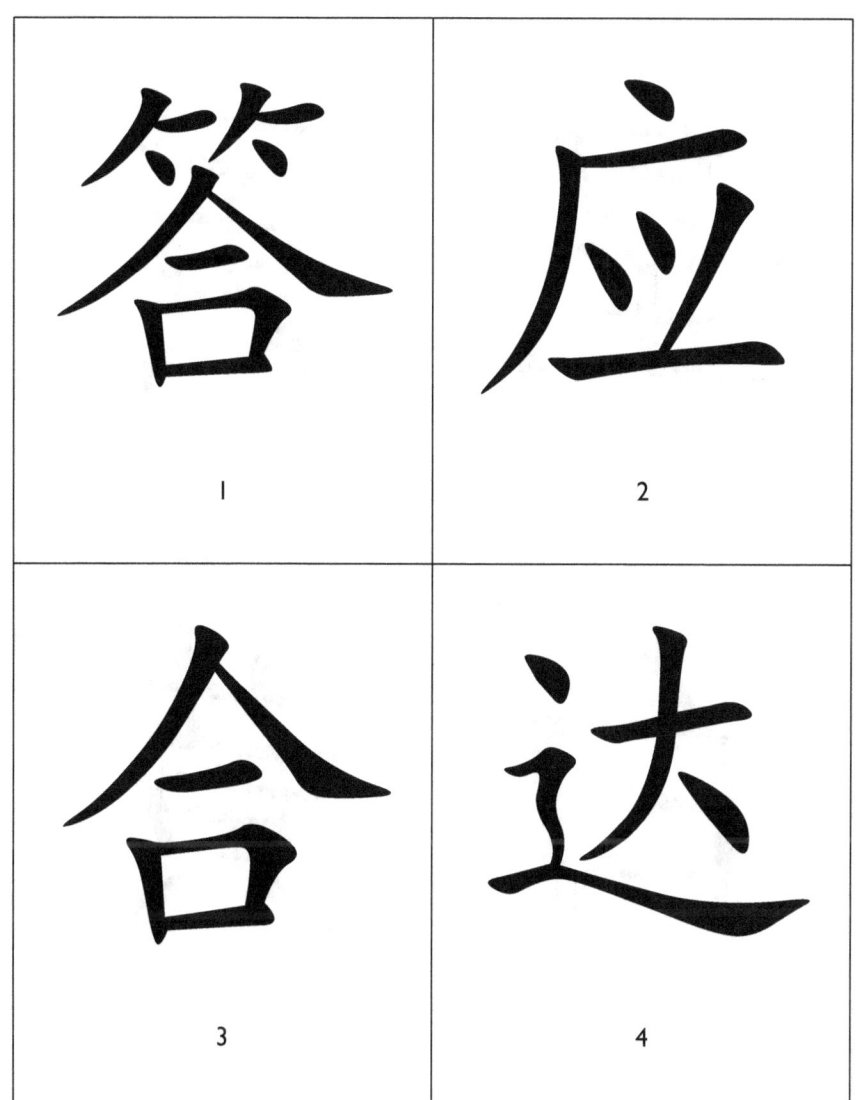

测验B：听音指字，项目14

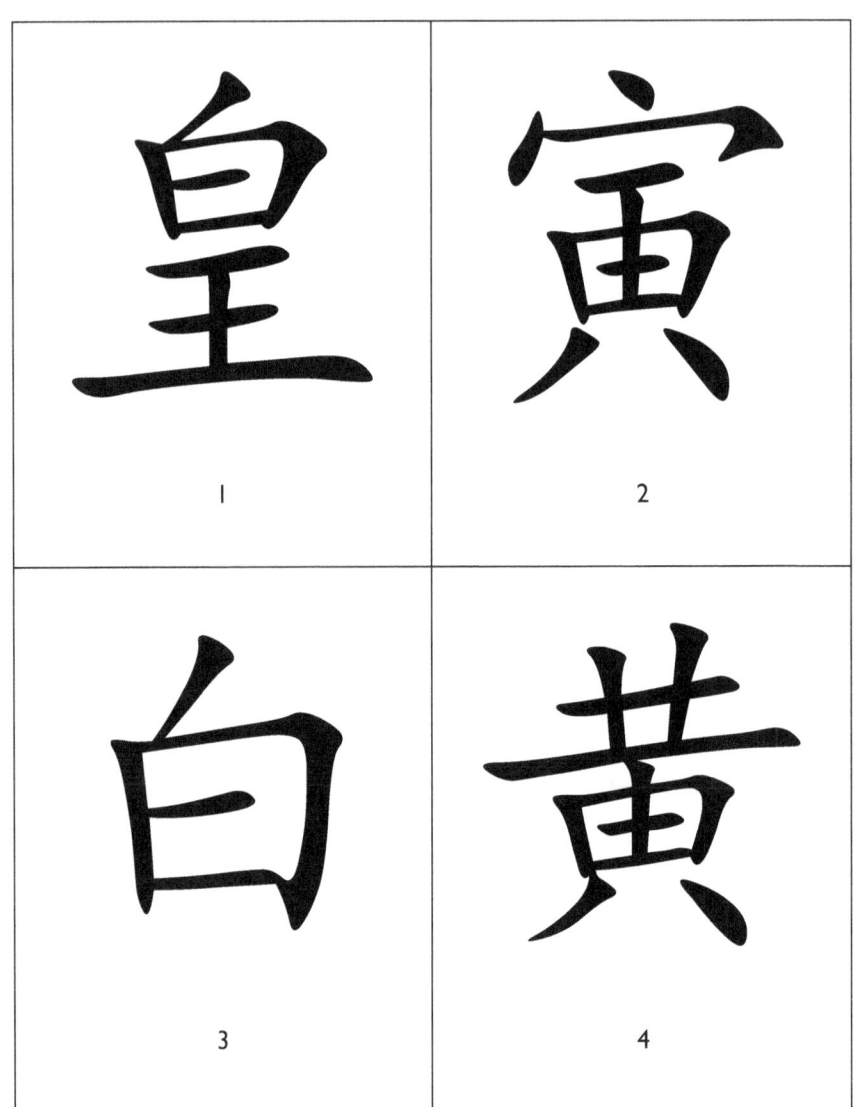

测验B：听音指字，项目15

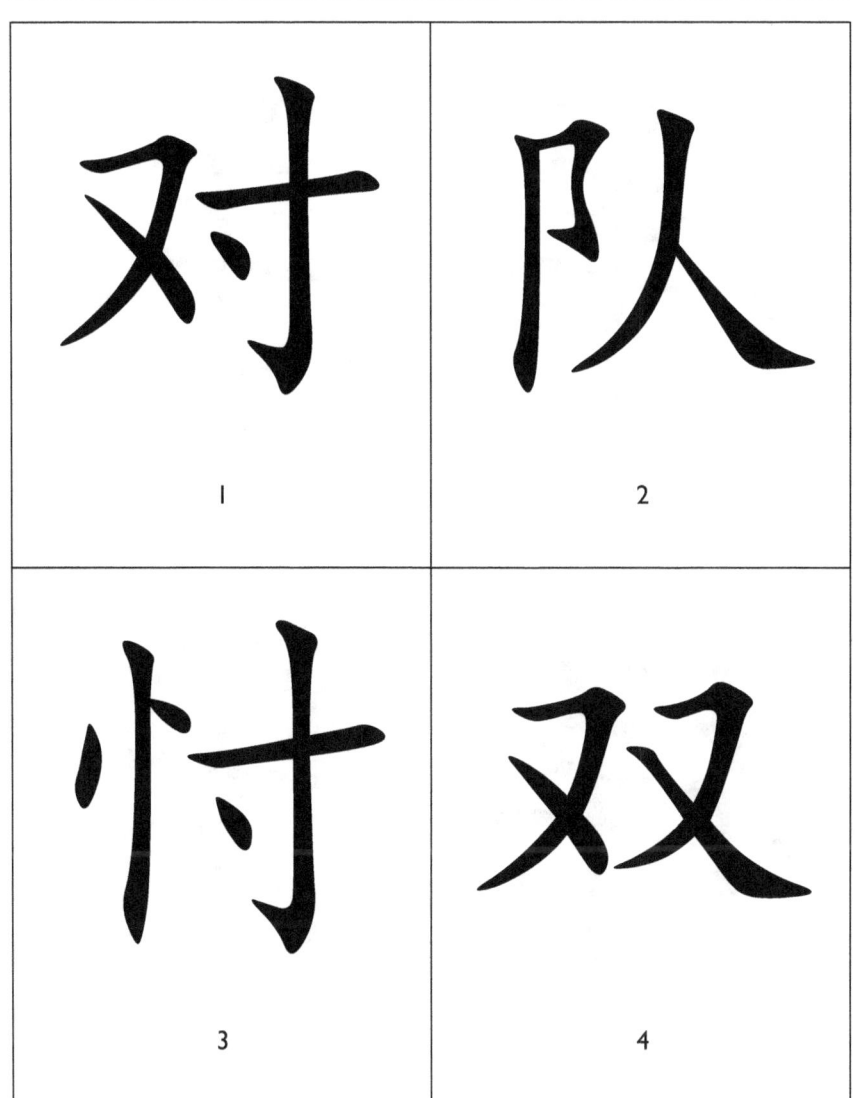

测验B：听音指字，项目16

测验B：听音指字，项目17

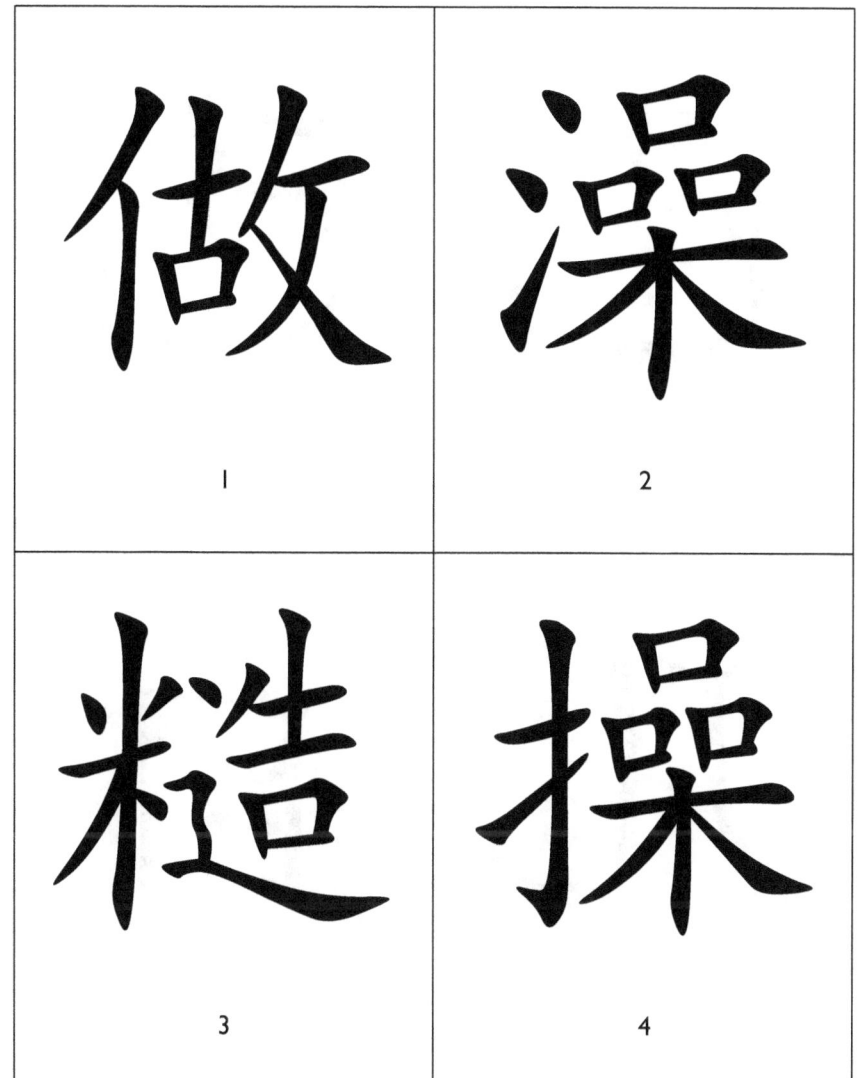

测验B：听音指字，项目18

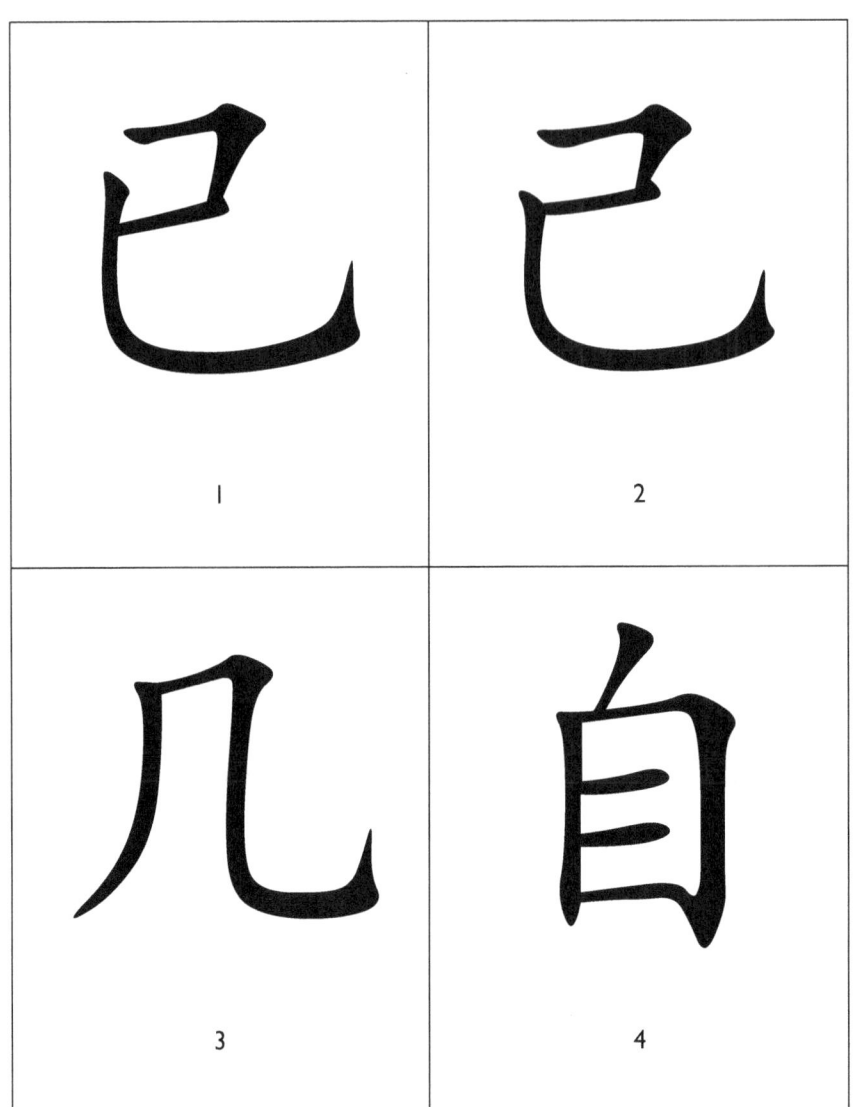

测验B：听音指字，项目19

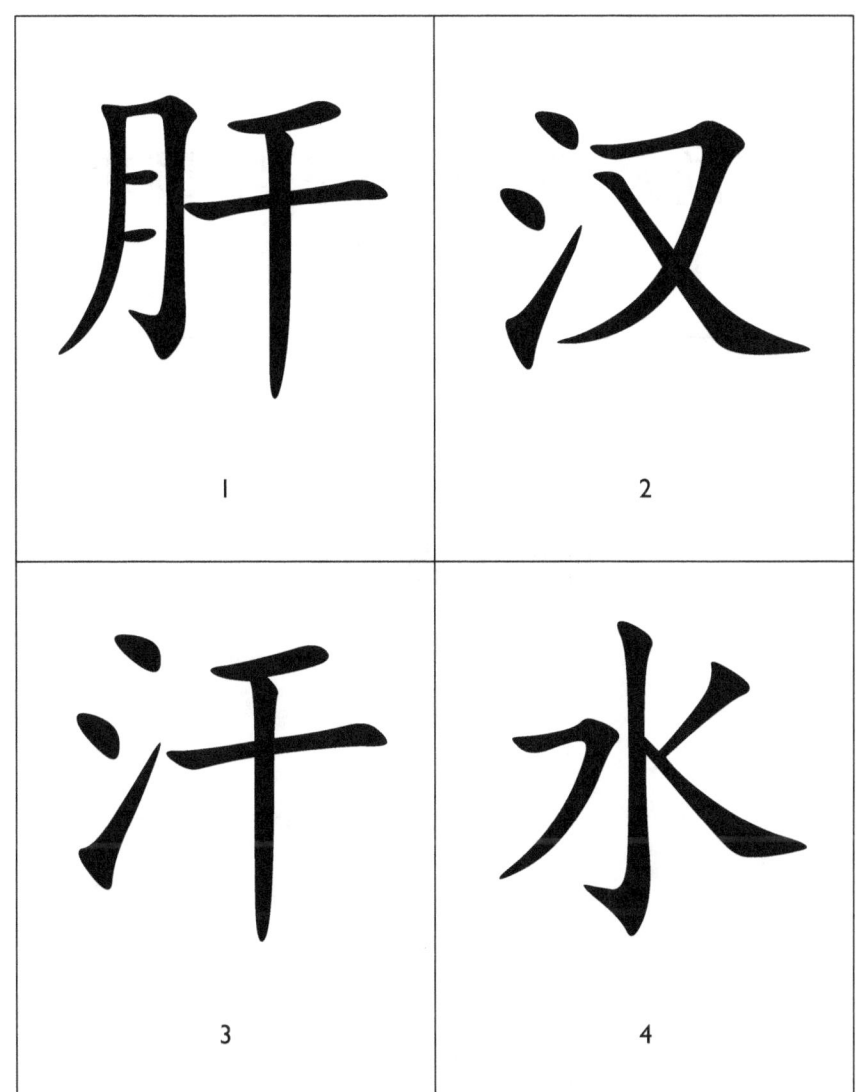

测验B：听音指字，项目20

Appendix 1D

Preschool and Primary Chinese Literacy Scale – Test C

学前及初小中文识字量表
（简体字版）

测验C：指字认字

本量表在制作过程中得到啬色园教育基金鼎力资助，在此谨致谢忱。
Special acknowledgments go to the **Sik Sik Yuen Education Research Fund** for its financial support.

一 1	三 2	多 3
病 4	忽 5	容 6
胜 7	父 8	幼 9
别 10	抄 11	呼 12
怎 13	美 14	旅 15

带 16	备 17	惰 18
然 19	间 20	暖 21
装 22	图 23	裳 24
播 25	整 26	迟 27
颜 28	斤 29	套 30

茎	厉	士
31	32	33
未	局	周
34	35	36
版	威	副
37	38	39
淡	丝	摩
40	41	42
据	隧	仇
43	44	45

刊 46	何 47	侍 48
舍 49	洲 50	胡 51
兼 52	庫 53	核 54
翁 55	袍 56	渠 57
雅 58	署 59	瑰 60

亿 61	毅 62	荫 63
伶 64	俐 65	剖 66
聊 67	绒 68	煎 69
弊 70	奋 71	瓣 72
肪 73	恃 74	脊 75

Appendix 1E

Preschool and Primary Chinese Literacy Scale – Test D

学前及初小中文识字量表

(简体字试用版)

测验D：认字说话

本量表在制作过程中得到啬色园教育基金鼎力资助，在此谨致谢忱。
Special acknowledgments go to the **Sik Sik Yuen Education Research Fund** for its financial support.

汇 1	皱 2
宪 3	矫 4
蜡 5	抹 6
耕 7	讨 8

飘	欺
9	10
脑	蕉
11	12
扣	究
13	14
台	突
15	16

展 17	栽 18
脆 19	將 20
羞 21	陪 22
愉 23	渡 24

闲	愁
25	26
痰	诗
27	28
嘈	需
29	30
躺	医
31	32

涯	终
41	42
喂	惶
43	44
舒	晕
45	46
违	寿
47	48

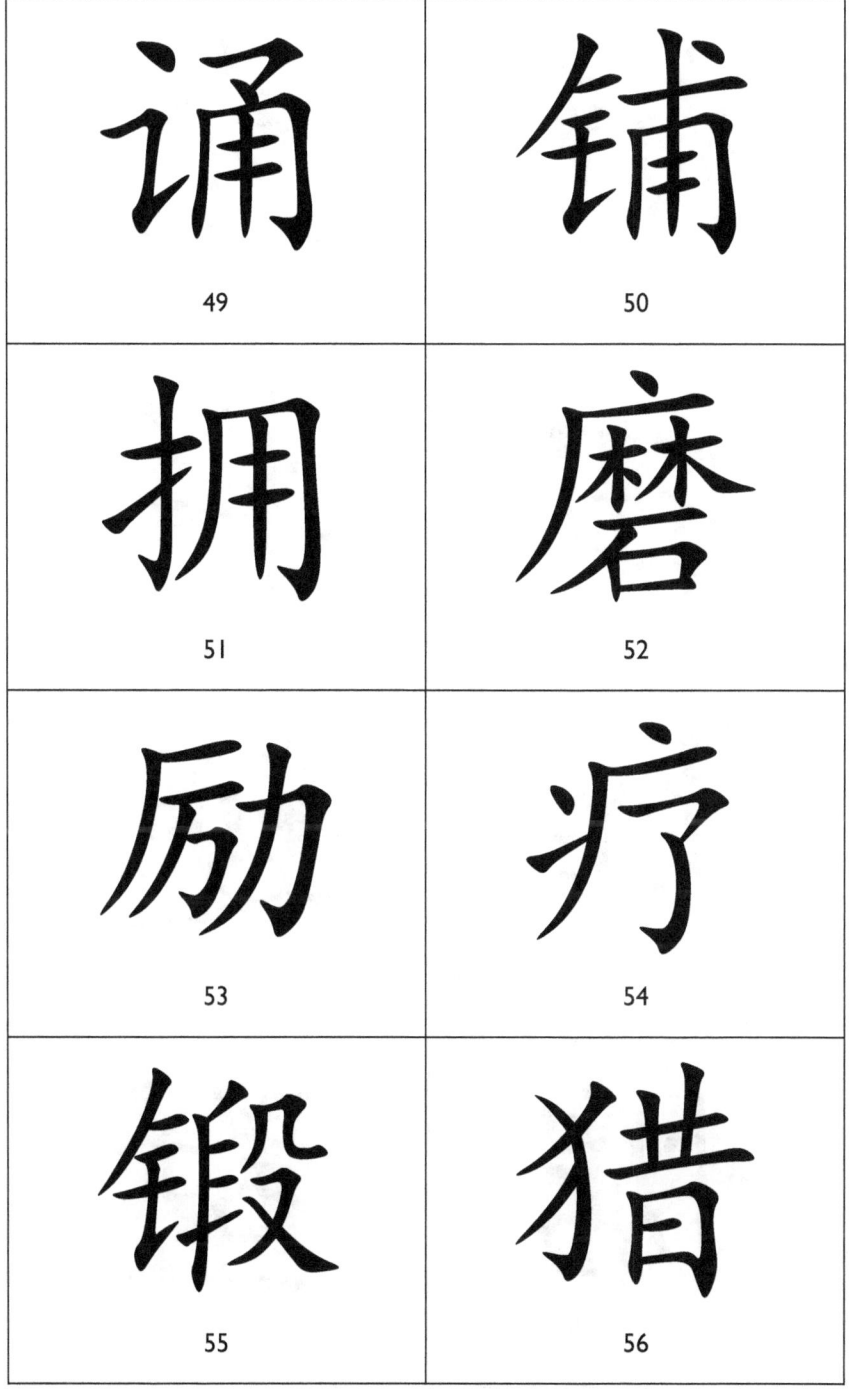

辩	允
57	58
扭	拼
59	60
炸	逆
61	62
惦	墅
63	64

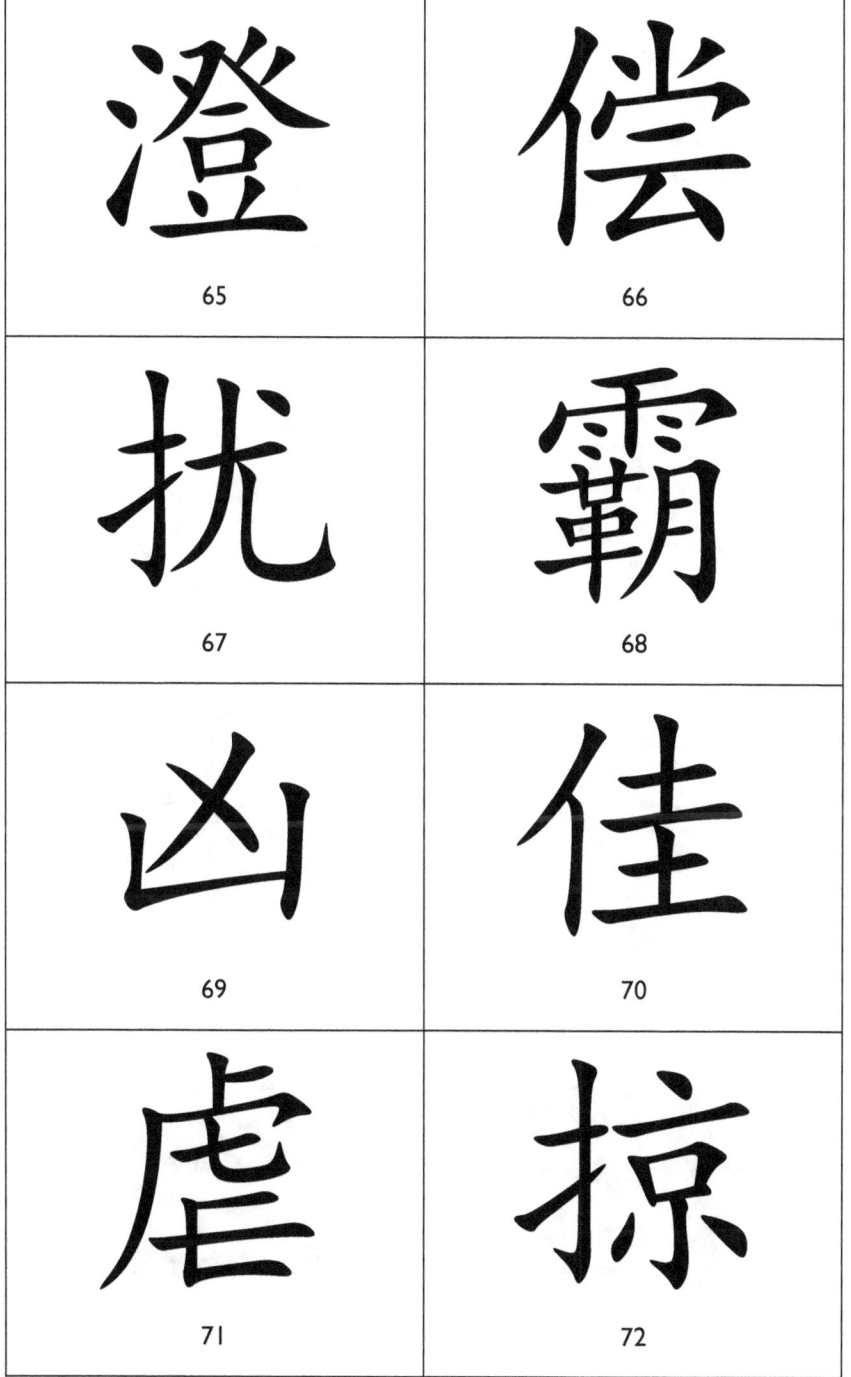

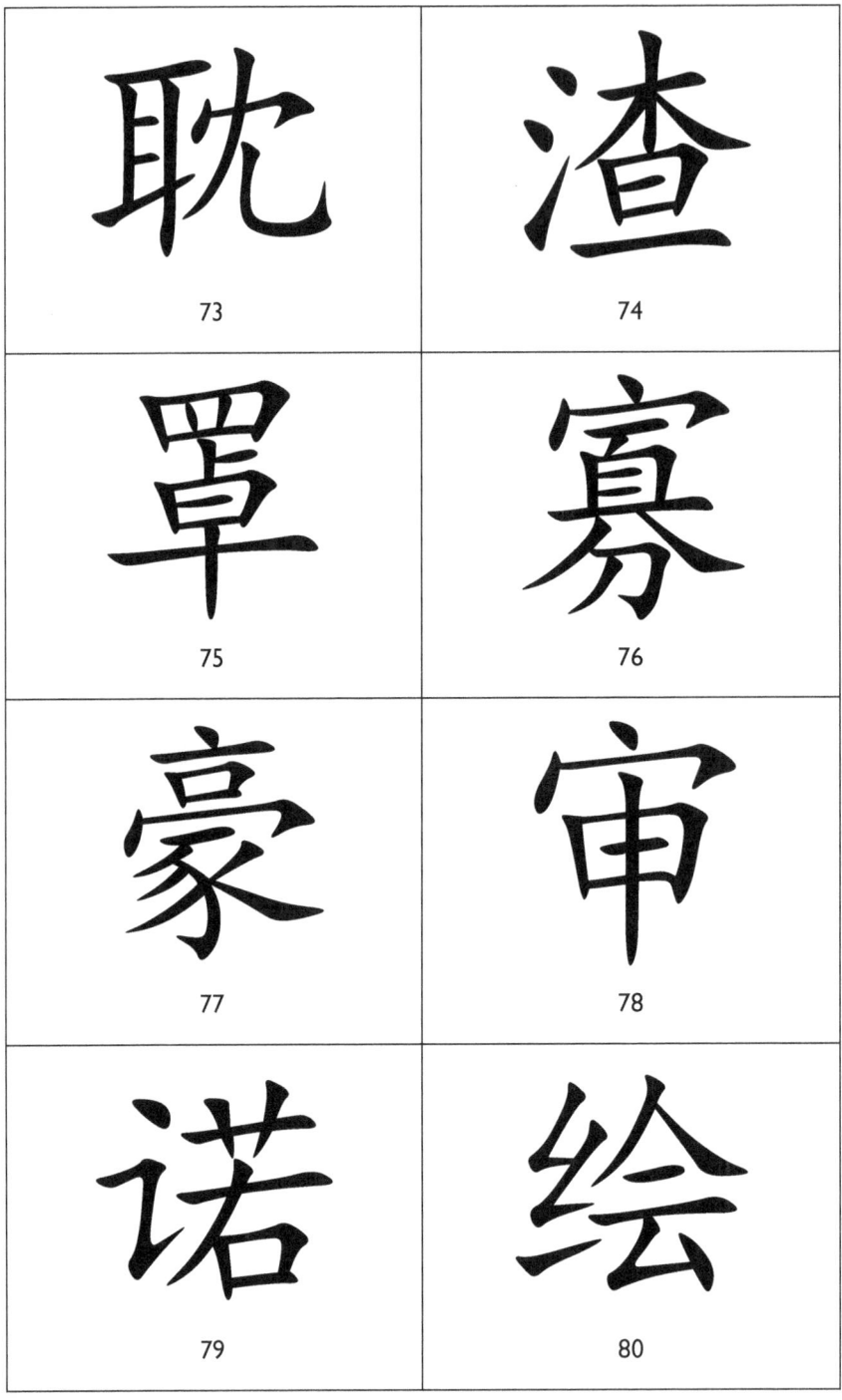

Appendix 1F

Preschool and Primary Chinese Literacy Scale Record Form

学前及初小儿童中文识字测验量表

(简体字版)

测验记录纸

被试姓名：_____

现就读于：_____

班　　级：_____

教师姓名：_____

主试姓名：_____

测验日期：_____年_____月_____日

出生日期：_____年_____月_____日

实足年龄：_____年_____个月。

测验A：字-图匹配（25项，每项1分）

项目	正确答案	被试幼儿的答案	正确与否
1. 车	(1)	_____	○
2. 河	(4)	_____	○
3. 雨	(1)	_____	○
4. 叶	(3)	_____	○
5. 树	(4)	_____	○
6. 竹	(3)	_____	○
7. 扇	(1)	_____	○
8. 帽	(2)	_____	○
9. 脚	(1)	_____	○
10. 表	(4)	_____	○
11. 蚊	(2)	_____	○
12. 伞	(4)	_____	○
13. 窝	(3)	_____	○
14. 钉	(1)	_____	○
15. 湖	(2)	_____	○
16. 剪	(3)	_____	○
17. 唇	(4)	_____	○
18. 剑	(2)	_____	○
19. 箱	(4)	_____	○
20. 锁	(1)	_____	○
21. 砖	(3)	_____	○
22. 龟	(2)	_____	○
23. 斧	(4)	_____	○
24. 炮	(1)	_____	○
25. 须	(4)	_____	○

测验A得分：_____分

测验B：听音指字测验（共计20项，每项1分）

项目	正确答案	被试幼儿的答案	正确与否
1. 今	(3)	_____	○
2. 出	(3)	_____	○
3. 左	(2)	_____	○
4. 光	(3)	_____	○
5. 坐	(4)	_____	○
6. 身	(1)	_____	○
7. 姐	(4)	_____	○
8. 后	(1)	_____	○
9. 红	(2)	_____	○
10. 夏	(3)	_____	○
11. 只	(1)	_____	○
12. 得	(4)	_____	○
13. 喜	(3)	_____	○
14. 答	(1)	_____	○
15. 黄	(4)	_____	○
16. 对	(1)	_____	○
17. 样	(3)	_____	○
18. 操	(4)	_____	○
19. 己	(2)	_____	○
20. 汗	(3)	_____	○

测验B得分：_____分

测验C：指字认字测验（共计75项，每项1分，请在符号上划"/"表示正确）

1. ○	2. ○	3. ○	4. ○	5. ○
6. ○	7. ○	8. ○	9. ○	10. ○
11. ○	12. ○	13. ○	14. ○	15. ○
16. ○	17. ○	18. ○	19. ○	20. ○
21. ○	22. ○	23. ○	24. ○	25. ○
26. ○	27. ○	28. ○	29. ○	30. ○
31. ○	32. ○	33. ○	34. ○	35. ○
36. ○	37. ○	38. ○	39. ○	40. ○
41. ○	42. ○	43. ○	44. ○	45. ○
46. ○	47. ○	48. ○	49. ○	50. ○
51. ○	52. ○	53. ○	54. ○	55. ○
56. ○	57. ○	58. ○	59. ○	60. ○
61. ○	62. ○	63. ○	64. ○	65. ○
66. ○	67. ○	68. ○	69. ○	70. ○
71. ○	72. ○	73. ○	74. ○	75. ○

测验C得分：_____分

测验D：读字说话测验（共计80项，每项1分，
　　　　请在符号上划"/"表示正确）

1. ○	2. ○	3. ○	4. ○	5. ○
6. ○	7. ○	8. ○	9. ○	10. ○
11. ○	12. ○	13. ○	14. ○	15. ○
16. ○	17. ○	18. ○	19. ○	20. ○
21. ○	22. ○	23. ○	24. ○	25. ○
26. ○	27. ○	28. ○	29. ○	30. ○
31. ○	32. ○	33. ○	34. ○	35. ○
36. ○	37. ○	38. ○	39. ○	40. ○
41. ○	42. ○	43. ○	44. ○	45. ○
46. ○	47. ○	48. ○	49. ○	50. ○
51. ○	52. ○	53. ○	54. ○	55. ○
56. ○	57. ○	58. ○	59. ○	60. ○
61. ○	62. ○	63. ○	64. ○	65. ○
66. ○	67. ○	68. ○	69. ○	70. ○
71. ○	72. ○	73. ○	74. ○	75. ○
76. ○	77. ○	78. ○	79. ○	80. ○

测验D得分：_____分

本次测验总得分 = 测验A + 测验B + 测验C + 测验D = _____分

Appendix 2
Primary Chinese Reading Literacy Scale (PCRLS)

Primary Chinese Reading Literacy Scale (PCRLS)
小学生中文阅读能力测验

考生姓名：_____

就读班级：_____

测评日期：_____

测评结果：_____

一、读文答问（圈出正确答案，每题2分，共10分）

捉迷藏

李辉（香港）

花园里，假山旁，小朋友们捉迷藏。
"手心、手背，手心、手—背！"
"谁先来？""李康康！"
捉呀捉，捉到一个摸一摸。
猜猜看，这是谁？头发长得这么长？
"是我呀！王小芳"
小芳去捉小朋友，跑呀跑，捉呀捉！
捉到一个摸一摸。
"谁的鼻子这么长？"
"哈哈！是我，张小邦！"
小邦去捉小朋友，东跑跑，西摸摸！
捉到一个摸一摸，摸到两只大耳朵。
"谁的耳朵这么长？"
"是我呀！我是灰太狼！"
大家一起说："那—
我们就是喜羊羊！"

1、谁先开始捉的？

  A 李康康 B 王小芳 C 张小邦 D 灰太狼

2、谁最后一个被捉？

  A 李康康 B 王小芳 C 张小邦 D 灰太狼

3、谁自称是"喜羊羊"？

  A 李康康 B 王小芳
  C 张小邦 D 除"灰太狼"以外的人

4、谁自称是"灰太狼"？

  A 李康康 B 王小芳
  C 张小邦 D 反正不是康康、小芳和小邦

5、这首儿童诗的作者是哪里人？

  A 湖北人 B 深圳人 C 北京人 D 中国人

二、这是什么广告？（圈出正确答案，每题2分，共10分）

1、有酸有甜，有滋有味。

   A 食品饮料　　B 品牌宣传　　C 服装和鞋　　D 药品广告

2、天上彩虹，人间长虹！

   A 食品饮料　　B 品牌宣传　　C 服装和鞋　　D 药品广告

3、自我自主，任你摆步。

   A 食品饮料　　B 品牌宣传　　C 服装和鞋　　D 药品广告

4、穿衣重品牌，吃药求正宗！

   A 食品饮料　　B 品牌宣传　　C 服装和鞋　　D 药品广告

5、今年过年不送礼，送礼要送脑白金。

   A 食品饮料　　B 品牌宣传　　C 服装和鞋　　D 药品广告

三、这是什么经典名句？（圈出正确答案，每题2分，共20分）

1、"白毛浮绿水，红掌拨清波。"出自哪首诗？

   A 咏鸡　　B 咏鹅　　C 骆宾王　　D 鹅鹅鹅

2、"欲穷千里目，更上一层楼。"出自哪首诗？

   A 风　　B 咏柳　　C 凉州词　　D 登鹳雀楼

3、"两岸猿声啼不住"下一句应该是？

   A 轻舟已过万重山　　B 孤帆一片日边来
   C 天下谁人不识君　　D 门泊东吴万里船

4、"日出江花红胜火" 下一句应该是？

   A 同到牵牛织女家　　B 霜叶红于二月花
   C 两山排闼送青来　　D 春来江水绿如蓝

5、"横看成岭侧成峰，远近高低各不同"写的是哪处风景？

   A 黄山　　B 华山　　C 庐山　　D 泰山

6、"卷地风来忽吹散,望湖楼下水如天。"写的是哪处风景?

    A 东湖   B 西湖   C 杭州   D 望湖

7、"蒌蒿满地芦芽短,正是河豚欲上时"中的"河豚"是什么?

    A 河里的猪   B 会游泳的猪   C 一种有毒的鱼   D 河里的豚

8、"昼出耘田夜绩麻,村庄儿女各当家"中的"绩麻"是什么?

    A 搓麻线   B 打麻将   C 织麻布   D 做麻酱

9、"儿童散学归来早,忙趁东风放纸鸢"作者是哪朝人?

    A 唐朝   B 宋朝   C 明朝   D 清朝

10、"粉身碎骨浑不怕,要留清白在人间"一句是什么意思?

    A 将石灰石烧成石灰粉的过程
    B 作者立志要做纯洁清白的人
    C 作者不怕粉身碎骨
    D 以石灰自喻,表达作者为国尽忠、坚守高洁的决心

四、新作赏析(圈出正确答案,每题2分,共10分)

毛毛虫的梦想

第1段

春天来了,大地开满美丽的花朵。一条毛毛虫爬到池塘边,照照自己的样子,说:"我这么丑,谁愿意和我做朋友呢?"话音刚落,池塘里就有人说:"你很可爱,我想跟你做朋友!"是水怪吗?不,原来是一只黑色的小蝌蚪!

第2段

花蝴蝶决定去找毛毛虫。她看见路上有一只小青蛙,就向它打听:"请问,你有没有见过原来住在这个池塘里的小蝌蚪呢?"小青蛙说:"我就是啊!你是谁呀?"花蝴蝶惊讶地说:"我是毛毛虫啊!你也怎么变了样呢?"小青蛙说:"蝌蚪长大了会变成青蛙,而青蛙同时可以在水里和陆地上生活啊!所以,人们说我们是两栖动物呀!"

第3段

　　毛毛虫和小蝌蚪都有一个梦想。毛毛虫希望变得漂亮些，而小蝌蚪却想冲出水面，到陆地上与毛毛虫一起赏花……

第4段

　　于是，小蝌蚪就成了毛毛虫的第一个好朋友。它还介绍了小蜜蜂、小甲虫、小蜗牛给毛毛虫认识，这些新朋友都各有本领啊！有的会飞，有的善爬，有的会背着自己的房子四处走。

第5段

　　毛毛虫和小蝌蚪都达成了自己的梦想。于是，它们一起唱歌、跳舞，庆祝春天的来临。

第6段

　　此后好几个星期，小蝌蚪都没有见过毛毛虫，它很担心。毛毛虫生病了吗？它去旅行了吗？它在哪里呢？原来，毛毛虫一直躲在蛹中。经过一段时间以后，它变成了一只美丽的花蝴蝶！它兴奋地飞到池塘边去找小蝌蚪，可是小蝌蚪却失踪了！它去了哪儿呢？

答问：

1、毛毛虫的梦想是什么？

　　A 变漂亮　　B 在天上飞　　C 交朋友　　D 找回小蝌蚪

2、谁是毛毛虫的第一个好朋友？

　　A 小蝌蚪　　B 小蜜蜂　　C 小甲虫　　D 小蜗牛

3、毛毛虫躲在蛹中干什么？

　　A 它生病了　　B 它在睡觉　　C 它在蜕变　　D 它在穿花衣裳

4、故事里有几种小动物？

　　A 4种　　B 5种　　C 6种　　D 7种

5、本文的正确排列顺序应该是：

　　A 123456　　B 13465　　C 146325　　D 143625

五、快速阅读（圈出正确答案，每题2分，共20分）

神奇的食物之旅

东东和妈妈坐在餐桌旁，开开心心地吃饭。可是，不知道为什么，每次吃饭时，总有不少饭粒从东东的嘴里掉出来，弄得桌上、地上到处都是。妈妈皱着眉头说："哎哟！东东的下巴好像有个洞啊！"东东连忙伸手摸摸自己的下巴说："洞？在哪里？我怎么摸不着？"妈妈看到东东那副紧张的样子，禁不住笑了起来，摸着东东的头说："妈妈是说，你吃东西时不小心，食物时常从嘴里掉出来，这样很浪费啊！"

于是，妈妈决定趁着假期带东东回乡探外婆。东东的外婆住在农村，她知道东东和妈妈要来，一早就站在门外欢迎他们。东东远远看见外婆，便跑上前向外婆问好。外婆说："东东，你长高了不少呢！"东东说："因为妈妈每天都会煮有营养的食物给我吃嘛！"外婆说："这里的食物新鲜，种类又多，东东吃了后，一定会长得更高更壮。来，陪外婆去地里摘菜和买鱼，准备今天的晚餐。"说罢便带东东到处参观。

走了一会儿，外婆忽然说："我们到田里看地里的宝藏，好吗？"东东听说要去看宝藏，十分兴奋。外婆带东东来到一片水稻田，东东看见农民伯伯弯下身子，好像在田里寻找什么似的，便问外婆："农民伯伯在寻宝吗？"外婆说："农民伯伯不是在寻宝，而是在耕种。我们吃的米饭，便是农民伯伯种出来的。"东东问："外婆，这里明明没有米饭啊！为什么你会说我最爱吃的米饭是从这里来呢？"外婆笑着说："东东，秧苗还没有长成稻米呢！农民伯伯要一直辛勤地工作，待稻米收成后，我们才有饭吃啊。"

东东知道田里的秧苗会变成米饭后，觉得很神奇。他问外婆："秧苗是怎样变成米饭的呢？"外婆说："农民伯伯首先要翻松泥土，然后插秧。他们会定时到田里灌溉、除虫和施肥，直到秧苗长成稻谷后，便会收割。"东东问："收割之后就有饭吃吗？"外婆说："不，刚割下来的稻谷有一个谷壳包着，要用机器把谷壳脱掉，才会变成我们平常吃的白米啊！"东东说："哇，工序真多！"外婆说："对呀，农民伯伯的工作十分辛劳，所以我们要珍惜米饭，不要浪费啊！"

东东觉得农民伯伯很伟大，他说："长大了我要做农民，为大家种稻米！"外婆笑着说："好啊，不如你和外婆到田里摘些新鲜的蔬菜吧！"东东高兴地答应。"哇，田里种了很多白菜啊！"东东拔起一棵白菜，交给外婆，你看他像不像一个小农民？

回家后，外婆说要摸几个鸡蛋炒菜。可是，她并不是去厨房。东东觉得很奇怪，于是便悄悄地跟在外婆身后，看看她到底去哪里摸鸡蛋。

　　原来，外婆的家很大，后院还有猪圈和鸡窝。东东跟着外婆来到鸡窝，看见鸡窝里有两堆鸡蛋，心想："哦，原来鸡蛋都藏在这里！"这时，外婆看见东东，便问他想不想喂母鸡吃东西，东东连忙答应。你看，母鸡一边啄食谷糠，一边咯咯地唱"个个大！个个个大！"，好像是在夸自己下的蛋个个都很大！

　　妈妈和外婆在厨房里准备晚餐，不一会儿便传来阵阵香味。"咕噜咕噜"东东的肚子开始作响呢！"开饭了！"妈妈说。东东洗了手，便帮忙摆放餐具。他看见桌上有炒白菜、白切鸡、蒸鱼和蕃茄炒蛋，却没有他最喜欢吃的炸鸡块，觉得有点儿失望。

　　吃饭时，外婆挟了一块鸡肉给东东，说："这是新鲜的鸡肉，很好吃的！"妈妈看见东东有点儿不高兴，便对他说："妈妈知道你爱吃炸鸡块，但是吃太多煎炸食物对身体不好，不如你就尝尝外婆为你预备的新鲜鸡肉吧！"东东咬了一口，发觉很好吃，一点也不比炸鸡块差。他谢了外婆，然后开心地吃晚餐。

　　晚饭后，妈妈准备了西瓜，与东东一起吃。东东说："妈妈，我的肚子真神奇！"妈妈笑着问："你的肚子怎样神奇呢？"东东说："它是一个百宝袋，可以放很多东西。我今天吃了那么多食物，它全部都能装下去。"东东一边说，一边神气地指着自己的肚皮。"不过真奇怪！我的肚子明明放了那么多食物，为什么到第二天还是觉得饿呢？"妈妈说："那是因为食物不会一直留在肚子里啊！"东东问："肚子里的食物会去哪里呢？"妈妈说："其实，吃进肚子里的食物，会经历一个奇妙的旅程。首先，食物会被牙齿咬碎，然后从长长的食道滑梯滑进胃里。胃里住了很多胃液精灵，一看见食物，便会把它们分解成糊状。""然后呢？"东东问。"变成糊状的食物会和蔬菜里的纤维精灵混在一起，落到小肠。小肠里有很多神奇的吸管，能吸收食物里的养分，送到我们身体各部分，为我们提供能量，帮助我们成长。"

　　"食物是不是最后都变成了养分呢？"东东问。"不全是。神奇吸管吸了食物的养份后，还会剩下一些残渣。这些残渣最后去到大肠，水分被吸收后，便会变成大便，在你上厕所时排出体外。"

　　东东说："原来食物不光来之不易，去之也不易呀！""对呀！"妈妈和外婆都笑了。

答问：

1、 妈妈为什么说东东的下巴有个洞呢？

    A 他长虫牙了　　B 食物常从嘴里掉出来
    C 妈妈捉弄他　　D 他下巴真有个洞

2、 外婆所说"田里的宝藏"是什么？

    A 稻米　　B 泥土　　C 白米　　D 白菜

3、 外婆为什么说要"摸"几个鸡蛋？

    A 外婆家很大　　B 鸡蛋在猪圈里
    C 鸡蛋在鸡窝里　　D 母鸡保护着鸡蛋

4、 农民伯伯要经过多少道工序才能得到白米呢？

    A 五道　　B 六道　　C 七道　　D 八道

5、 东东最喜欢吃的食物是？

    A 炒白菜　　B 白切鸡　　C 蕃茄炒蛋　　D 对身体不好的食物

6、 为什么东东会说自己的肚子很神奇呢？

    A 是一个百宝袋　　B 可以装下很多食物
    C 能大能小　　D 能够消化食物

7、 是什么东西在胃里帮助消化食物呢？

    A 牙齿　　B 食道　　C 胃液　　D 小肠

8、 食物消化后剩下的残渣最终会去哪里？

    A 大肠　　B 大便　　C 厕所马桶里　　D 化粪池

9、 东东为什么说食物"来之不易，去之也不易"？

    A 获取和消化食物都需要人力物力
    B 食物不易生长也不易消化
    C 食物不会自己长出来也不会自己消失
    D 食物要经过神奇之旅才能完成使命。

10、 这篇文章想要表达什么主题思想？

    A 食物来之不易　　　　　　　　B 食物消化也不易
    C 食物从生长到消化要经过一个神奇之旅　　D 食物是生存之本

六、天气预报（圈出正确答案，每题2分，共20分）

每日天气预报

　　新的一周，冷空气再度南下，我国中东部地区将又一次吹响"大风降温进行曲"。与此同时，雨雪也不甘寂寞，未来三天，江淮、江南以及东北地区等地将有明显的降水天气。

　　预计今天白天到夜间，我国西北、东北、华北、青藏高原等地有小雪或雨夹雪；黄淮、江淮、江汉南部、江南北部、广西北部、广东东南部等地有小到中雨或阵雨。

　　预计此次冷空气带来的影响将一直持续到16日，中东部大部地区降温4～8℃，东北南部、江南北部局部降温可达10℃。其中降水最强的时段出现在明日（14日），在此提醒外出的朋友要多注意防风保暖，雨雪天气路滑，驾车时需格外小心。

根据文章判断下列句子对与错，并请在对的句子后面划 ✓；错的句子后面划 ✗。

1、今天是13日。（　　）

2、未来三天，江淮、江南以及东北地区等地将有明显的雨雪天气。（　　）

3、13日白天到夜间，我国广西、广东两省等局部地区有小到中雨或阵雨。（　　）

4、此次冷空气影响将一直持续到16日，河南省降温在4～8℃之间。（　　）

5、降水最强的时段是在14日。（　　）

6、今天夜间，北京市可能会有小雪。（　　）

7、根据天气预告可以判断，这是9月13日发布的。（　　）

8、未来三天，南京可能会有小到中雨或阵雨。（　　）

9、在本周之前，冷空气曾经造访过我国部分地区。（　　）

10、"大风降温进行曲"是由南下冷空气吹响的。（　　）

七、请你填写对联（圈出正确答案，每题2分，共10分）

1、上联：山寨炊烟撩牧笛；下联：水乡图画带____。

　　A 渔歌　　B 七彩　　C 杨柳　　D 渔童

2、上联：磊落为人书正气；下联：____办案秉公心。

　　A 廉洁　　B 秉公　　C 清风　　D 公正

3、上联：长空展卷风云画；下联：____扬声潮浪歌。

　　A 海涛　　B 大海　　C 轮船　　D 渔夫

4、上联：清风梦我春天里；下联：皓月圆谁____中。

　　A 秋风　　B 秋夜　　C 秋梦　　D 秋水

5、上联：掬来秋水千江月；下联：拾得____一壑云 。

　　A 春山　　B 春花　　C 春梦　　D 春水

（全卷完！谢谢参与！）

标准答案

满分：100分

一、读文答问（圈出正确答案，每题2分，共10分）

　　1A　2D　3D　4D　5D

二、这是什么广告？（圈出正确答案，每题2分，共10分）

　　1A　2B　3C　4D　5B

三、这是什么经典名句？（圈出正确答案，每题2分，共20分）

　　1B　2D　3A　4D　5C　6B　7C　8A　9D　10D

四、新作赏析（圈出正确答案，每题2分，共10分）

　　1A　2A　3C　4B　5D

五、快速阅读（圈出正确答案，每题2分，共20分）

　　1B　2A　3C　4C　5D　6B　7C　8D　9A　10C

六、天气预报（圈出正确答案，每题2分，共20分）

　　1✓　2✓　3✓　4✓　5✓　6✓　7✗　8✓　9✓　10✓

七、请你填写对联（圈出正确答案，每题2分，共10分）

　　1A　2A　3B　4B　5A

References

Adams, M. J. (1990). *Beginning to read: Thinking and learning about print*. Cambridge, MA: MIT Press.
Alexander, J. D. (1988). The erosion of English. *English Today*, 4(2), 17–20.
Allen, J. R. (2008). Why learning to write Chinese is a waste of time: A modest proposal. *Foreign Language Annals*, 41(2), 237–251.
Ang, R. P. (2008). Dysfunctional parenting behaviors and parenting stress among mothers of aggressive boys. *Child and Family Behavior Therapy*, 30(4), 319–336.
Angel, L., Fay, S., Bouazzaoui, B., and Isingrini, M. (2011). Two hemispheres for better memory in old age: Role of executive functioning. *Journal of Cognitive Neuroscience*, 23(12), 3767–3777.
Aram, D. and Korat, O. (2010). *Literacy development and enhancement across orthographies and cultures*. New York, NY: Springer.
Asher, J. (1977). Children learning another language: A developmental hypothesis. *Child Development*, 48, 1040–1048.
Asher, James J. (2003). *Learning another language through actions* (6th edition). Los Gatos, CA: Sky Oaks Productions Incorporation.
Baddeley, A. (1992). Working memory. *Science*, 255(5044), 556–559.
Baddeley, A. (2000). The episodic buffer: a new component of working memory? *Trends in cognitive sciences*, 4(11), 417–423.
Baddeley, A. (2003). Working memory and language: An overview. *Journal of communication disorders*, 36(3), 189–208.
Bae-Suh, S. (2007). Investigating changes of early childhood teacher candidates' dispositions: Within one-year time frame. *Asia-Pacific Journal of Research in Early Childhood Education*, 1(2), 47–66.
Bai, X., Yan, G., Liversedge, S. P., Zang, C., and Rayner, K. (2008). Reading spaced and unspaced Chinese text: Evidence from eye movements. *Journal of Experimental Psychology: Human Perception and Performance*, 34(5), 1277.
Balconi, M. and Vitaloni, S. (2012). The tDCS effect on alpha brain oscillation for correct versus incorrect object use. The contribution of the left DLPFC. *Neuroscience Letters*, 517(1), 25–29.
Bandettini, P. A., Wong, E. C., Hinks, R. S., Tikofsky, R. S., and Hyde, J. S. (1992). Time course EPI of human brain function during task activation. *Magnetic Resonance in Medicine*, 25(2), 390–397.
Baron, J. and Strawson, C. (1976). Use of orthographic and word-specific knowledge in reading words aloud. *Journal of Experiment Psychology: Human Perception and Performance*, 2, 386–393.

Barton, D. (1994). *Literacy: An introduction to the ecology of written language*. Oxford, UK: Blackwell.

Bateson, G. (1972). *Steps to an ecology of mind*. New York, NY: Ballantine Books.

Bi, Y., Han, Z., Shu, H., and Caramazza, A. (2007). Nouns, verbs, objects, actions, and the animate/inanimate effect. *Cognitive neuropsychology*, 24(5), 485–504.

Bogard, K. and Takanishi, R. (2005). PK-3: An aligned and coordinated approach to education for children 3 to 8 years old. *Social Policy Report*, 19(3), 1–24.

Booth, J. R., Burman, D. D., Meyer, J. R., Gitelman, D. R., Parrish, T. B., and Mesulam, M. M. (2002). Modality independence of word comprehension. *Human Brain Mapping*, 16(4), 251–261.

Booth, J. R., Burman, D. D., Meyer, J. R., Gitelman, D. R., Parrish, T. B., and Mesulam, M. M. (2004). Development of brain mechanisms for processing orthographic and phonologic representations. *Journal of Cognitive Neuroscience*, 16(7), 1234–1249.

Booth, J. R., Lu, D., Burman, D. D., Chou, T. L., Jin, Z., Peng, D. L., and Liu, L. (2006). Specialization of phonological and semantic processing in Chinese word reading. *Brain Research*, 1071(1), 197–207.

Bowman, B. T., Donovan, M. S., and Burns, M. S. (eds) (2001). *Eager to learn: Educating our preschoolers*. Washington, DC: National Academy Press.

Bronfenbrenner, U. (1979). Contexts of child rearing: Problems and prospects. *American Psychologist*, 34(10), 844.

Burzynska, A. Z., Nagel, I. E., Preuschhof, C., Li, S. C., Lindenberger, U., Bäckman, L., and Heekeren, H. R. (2011). Microstructure of frontoparietal connections predicts cortical responsivity and working memory performance. *Cerebral Cortex*, 21(10), 2261–2271.

Bus, A., Van IJzendoorn, M., and Pellegrini, A. (1995). Joint book reading makes for success in learning to read: A meta-analysis on intergenerational transmission of literacy. *Review of Educational Research*, 65, 1–21.

Butcher, L. S. (1995). *Mother tongue literacy maintenance among the children of recent Chinese immigrants in Brisbane*. Adelaide, South Australia: Helios Art and Book Company.

Cannella, G. S., Swadener, B. B., and Che, Y. (2007). Entry: Reconceptualizing early childhood education. In R. New (ed.), *International Encyclopedia of Early Childhood Education*. Westport, CT: Praeger Publishers.

Cao, C. Y. and Shen, Y. (1963). The recognition of Chinese characters by primary school children under tachistoscopic conditions II. The effect of the structure of characters (in Chinese). *Acta Psychologica Sinica*, 4, 271–279.

Cao, F., Lee, R., Shu, H., Yang, Y., Xu, G., Li, K., and Booth, J. R. (2010). Cultural constraints on brain development: Evidence from a developmental study of visual word processing in Mandarin Chinese. *Cerebral Cortex*, 20(5), 1223–1233.

Cao, F., Peng, D., Liu, L., Jin, Z., Fan, N., Deng, Y., and Booth, J. R. (2009). Developmental differences of neurocognitive networks for phonological and semantic processing in Chinese word reading. *Human Brain Mapping*, 30(3), 797–809.

Cao, F., Vu, M., Chan, L., Ho, D., Lawrence, J. M., Harris, L. N., and Perfetti, C. A. (2012). Writing affects the brain network of reading in Chinese: A functional magnetic resonance imaging study. *Human Brain Mapping*, 34(7), 1670–1684.

Caramazza, A. and Mahon, B. Z. (2006). The organisation of conceptual knowledge in the brain: The future's past and some future directions. *Cognitive Neuropsychology*, 23(1), 13–38.

Carter, R. (1995). *Keywords in language and literacy*. London: Routledge Press.
Castle, J. M., Riach, J., and Nicholson, T. (1994). Getting off to a better start in reading and spelling: The effects of phonemic awareness instruction within a whole language program. *Journal of Educational Psychology*, 86(3), 350.
Chall, J. (1983). *Stages of reading development*. New York: McGraw-Hill.
Chall, J. (1992). The new reading debates: Evidence from science, art, and ideology. *The Teachers College Record*, 94(2), 315–328.
Chall, J. S. (1996). *Learning to read: The great debate* (revised, with new foreword). Orlando, FL: Harcourt Brace.
Chan, D. W., Ho, C. S. H., Tsang, S. M., Lee, S. H., and Chung, K. K. (2006). Exploring the reading–writing connection in Chinese children with dyslexia in Hong Kong. *Reading and Writing*, 19(6), 543–561.
Chan, M. Y. (1982). Statistics on the strokes of present-day Chinese script. *Chinese Linguistics*, 10, 281–358.
Chan, P. L., Lau, C. K., and Poon, L. M. (1999). *Study on the adjustment issues of primary one pupils in Sha Tin* (in Chinese). Hong Kong: Sha Tin Provisional District Council.
Cheah, Y. M. and Lim, S. E. (1996). Literacy and biliteracy issues in Singapore. In E. F. K. Lai (ed.), *Reading Research Symposium 1996: Asian perspectives on biliteracy research: Facts, issues and action* (pp. 23–40). Hong Kong: Hong Kong Reading Association.
Chee, M. W., Hon, N., Lee, H. L., and Soon, C. S. (2001). Relative language proficiency modulates BOLD signal change when bilinguals perform semantic judgments. *Neuroimage*, 13(6), 1155–1163.
Chee, M. W., Tan, E. W., and Thiel, T. (1999). Mandarin and English single word processing studied with functional magnetic resonance imaging. *Journal of Neuroscience*, 19(8), 3050–3056.
Chee, M. W., Weekes, B., Lee, K. M., Soon, C. S., Schreiber, A., Hoon, J. J., and Chee, M. (2000). Overlap and dissociation of semantic processing of Chinese characters, English words, and pictures: Evidence from fMRI. *Neuroimage*, 12(4), 392–403.
Chen, F., Fu, S., Iversen, S. D., Smith, S. M., and Matthews, P. M. (2002). Testing for dual brain processing routes in reading: A direct contrast of Chinese character and Pinyin reading using fMRI. *Journal of Cognitive Neuroscience*, 14, 1088–1098.
Chen, H. C. (1992). Reading comprehension in Chinese: Implications form character reading times (in Chinese). In H. C. Chen and O. J. L. Tzeng (eds), *Language Processing* (pp. 175–205). Amsterdam: Elsevier Science Publishers B.V.
Chen, M. J. and Wong, A. (1991). Component skills as predictors of Chinese reading proficiency in primary school children. *International Journal of Psychology*, 26(1), 53–70.
Chen, M. J., Lau, L. L., and Yung, Y. F. (1993). Development of component skills in reading Chinese. *International Journal of Psychology*, 28(4), 481–507.
Chen, X. and Kao, H. S. R. (2002). Visual–spatial properties and orthographic processing of Chinese characters. In H. S. R. Kao, C. K. Leong, and D. G. Gao (eds), *Cognitive neuroscience studies of the Chinese language* (pp. 175–194). Hong Kong: Hong Kong University Press.
Chen, X., Shu, H., Wu, N., and Anderson, R. C. (2003). Stages in learning to pronounce Chinese characters. *Psychology in the Schools*, 40(1), 115–124.
Chen, Y., Fu, S., Iversen, S. D., Smith, S. M., and Matthews, P. M. (2002). Testing for dual brain processing routes in reading: a direct contrast of Chinese character and pinyin reading using fMRI. *Journal of Cognitive Neuroscience*, 14(7), 1088–1098.

Chen, Y. P., Allport, D. A., and Marshall, J. C. (1996). What are the functional orthographic units in Chinese word recognition: The stroke or the stroke pattern? *The Quarterly Journal of Experimental Psychology*, 49A, 1024–1043.

Cheng, C. M. (1982). Analysis of present-day Mandarin. *Journal of Chinese Linguistics*, 10, 281–358.

Cheng, C. M. and Huang, H. M. (1995). *The acquisition of general lexical knowledge of Chinese characters in school children*. Paper presented at the Seventh International Conference on the Cognitive Processing of Chinese and Other Asian Languages, Hong Kong.

Cheng, D. P. W. (2006). The translation of Western teaching approaches in the Hong Kong early childhood curriculum: A promise for effective teaching? *Contemporary Issues in Early Childhood*, 7(3), 228–237.

Cheng, P. W. D. (2001). Difficulties of Hong Kong teachers' understanding and implementation of play in the curriculum. *Teaching and Teacher Education*, 17(7), 857–869.

Cheung, H., Chen, H. C., Lai, C. Y., Wong, O. C., and Hills, M. (2001). The development of phonological awareness: Effects of spoken language experience and orthography. *Cognition*, 81(3), 227–241.

Cheung, H., McBride-Chang, C., and Chow, B. W. Y. (2006). Reading Chinese. In R. M. Joshi and P. G. Aaron (eds), *Handbook of Orthography and Literacy* (pp. 421–438). Mahwah, NJ: Erlbaum.

Cheung, S. K. and McBride-Chang, C. (2011). Relations of gender, gender-related personality characteristics, and dating status to adolescents' cross-sex friendship quality. *Sex Roles*, 64(1), 59–69.

China Preschool Education Research Society. (1999). *Collection of important documentations on early childhood education in the People's Republic of China* (in Chinese). Beijing: Beijing Normal University Press.

Chow, B. W. Y. and McBride-Chang, C. (2003). Promoting language and literacy development through parent-child reading in Hong Kong preschoolers. *Early Education and Development*, 14(2), 233–248.

Chow, B. W. Y., McBride-Chang, C., and Burgess, S. (2005). Phonological processing skills and early reading abilities in Hong Kong Chinese kindergarteners learning to read English as an L2. *Journal of Educational Psychology*, 97, 81–87.

Chow, B. W. Y., McBride-Chang, C., Cheung, H., and Chow, C. S. L. (2008). Dialogic reading and morphology training in Chinese children: Effects on language and literacy. *Developmental Psychology*, 44(1), 233.

Chow, B. W. Y., Ho, C. S. H., Wong, S. W. L., Waye, M. M., and Bishop, D. V. (2011). Genetic and environmental influences on Chinese language and reading abilities. *PloS one*, 6(2), e16640.

Chow, Y. H. (1993). Kindergarten and primary school teachers' expectations of school readiness skills in young children. In S. Opper (ed.), *Early childhood education in Hong Kong* (pp. 67–90). Hong Kong: University of Hong Kong, Faculty of Education.

Chung, K. K. and McBride-Chang, C. (2011). Executive functioning skills uniquely predict Chinese word reading. *Journal of Educational Psychology*, 103(4), 909–921.

Chung, K. K., Ho, C. S. H., Chan, D. W., Tsang, S. M., and Lee, S. H. (2011). Cognitive skills and literacy performance of Chinese adolescents with and without dyslexia. *Reading and Writing*, 24(7), 835–859.

Chung, K. K., Ho, C. S. H., Chan, D. W., Tsang, S. M., and Lee, S. H. (2013). Contributions of syntactic awareness to reading in Chinese-speaking adolescent readers with and without dyslexia. *Dyslexia*, *19*(1), 11–36.

Chung, K. K. H. (2002). Effective use of hanyu pinyin and English translation as extra stimulus prompts on learning of Chinese characters. *Educational Psychology*, *22*, 149–164.

Chung, K. K. H. (2008). What effect do mixed sensory mode instructional formats have on both novice and experienced learners of Chinese characters? *Learning and Instruction*, *18*, 96–108.

Chung, K. K. H., Tong, X., and McBride-Chang, C. (2012). Evidence for a deficit in orthographic structure processing in Chinese character recognition among developmental dyslexics: An Event-Related Potentials (ERP) study. *Brain Research*, *1472*, 20–31.

Clay, M. M. (1966). *Emergent reading behavior*. Unpublished doctoral dissertation, University of Auckland, New Zealand.

Cormier, P. and Dea, S. (1997). Distinctive patterns of relationship of phonological awareness and working memory with reading development. *Reading and Writing*, *9*(3), 193–206.

Coulmas, F. (1989). *The writing systems of the world*. Oxford: Basil Blackwell.

Crawford, P. A. (1995). Early literacy: Emerging perspectives. *Journal of Research in Childhood Education*, *10*(1), 71–86.

Curriculum Development Council. (2006). *Guide to the pre-primary curriculum*. Hong Kong: Government Printer.

Daneman, M. and Carpenter, P. A. (1980). Individual differences in working memory and reading. *Journal of Verbal Learning and Verbal Behavior*, *19*(4), 450–466.

DeFrancis, J. (1984). *The Chinese language: Fact and fantasy*. Honolulu: University of Hawaii Press.

DeFrancis, J. (1989). *Visible speech: The diverse oneness of writing systems*. Honolulu: University of Hawaii Press.

DeGroff, L. J. C. (1985). Review of readings on reading instruction. *Literacy Research and Instruction*, *24*(3), 106–108.

Dehaene, S. and Cohen, L. (2007). Cultural recycling of cortical maps. *Neuron*, *56*(2), 384–398.

Dickinson, D. and Smith, M. (1994). Long-term effects of preschool teachers' book readings on low-income children's vocabulary and story comprehension. *Reading Research Quarterly*, *29*(2), 104–122.

Duncan, J. and Owen, A. M. (2000). Common regions of the human frontal lobe recruited by diverse cognitive demands. *Trends in neurosciences*, *23*(10), 475–483.

Durkin, D. (1966). *Children who read early: Two longitudinal studies*. New York: Teachers College Press.

Durkin, D. (1987). A classroom-observation study of reading instruction in kindergarten. *Early Childhood Research Quarterly*, *2*(3), 275–300.

Dyson, A. H. (1988). Appreciate the drawing and dictating of young children. *Young Children*, *43*(3), 25–32.

Education Commission. (2000). *Review of the education system: Reform proposals*. Hong Kong: Government Printer.

Education Department. (1984). *Manual of Kindergarten Practice*. Hong Kong: Government Printer.

Education Department. (1993). *A study on the continuity of curriculum and teaching practices between the kindergarten and primary school levels of education*. Hong Kong: Government Printer.

Education Department. (1996). *Guide to the preprimary curriculum*. Hong Kong: Government Printer.
Ehri, L. C., Nunes, S. R., Stahl, S. A., and Willows, D. M. (2001). Systematic phonics instruction helps students learn to read: Evidence from the National Reading Panel's meta-analysis. *Review of Educational Research*, 71(3), 393–447.
Elkind, D. (2001). Much too early. *Education Matters*, 1, 9–15.
Evans, M. A., Shaw, D., and Bell, M. (2000). Home literacy activities and their influence on early literacy skills. *Canadian Journal of Experimental Psychology*, 54(2), 65–75.
Everson, M. E. (1994). Toward a process view of teaching reading in the second language Chinese curriculum. *Theory into Practice*, 33(1), 4–9.
Everson, M. E. (1998). Word recognition among learners of Chinese as a foreign language: Investigating the relationship between naming and knowing. *The Modern Language Journal*, 82(2), 194–204.
Everson, M. E. (2011). Best practices in teaching logographic and non-roman writing systems to L2 learners. *Annual Review of Applied Linguistics*, 31(1), 249–274.
Everson, M. E. and Xiao, Y. (2009). *Teaching Chinese as a foreign language: Theories and applications*. Boston, MA: Cheng and Tsui Company.
Fabian, H. (2002). Empowering children for transitions. In H. Fabian and A. W. Dunlop (eds), *Transitions in the early years: Debating progression and continuity for children in early education* (pp. 123–134). London: Routledge Falmer.
Fan, K. Y., Gao, J. Y., and Ao, X. P. (1984). On the pronunciation of characters and pinyin alphabet. *Language Construction*, 3, 19–22.
Fan, M. H-M. (2010). *Developing Chinese orthographic awareness: What insights into characters do beginning level Chinese as a foreign language textbooks provide?* Saarbrücken, Germany: Lap Lambert Academic Publishing.
Federmeier, K. D. (2007). Thinking ahead: The role and roots of prediction in language comprehension. *Psychophysiology*, 44(4), 491–505.
Feng, G., Miller, K., Shu, H., and Zhang, H. (2001). Rowed to recovery: The use of phonological and orthographic information in reading Chinese and English. *Journal of Experimental Psychology: Learning, Memory, and Cognition*, 27(4), 1079–1100.
Feng, Z. W. (1999). *On Chinese applied linguistics*. Guangzhou, China: Guangdong Publishing House.
Flores d'Aracis, G. B. (1994). Order of strokes writing as a cue for retrieval in reading Chinese characters. *European Journal of Cognitive Psychology*, 6(4), 337–355.
Fox, P. T. and Raichle, M. E. (1986). Focal physiological uncoupling of cerebral blood flow and oxidative metabolism during somatosensory stimulation in human subjects. *Proceedings of the National Academy of Sciences*, 83(4), 1140–1144.
Fox, P. T., Mintun, M. A., Raichle, M. E., Miezin, F. M., Allman, J. M., and Van Essen, D. C. (1986). Mapping human visual cortex with positron emission tomography. *Nature*, 323, 806–809.
Frerichs, L. C. (1993, December). *Kindergarten teachers' perceptions and practices in reading/language arts*. Paper presented at the annual meeting of the National Reading Conference, Charleston, SC.
Fu, S., Chen, Y., Smith, S., Iversen, S., and Matthews, P. M. (2002). Effects of word form on brain processing of written Chinese. *Neuroimage*, 17(3), 1538–1548.
Gallese, V., Fadiga, L., Fogassi, L., and Rizzolatti, G. (1996). Action recognition in the premotor cortex. *Brain*, 119(2), 593–609.

Gandour, J., Wong, D., Dzemidzic, M., Lowe, M., Tong, Y., and Li, X. (2003b). A cross-linguistic fMRI study of perception of intonation and emotion in Chinese. *Human Brain Mapping*, *18*(3), 149–157.

Gandour, J., Wong, D., Hsieh, L., Weinzapfel, B., Van Lancker, D., and Hutchins, G. D. (2000). A crosslinguistic PET study of tone perception. *Journal of Cognitive Neuroscience*, *12*(1), 207–222.

Gandour, J., Dzemidzic, M., Wong, D., Lowe, M., Tong, Y., Hsieh, L., and Lurito, J. (2003a). Temporal integration of speech prosody is shaped by language experience: An fMRI study. *Brain and Language*, *84*(3), 318–336.

Gandour, J., Xu, Y., Wong, D., Dzemidzic, M., Lowe, M., Li, X., and Tong, Y. (2003c). Neural correlates of segmental and tonal information in speech perception. *Human Brain Mapping*, *20*(4), 185–200.

Gao, L. Q. and Meng, L. (2000). The role of the phonetic code and orthographic code of Chinese character recognition by foreign learners. *Chinese Teaching in the World*, *4*, 67–76.

Gates, A. I. (1947). *The improvement of reading: A program of diagnostic and remedial methods* (3rd edition). New York: The Macmillan Company.

Genishi, C. (1993). Assessing young children's language and literacy: Tests and their alternatives. In B. Spodek and O. N. Saracho (eds), *Language and literacy in early childhood education* (pp. 61–81). New York: Teachers College Press.

GOC, Government of the People's Republic of China, Ministry of Education. (2001). Guidance for kindergarten education (in Chinese). *Early Childhood Education*, *237*(9), 4–7.

Goodman, K. S. (1998). *In defense of good teaching: what teachers need to know about the "reading wars"*. Teachers Pub Group Incorporation.

Goodman, Y. M. (1986). Children coming to know literacy. In W. H. Teale and E. Sulzby (eds), *Emergent literacy: Writing and reading*. Norwood, New Jersey: Ablex Publishing Corporation.

Goodman, Y. M. (1989). Roots of the whole-language movement. *The Elementary School Journal*, *90*, 113–127.

Gottardo, A., Yan, B., Siegel, L. S., and Wade-Woolley, L. (2001). Factors related to English reading performance in children with Chinese as a first language: More evidence of cross-language transfer of phonological processing. *Journal of Educational Psychology*, *93*(3), 530.

Gray, W. S. (1925). Reading activities in school and in social life. In G. M. Whipple (ed.), *The Twenty-Fourth Yearbook of the National Society for the Study of Education: Part I* (pp. 1–8). Bloomington, IL: Public School Publishing Company.

Grunwald, M. (2006). The education issue. *Education*, *11*, 03.

Guan, C. Q., Liu, Y., Chan, D. H. L., Ye, F., and Perfetti, C. A. (2011). Writing strengthens orthography and alphabetic-coding strengthens phonology in learning to read Chinese. *Journal of Educational Psychology*, *103*(3), 509.

Haith, M. M. (1990). Progress in the understanding of sensory and perceptual processes in early infancy. *Merill-Palmer Quarterly*, *36*, 1–26.

Hall, N. (1987). *The emergence of literacy*. Portsmouth: Heinemann Educational Books Incorporation.

Hall, N. (1994). The emergence of literacy. In B. Stierer and J. Maybin (eds), *Language, literacy and learning in educational practice: A reader* (pp. 15–29). Clevedon, Avon: Multilingual Matters.

Halpern, C., McMillan, C., Moore, P., Dennis, K., and Grossman, M. (2003). Calculation impairment in neurodegenerative diseases. *Journal of the Neurological Sciences*, 208(1), 31–38.

Han, B. X. (1994). Development of database of Chinese constituents information: Statistical analysis of the frequency of the constituents and their combination. *ACTA Psychologica Sinca*, 26(2), 147–152.

Han, Z., Zhang, Y., Shu, H., and Bi, Y. (2007). The orthographic buffer in writing Chinese characters: Evidence from a dysgraphic patient. *Cognitive neuropsychology*, 24(4), 431–450.

Hanley, J. R. and Huang, H. S. (1997). Phonological awareness and learning to read Chinese. In C. K. Leong and R. M. Joshi (eds), *Cross-language studies of learning to read and spell: Phonologic, orthographic processing* (pp. 361–378). Dordrecht: Kluwer Academic Publishers.

Hansen, J. S. (1969). *The impact of the home literacy environment on reading attitude.* Elementary English, 46, 17–24.

Harris, A. J. and Sipay, E. R. (1985). How to increase reading ability: A guide to developmental and remedial methods (8th edition). New York: Longman.

Harris, T. L. and Hodges, R. E. (eds). (1995). *The literacy dictionary: The vocabulary of reading and writing.* Newark, DE: International Reading Association.

Hayhoe, R. (1984). *Contemporary Chinese Education.* Armonk, NY: ME Sharpe.

He, A. G., Tan, L. H., Tang, Y., James, A., Wright, P., Eckert, M. A., Fox, P. T., and Liu, Y. J. (2003). Modulation of neural connectivity during tongue movement and reading. *Human Brain Mapping*, 18, 222–232.

Heath, S. B. (1983). *Ways with words: Language, life and work in communities and Classrooms.* Cambridge University Press, Cambridge.

Hedden, T. and Gabrieli, J. D. (2004). Insights into the ageing mind: a view from cognitive neuroscience. *Nature reviews neuroscience*, 5(2), 87–96.

Ho, C. S. H. and Lai, D. N. C. (1999). Naming-speed deficits and phonological memory deficits in Chinese developmental dyslexia. *Learning and Individual Differences*, 11(2), 173–186.

Ho, C. S. H., Law, T. P. S., and Ng, P. M. (2000). The phonological deficit hypothesis in Chinese developmental dyslexia. *Reading and Writing*, 13(1–2), 57–79.

Ho, C. S. H., Chan, D. W. O., Lee, S. H., Tsang, S. M., and Luan, V. H. (2004). Cognitive profiling and preliminary subtyping in Chinese developmental dyslexia. *Cognition*, 91(1), 43–75.

Ho, S. H. C. and Bryant, P. (1997a). Phonological skills are important in learning to read Chinese. *Developmental Psychology*, 33(6), 946–951.

Ho, S. H. C. and Bryant, P. (1997b). Learning to read Chinese beyond the logographic phase. *Reading Research Quarterly*, 32(3), 276–290.

Ho, S. H. C. and Bryant, P. (1999). Different visual skills are important in learning to read English and Chinese. *Educational and Child Psychology*, 16(4), 4–14.

Ho, S. H. C. and Ma, N. L. (1999). Training in phonological strategies improves Chinese dyslexic children's character reading skills. *Journal of Research in Reading*, 22(2), 131–142.

Hoeft, F., Hernandez, A., McMillon, G., Taylor-Hill, H., Martindale, J. L., Meyler, A., and Gabrieli, J. D. (2006). Neural basis of dyslexia: a comparison between dyslexic and nondyslexic children equated for reading ability. *Journal of Neuroscience*, 26(42), 10700–10708.

Holdaway, D. (1984). *Stability and change in literacy learning*. Portsmouth, NH: Heinemann.

Hong Kong Census and Statistics Department. (2000, February 15). *End-year population for 1999*. Retrieved from http://www.info.gov.hk/gia/general/200002/15/0215129.htm.

Hong Kong Education Department. (1999). *Key Statistics*. Retrieved from http://www.info.gov.hk/ed/english/resource/key_statistics/index.htm.

Honorof, D. N. and Feldman, L. (2006). The Chinese character in psycholinguistic research: Form, structure, and the reader. In P. Li, L. H. Tan, E. Bates, and O. J. L. Tzeng (eds), *The handbook of east Asian psycholinguistics:* Chinese (pp. 195–208). New York, NY: Cambridge University Press.

Hu, Bo. (2010). The challenge of Chinese: a preliminary study of UK learners' perceptions of difficulty. *Language Learning Journal*, 38, 99–118.

Hu, C. F. and Catts, H. W. (1998). The role of phonological processing in early reading ability: What we can learn from Chinese. *Scientific Studies of Reading*, 2(1), 55–79.

Hu, G. W. (2002). Potential Cultural Resistance to Pedagogical Imports: The Case of Communicative Language Teaching in China. *Language, Culture and Curriculum*, 15(2), 93–105.

Huang, H. S. and Hanley, J. R. (1995). Phonological awareness and visual skills in learning to read Chinese and English. *Cognition*, 54, 73–98.

Huang, J. T. and Wang, M. Y. (1992). From unit to Gestalt: Perceptual dynamics in recognizing Chinese characters. *Advances in Psychology*, 90, 3–35.

Hubel, D. H. and Wiesel, T. N. (1959). Receptive fields of single neurones in the cat's striate cortex. *The Journal of Physiology*, 148(3), 574–591.

Hubel, D. H. and Wiesel, T. N. (1962). Receptive fields, binocular interaction and functional architecture in the cat's visual cortex. *The Journal of Physiology*, 160(1), 106.

Ingulsrud, J. E. and Allen, K. (1999). *Learning to read in China: Sociolinguistic perspectives on the acquisition of literacy*. Lewiston, NY: The Edwin Mellen Press.

International Reading Association. (1986). *Guidelines for the specialized preparation of reading professionals*. The Association.

Ip, T. N. M. (2013). *Probing into the underlying neural basis of reading in Chinese*. PhD Dissertation Submitted to the University of Hong Kong.

Ito, A., Abe, N., Fujii, T., Hayashi, A., Ueno, A., Mugikura, S., and Mori, E. (2012). The contribution of the dorsolateral prefrontal cortex to the preparation for deception and truth-telling. *Brain Research*, 1464, 43–52.

Jackson, N. E., Everson, M. E., and Ke, C. (2003). Beginning readers' awareness of the orthographic structure of semantic-phonetic compounds: Lessons from a study of learners of Chinese as a foreign language. In C. McBride-Chang and H-C. Chen (eds), Reading Development in Chinese Children (pp. 141–153). Praeger Publishers: London.

James, K. H. and Atwood, T. P. (2009). The role of sensorimotor learning in the perception of letter-like forms: Tracking the causes of neural specialization for letters. *Cognitive Neuropsychology*, 26(1), 91–110.

James, K. H. and Gauthier, I. (2006). Letter processing automatically recruits a sensory–motor brain network. *Neuropsychologia*, 44(14), 2937–2949.

Jiang, X. (2003). The relationship between knowing pronunciation and knowing meaning of Chinese characters among CSL learners (in Chinese). *Language Teaching and Linguistics Studies*, 6, 51–7.

Jiang, X. and Zhao, G. (2001). A survey on the strategies for learning Chinese characters among CSL beginners (in Chinese). *Language Teaching and Linguistics Studies*, 4, 10–16.

Jin, H. G. (2006). Multimedia effects and Chinese character processing: An empirical study of CFL learners from three different orthographic backgrounds. *Journal of Chinese Teachers Association*, 41(3), 35.

John-Steiner, V. and Mahn, H. (1996). Sociocultural approaches to learning and development: A Vygotskian framework. *Educational Psychologist*, 31(3), 191–206.

Jones, J. (2003). *Early Literacy Assessment Systems: Essential Elements*. Princeton, NJ: Educational Testing Service.

Kagan, S. L. and Neuman, M. J. (1998). Lessons from three decades of transition research. *The Elementary School Journal*, 365–379.

Karmel, B. Z. (1969). The effect of age, complexity, and amount of contour on pattern preferences in human infants. *Journal of Experimental Child Psychology*, 7(2), 339–354.

Karmel, B. Z. and Maisel, E. B. (1975). A neuronal activity model for infant visual attention. In L. B. Cohen and P. Salapatek (eds), *Infant perception: From sensation to cognition* (pp. 78–131). New York: Academic Press.

Karweit, N. and Wasik, B. (1996). The effects of story reading programs on literacy and language development of disadvantaged pre-schoolers. *Journal of Education for Students Placed At Risk*, 4, 319–348.

Katz, L. and Frost, R. (1992). The reading process is different for different orthographies: The orthographic depth hypothesis. *Advances in Psychology*, 94, 67–84.

Katz, L. G. and Chard, S. C. (1989). *Engaging children's minds: The project approach*. Norwood, NJ: Ablex.

Katz, L. G. and Chard, S. C. (2000). *Engaging Children's Minds: The Project Approach*. Westport, CT: Praeger.

Kauerz, K. (2006). Ladders of learning: Fighting fade-out by advancing PK-3 alignment. *NAF Issue Brief No. 2*. New America Foundation: Early Education Initiative, Washington, DC.

Ke, C., Wen, X., and Kotenbeutel, C. (2001). Report on the 2000 CLTA articulation project. *Journal of Chinese Teachers Association*, 36(3), 25–60.

Kessler, S. A. and Swadener, B. B. (1992). *Reconceptualizing the early childhood curriculum: Beginning the dialogue*. Teachers College Press.

Kilgore, D. W. (2001). Critical and postmodern perspectives on adult learning. *New directions for adult and continuing education*, 2001(89), 53–62.

Kintgen, E. R., Kroll, B. M., and Rose, M. (1988). *Perspectives on literacy*. SIU Press.

Klein, D., Zatorre, R. J., Milner, B., and Zhao, V. (2001). A cross-linguistic PET study of tone perception in Mandarin Chinese and English speakers. *Neuroimage*, 13(4), 646–653.

Koda, K. (2008). Impacts of prior literacy experience on second-language learning to read. *Learning to read across languages: Cross-linguistic relationships in first- and second-language literacy development*, 68–96.

Kohler, E., Keysers, C., Umilta, M. A., Fogassi, L., Gallese, V., and Rizzolatti, G. (2002). Hearing sounds, understanding actions: Action representation in mirror neurons. *Science*, 297(5582), 846–848.

Kuo, E. C. Y. and Jernudd, B. H. (1993). Balancing macro- and micro-sociolinguistic perspectives in language management: The case of Singapore. *Language Problems and Language Planning*, 17(1), 1–21.

Kuo, W. J., Yeh, T. C., Duann, J. R., Wu, Y. T., Ho, L. T., Hung, D., and Hsieh, J. C. (2001). A left-lateralized network for reading Chinese words: a 3 T fMRI study. *Neuroreport*, 12(18), 3997–4001.

Lakoff, G. (1987). *Women, fire, and dangerous things: What categories reveal about the mind*. Chicago: University of Chicago Press.

Lasaga, M. I. and Garner, W. R. (1983). Effect of line orientation on various information-processing tasks. *Journal of Experimental Psychology: Human Perception and Performance*, 9, 215–225.

Lau, E. Y., Li, H., and Rao, N. (2011). Parental involvement and children's readiness for school in China. *Educational Research*, 53(1), 95–113.

Law, F. (1999). Quality early childhood education for the 21st century. *OMEP-Hong Kong Newsletter*, 11, 8.

Law, S. P. and Leung, M. T. (2000). Sentence processing deficits in two Cantonese aphasic patients. *Brain and Language*, 72(3), 310–342.

Law, S. P. and Or, B. (2001). A case study of acquired dyslexia and dysgraphia in Cantonese: Evidence for nonsemantic pathways for reading and writing in Chinese. *Cognitive Neuropsychology*, 18(8), 729–748.

Law, S. P., Yeung, O., Wong, W., and Chiu, K. M. (2005). Processing of semantic radicals in writing Chinese characters: Data from a Chinese dysgraphic patient. *Cognitive Neuropsychology*, 22(7), 885–903.

Lee, C. H. and Kalyuga, S. (2011). Effectiveness of on-screen pinyin in learning Chinese: An expertise reversal for multimedia redundancy effect. *Computers in Human Behavior*, 27(1), 11–15.

Lee, C. Y., Huang, H. W., Kuo, W. J., Tsai, J. L., and Tzeng, J. L. (2010). Cognitive and neural basis of the consistency and lexicality effects in reading Chinese. *Journal of Neurolinguistics*, 23(1), 10–27.

Lee, I. F. and Tseng, C. L. (2008). Cultural conflicts of the child-centered approach to early childhood education in Taiwan. *Early Years*, 28(2), 183–196.

Leong, C. K. (1991). From phonemic awareness to phonological processing to language access in children developing reading proficiency. In D. J. Sawyer and B. J. Fox (eds), *Phonological awareness in reading: The evolution of current perspectives* (pp. 217–254). New York: Springer-Verlag.

Leong, C. K. (1997). Paradigmatic analysis of Chinese word reading: Research findings and classroom practices. In C. K. Leong and R. M. Joshi (eds), Cross-language studies of learning to reading and spell: Phonological and orthographic processing (pp. 379–417). Amsterdam, the Netherlands: Kluwer Academic.

Leong, C. K., Hau, K. T., Cheng, P. W., and Tan, L. H. (2005). Exploring two-wave reciprocal structural relations among orthographic knowledge, phonological sensitivity, and reading and spelling of English words by Chinese students. *Journal of Educational Psychology*, 97(4), 591.

Leong, C. K., Tse, S. K., Loh, K. Y., and Hau, K. T. (2008). Text comprehension in Chinese children: Relative contribution of verbal working memory, pseudoword reading, rapid automatized naming, and onset-rime phonological segmentation. *Journal of Educational Psychology*, 100(1), 135.

Li, H. (1998). Advances and quandaries in contemporary Chinese cognitive research (in Chinese). *Nantah Journal of Chinese Language and Culture*, 3(1), 1–32.

Li, H. (1999). Development and Validation of the Preschool and Primary Chinese Literacy Scale (in Chinese). *Psychological Development and Education*, 15(3), 18–24.

Li, H. (2000). *Contributors to Chinese literacy development: A longitudinal study of preschoolers in Beijing, Hong Kong and Singapore*. Unpublished doctoral dissertation, University of Hong Kong, Hong Kong.

Li, H. (2002). Reforming the early childhood curriculum in Hong Kong (in Chinese). *Hong Kong Journal of Early Childhood*, *1*(1), 44–49.

Li, H. (2003). Response errors in reading Chinese characters: A developmental and sociocontextual perspective. In C. McBride-Chang and H. C. Chen (eds), *Reading Development in Chinese Children* (pp. 77–85). Westport, CT: Greenwood Publishing Group.

Li, H. (2004). *Story approach to integrated learning (SAIL 1.0) Learning Package*. Hong Kong: Oxford University Press.

Li, H. (2005). Development and validation of the preschool and primary Chinese literacy scale. In B. Kozuh, T. Beran, A. Kozioska, and P. Bayliss (eds), *Measurement and assessment in educational and social research*. Krakow: Oficyna Wydawnicza AFM.

Li, H. (2007a). *Story Approach to Integrated Learning: The Curricula and Pedagogies*. Hong Kong: Oxford University Press.

Li, H. (2007b). Universalism or relativism: Rethinking Chinese early childhood education reform from a cultural perspective. In J. X. Zhu (ed.), *Chinese perspectives on early childhood education*. Shanghai: East China Normal University Press.

Li, H. (2008). A comparison of mainstream contemporary perspectives on early childhood curriculum. *Early Childhood Education (Education Science Edition)*, *424*(12), 17–20.

Li, H. (2013a). Teaching Chinese literacy in the early years: A comparison of L1 and L2 preschool classrooms in Shenzhen and Singapore. *Asia-Pacific Journal of Research in Early Childhood Education*, *7*(3), 19–43.

Li, H. (2013b). *Story Approach to Integrated Learning (SAIL 3.0) Learning Package*. Hong Kong: Oxford University Press.

Li, H. and Li, P. M. (2003). Lessons from implanting Reggio Emilia and Montessori curriculum in China (in Chinese). *Early Childhood Education*, *9*, 4–5.

Li, H. and Rao, N. (2000). Parental influences on Chinese literacy development: A comparison of preschoolers in Beijing, Hong Kong and Singapore. *International Journal of Behavioral Development*, *24*(1), 82–90.

Li, H. and Rao, N. (2005). Curricular and instructional influences on early literacy attainment: Evidence from Beijing, Hong Kong and Singapore. *International Journal of Early Years Education*, *13*(3), 235–253.

Li, H. and Wang, X. C. (2014). International perspectives on early childhood education in Chinese societies. In N. Rao, J. Zhou, and J. Sun (eds), *Early Childhood Development in Chinese Societies*. Springer.

Li, H. and Wu, Y. X. (1996). *The TPR Chinese literacy education programme* (in Chinese). Beijing: Press of Science.

Li, H., Corrie, L. F., and Wong, B. K. M. (2008). Early teaching of Chinese literacy skills and later literacy outcomes. *Early Child Development and Care*, *178*(5), 441–459.

Li, P., Jin, Z., and Tan, L. H. (2004). Neural representations of nouns and verbs in Chinese: An fMRI study. *Neuroimage*, *21*(4), 1533–1541.

Li, H., Peng, H., and Shu, H. (2006). A study on the emergence and development of Chinese orthographic awareness in preschool and school children (in Chinese). *Psychological Development and Education*, *18*(1), 35–38.

Li, H., Rao, N., and Tse, S. K. (2011). Bridging the gap: a longitudinal study of the relationship between pedagogical continuity and early Chinese literacy acquisition. *Early Years*, *31*(1), 57–70.

Li, H., Rao, N., and Tse, S. K. (2012). Adopting western pedagogies into teaching Chinese literacy: Comparison of Hong Kong, Shenzhen and Singapore preschool classrooms. *Early Education and Development*, *23*(4), 1–19.

Li, H., Wang, X. C., and Wong, J. M. S. (2011). Early Childhood Curriculum Reform in China. *Chinese Education and Society*, 44(6), 5–23.

Li, H., Wong, M. S., and Wang, C. X. (2010). Affordability, accessibility, and accountability: Perceived impacts of the Pre-primary Education Vouchers in Hong Kong. *Early Childhood Research Quarterly*, 25(1), 125–138.

Li, X. S., Gu, J. J., Liu, P. P., and Rayner, K. (2012). The psychological reality of words in Chinese reading: Evidence from eye movements. *Manuscript submitted for publication*.

Li, X. S., Gu, J., Liu, P. P., and Rayner, K. (2013). The advantage of word-based processing in Chinese reading: Evidence from eye movements. *Journal of Experimental Psychology: Learning, Memory, and Cognition*, 39(3), 879.

Liang, Z. S., Li, H., and Wu, Y. X. (1997). Essential problems of Chinese literacy education in kindergartens (in Chinese). *Preschool Education (Beijing)*, 1, 2–4.

Liberman, A. M., Cooper, F. S., Shankweiler, D. P., and Studdert-Kennedy, M. (1967). Perception of the speech code. *Psychological review*, 74(6), 431.

Liu, I. M. (1995). Script factors that affect literacy: alphabetic vs. logographic languages. In I. Taylor and D. R. Olson (eds), *Scripts and literacy: reading and learning to read alphabets, syllabaries, and characters* (pp. 145–162). Netherlands: Kluwer Academic Publishers.

Liu, W., Inhoff, A. W., Ye, Y., and Wu, C. (2002). Use of parafoveally visible characters during the reading of Chinese sentences. *Journal of Experimental Psychology: Human Perception and Performance*, 28(5), 1213.

Liu, Y. and Feng, X. X. (2005). Kindergarten educational reform during the past two decades in Mainland China: Achievements and problems. *International Journal of Early Years Education*, 13(2), 93–99.

Liu, Y. and Perfetti, C. A. (2003). The time course of brain activity in reading English and Chinese: an ERP study of Chinese bilinguals. *Human brain mapping*, 18(3), 167–175.

Liu, Y., Perfetti, C. A., and Hart, L. (2003). ERP evidence for the time course of graphic, phonological, and semantic information in Chinese meaning and pronunciation decisions. *Journal of Experimental Psychology: Learning, Memory, and Cognition*, 29(6), 1231.

Liu, Y., Dunlap, S., Fiez, J., and Perfetti, C. (2007). Evidence for neural accommodation to a writing system following learning. *Human Brain Mapping*, 28(11), 1223–1234.

Liu, Y., Kotov, R., Rahim, R. A. B. D., and Goh, H. H. (2005). *Mandarin pedagogical practice: A snapshot description of Singaporean Chinese language classrooms*. Singapore: CRPP, National Institute of Education.

Liu, Y. L. and Song S. Z. (1992). Vocabulary guideline for Chinese proficiency test. Beijing: Beijing Language and Culture University Press.

Liu, Y. M. (2009). An experimental study of the necessity, teachability and effectiveness of strategy training for Chinese character learning. *Chinese Teaching in the World*, 2, 280.

Liu, Y. M. and Jiang, X. (2003). An experimental study on the methods of Chinese characters learning by European and American learners. *Chinese Teaching in the World*, 1, 1–9.

Longcamp, M., Anton, J. L., Roth, M., and Velay, J. L. (2003). Visual presentation of single letters activates a premotor area involved in writing. *Neuroimage*, 19(4), 1492–1500.

Longcamp, M., Anton, J. L., Roth, M., and Velay, J. L. (2005). Premotor activations in response to visually presented single letters depend on the hand used to write: a study on left-handers. *Neuropsychologia*, 43(12), 1801–1809.

Longcamp, M., Boucard, C., Gilhodes, J. C., Anton, J. L., Roth, M., Nazarian, B., and Velay, J. L. (2008). Learning through hand or typewriting influences visual recognition of new graphic shapes: Behavioral and functional imaging evidence. *Journal of Cognitive Neuroscience*, 20(5), 802–815.

Luke, A., Freebody, P., Shun, L., and Gopinathan, S. (2005). Towards research-based innovation and reform: Singapore schooling in transition. *Asia Pacific Journal of Education*, 25(1), 5–28.

Luke, K. K., Liu, H. L., Wai, Y. Y., Wan, Y. L., and Tan, L. H. (2002). Functional anatomy of syntactic and semantic processing in language comprehension. *Human Brain Mapping*, 16(3), 133–145.

Luo, C. R., Ji, G. P., and Fang, L. J. (1987). The global precedence in visual information extraction (in Chinese). *Acta Psychologica Sinica*, 2, 184–189.

Madison, S. G. and Speaker. R. B. (1994). *The construction of literacy environments in early childhood classrooms: Spectrum of approaches.* New Orleans. LA: American Educational Research Association.

Mahon, B. Z. and Caramazza, A. (2005). The orchestration of the sensory-motor systems: Clues from neuropsychology. *Cognitive Neuropsychology*, 22(3), 480–494.

Mahon, B. Z. and Caramazza, A. (2008). A critical look at the embodied cognition hypothesis and a new proposal for grounding conceptual content. *Journal of Physiology-Paris*, 102(1), 59–70.

Martin, A., Haxby, J. V., Lalonde, F. M., Wiggs, C. L., and Ungerleider, L. G. (1995). Discrete cortical regions associated with knowledge of color and knowledge of action. *Science*, 270(5233), 102–105.

Martin, A., Ungerleider, L. G., and Haxby, J. V. (2000). Category specificity and the brain: The sensory/motor model of semantic representations of objects. *The New Cognitive Neurosciences*, 2, 1023–1036.

Mason, J. M. (1992). Reading stories to preliterate children: A proposed connection to reading. In P. B. Gough, L. C. Ehri, and R. Treiman (eds), *Reading acquisition* (pp. 215–243). Hillsdale, NJ: Erlbaum.

Mason, J. M. (1980). When do children begin to read: An exploration of four year old children's letter and word reading competencies. *Reading Research Quarterly*, 15, 203–227.

Mattingly, I. G. (1987). Morphological structure and segmental awareness. *Cahiers de Psychologie Cognitive*, 7, 488–493.

McBride-Chang, C. (2004). *Children's literacy development.* New York: Oxford University Press.

McBride-Chang, C. and Chang, L. (1995). Memory, print exposure, and metacognition: components of reading in Chinese children. *International Journal of Psychology*, 30, 607–616.

McBride-Chang, C. and Ho, C. S.-H. (2000). Developmental issues in Chinese children's character acquisition. *Journal of Educational Psychology*, 92(1), 50–55.

McBride-Chang, C. and Kail, R. V. (2002). Cross-cultural similarities in the predictors of reading acquisition. *Child Development*, 73(5), 1392–1407.

McBride-Chang, C., Bialystok, E., Chong, K., and Li, Y. P. (2004). Levels of phonological awareness in three cultures. *Journal of Experimental Child Psychology*, 89, 93–111.

McGraw, I., Yoshimoto, B., and Seneff, S. (2009). Speech-enabled card games for incidental vocabulary acquisition in a foreign language. *Speech Communication*, 51(10), 1006–1023.

McNaughton, S. (1995). *Patterns of emergent literacy: Process of development and transition.* Melbourne: Oxford University Press.

Meng, X., Sai, X., Wang, C., Wang, J., Sha, S., and Zhou, X. (2005). Auditory and speech processing and reading development in Chinese school children: Behavioural and ERP evidence. *Dyslexia, 11*(4), 292–310.

Miller, E. K. and Cohen, J. D. (2001). An integrative theory of prefrontal cortex function. *Annual Review of Neuroscience, 24*(1), 167–202.

Morrow, L. M. (1997). *Literacy Development in the Early Years: Helping children read and write.* Needham Heights, MA: Allyn and Bacon.

Morrow, L. M. (1988). Young children's responses to one-to-one readings in school settings. *Reading Research Quarterly, 23,* 89–107.

National Research Council. (2001). *Educating children with autism.* National Academies Press.

Navon, D. (1977). Forest before trees: The precedence of global features in visual perception. *Cognitive Psychology, 9*(3), 353–383.

Navon, D. (1981). Do attention and decision follow perception? Comment on Miller. Journal of Experimental Psychology: Human Perception and Performance, 7, 1175–1182.

Neuman, M. J. (2002). The wider context: An international overview of transition issues. In H. Fabian and A. W. A. Dunlop (eds), *Transition in the early years – Debating continuity and progression for young children in early education* (pp. 8–22). London: Routledge Falmer.

Ng, S. S. N. and Rao, N. (2008). Mathematics teaching during the early years in Hong Kong: A reflection of constructivism with Chinese characteristics? *Early Years, 28*(2), 159–172.

Ni, B. Y. (1995). *Chinese linguistics and language education.* Shanghai: Shanghai Education Publisher.

Norman, J. (2000). *Chinese.* Cambridge, United Kingdom: Cambridge University Press.

Nurss, J. R. (1992). Evaluation of language and literacy. In L. O. Ollila and M. I. Mayfield (eds), *Emerging literacy preschool, kindergarten, and primary grades* (pp. 229–252). Needham Heights, MA: Allyn and Bacon.

Opper, S. (1992). *Hong Kong's young children: Their preschools and families* (pp. 21–27). Hong Kong: Hong Kong University Press.

Palmer, B. C., Zhang, N., Taylor, S. H., and Leclere, J. T. (2010). Language proficiency, reading, and the Chinese-speaking English language learner: Facilitating the L1-L2 connection. *Multicultural Education, 17*(2), 44–51.

Pan, J., McBride-Chang, C., Shu, H., Liu, H., Zhang, Y., and Li, H. (2011). What is in the naming? A 5-year longitudinal study of early rapid naming and phonological sensitivity in relation to subsequent reading skills in both native Chinese and English as a second language. *Journal of Educational Psychology, 103*(4), 897–908.

Pan, Y. J. and Liu, Y. (2008). A Comparison of Curricular Practices in Chinese Kindergartens: The Influences of Curriculum Reform. *International Journal of Early Childhood, 40*(2), 33–48.

Pang, L. J. and Li, H. (1994). *Infant Psychology.* Zhejiang Education Press.

Passolunghi, M. C. and Siegel, L. S. (2004). Working memory and access to numerical information in children with disability in mathematics. *Journal of Experimental Child Psychology, 88*(4), 348–367.

Paulesu, E., Démonet, J. F., Fazio, F., McCrory, E., Chanoine, V., Brunswick, N., and Frith, U. (2001). Dyslexia: Cultural diversity and biological unity. *Science, 291*(5511), 2165–2167.

Pearson, E. and Rao, N. (2003). Socialization goals, parenting practices, and peer competence in Chinese and English preschoolers. *Early Child Development and Care*, *173*(1), 131–146.

Pearson, E. and Rao, N. (2006). Early Childhood Education Policy Reform in Hong Kong: Challenges in effecting change in practices. *Childhood Education*, *82*(6) 363–369.

Peng, D. L. and Li, Y. P. (1995). Orthographic information in identification of Chinese characters. Paper presented at the 7th International Conference of the Cognitive Processing of Chinese and other Asian Languages. Hong Kong.

Peng, D. L. and Wang, C. M. (1997). Basic processing unit of Chinese character recognition: Evidence from stroke number effect and radical number effect (in Chinese). *Acta Psychologica Sinica*, *1*, 8–15.

Peng, D. L., Guo, D. J., and Zhang, S. L. (1985). The retrieval of information of Chinese characters in making similarity judgment under recognition condition (in Chinese). *Acta Psychologica Sinica*, *3*, 227–233.

Peng, D. L., Guo, D. J., and Zhang, S. L. (1986). The retrieval of information of Chinese characters in making similarity judgment under recall conditions (in Chinese). *Acta Psychologica Sinica*, *3*, 264–271.

Peng, R. X. (1982). A preliminary report on statistical analysis of the structure of Chinese characters (in Chinese). *Acta Psychologica Sinica*, *4*, 285–390.

Perfetti, C. A. (1985). *Reading Ability*. New York: Oxford University Press.

Perfetti, C. A. and Tan, L. H. (2013). Write to read: The brain's universal reading and writing network. *Trends in cognitive sciences*, *17*(2), 56–57.

Perfetti, C. A. and Zhang, S. (1991). Phonological processes in reading Chinese characters, *Journal of Experimental Psychology: Learning, Memory and Cognition*, *17*, 633–643.

Perfetti, C. A., Cao, F., and Booth, J. (2013). Specialization and universals in the development of reading skill: How Chinese research informs a universal science of reading. *Scientific Studies of Reading*, *17*(1), 5–21.

Perfetti, C. A., Liu, Y., and Tan, L. H. (2005). The lexical constituency model: some implications of research on Chinese for general theories of reading. *Psychological Review*, *112*(1), 43.

Perfetti, C. A., Tan, L. H., and Siok, W. T. (2006). Brain-behavior relations in reading and dyslexia: Implications of Chinese results. *Brain and Language*, *98*(3), 344–346.

Perfetti, C. A., Zhang, S., and Berent, I. (1992). Reading in English and Chinese: Evidence for a "universal" phonological principle. In R. Frost and I. Katz (eds), *Orthography, phonology, morphology, and meaning* (pp. 227–248). Amsterdam: North-Holland.

Perfetti, C. A., Liu, Y., Fiez, J., Nelson, J., Bolger, D. J., and Tan, L. H. (2007). Reading in two writing systems: Accommodation and assimilation in the brains reading network. *Bilingualism: Language and Cognition*, *10*(2), 131–146. Special issue on Neurocognitive approaches to bilingualism: Asian languages, P. Li (ed.).

Perry, P. (2001). White means never having to say you're ethnic. *Journal of Contemporary Ethnography*, *30*, 56–91.

Petriwskyj, A., Thorpe, K. J., and Tayler, C. P. (2005). Trends in construction of transition to school in three western regions, 1990–2004. *International Journal of Early Years Education*, *13*(1), 55–69.

Pickering, M. J. and Garrod, S. (2007). Do people use language production to make predictions during comprehension? *Trends in Cognitive Sciences*, *11*(3), 105–110.

Pope, C. C. and O'Sullivan, M. (1998). Culture, pedagogy and teacher change in an urban high school: How would you like your eggs done?. *Sport, Education and Society*, 3(2), 201–226.

Pressley, M., Wharton-McDonald, R., Mistretta-Hampston, J., and Echevarria, M. (1998). Literacy instruction in 10 fourth-grade classrooms in upstate New York. *Scientific Studies of Reading*, 2(2), 159–194.

Pu, Y., Liu, H. L., Spinks, J. A., Mahankali, S., Xiong, J., Feng, C. M., and Gao, J. H. (2001). Cerebral hemodynamic response in Chinese (first) and English (second) language processing revealed by event-related functional MRI. *Magnetic Resonance Imaging*, 19(5), 643–647.

Rao, N. (2002). Early childhood education in Hong Kong: Moving towards child-friendly policies, curricula and practices. In V. Sollars (ed.), *Curricula, policies and practies in early childhood education* (pp. 76–88). Malta: P.E.G.

Rao, N. and Koong, M. (1999). *Early childhood education and care in Hong Kong*. Hong Kong: OMEP-Hong Kong.

Rao, N. and Li, H. (2009). Quality Matters: Early Childhood Education Policy in Hong Kong. *Early Child Development and Care*, 179(3), 233–245.

Rao, N., Ng, S. S. N., and Pearson, E. (2010). Preschool pedagogy: A fusion of traditional Chinese beliefs and contemporary notions of appropriate practice. In C. K. K. Chan and N. Rao (eds), *Revisiting the Chinese learner: Changing contexts, changing education* (pp. 255–280). The University of Hong Kong: Comparative Education Research Centre/Springer Academic Publishers.

Rao, N., Koong, M., Kwong, M., and Wong, M. (2003). Predictors of preschool process quality in a Chinese context. *Early Childhood Research Quarterly*, 18(3), 331–350.

Ren, G. (2004). Introducing OVAL writing: A new approach to Chinese character retention for secondary non-Chinese-speaking background learners. *Babel*, 39(1), 4–10.

Ren, G. Q. and Yang, Y. (2010). Syntactic boundaries and comma placement during silent reading of Chinese text: evidence from eye movements. *Journal of Research in Reading*, 33(2), 168–177.

Reutzel, D. R. and Cooter, R. B. (1992). *Teaching children to read: From basals to books*. New York: Merrill.

Reutzel, D. R., Oda, L. K., and Moore, B. H. (1989). Developing print awareness: The effect of three instructional approaches on kindergarteners' print awareness, reading readiness, and word reading. *Journal of Literacy Research*, 21(3), 197–217.

Reyhner, J. (2008). *The reading wars*. Retrieved December 18, 2009, from http://jan.ucc.nau.edu/~jar/Reading_Wars.html

Richards, J. C. and Rodgers, T. S. (2001). *Approaches and methods in language teaching*. Cambridge: Cambridge University Press.

Rogoff, B. (2003). The cultural nature of human development. New York, NY: Oxford University Press.

Rosenshine, B. V. and Stevens, R. (1984). Classroom instruction in reading. In P. D. Pearson (ed.), *Handbook of reading research* (pp. 745–798). New York: Longman.

Russell, D. H. (1961). Reading research that makes a difference. *Elementary English*, 38(2), 74–78.

Saji, N. and Imai, M. (2013). Evolution of verb meanings in children and L2 adult learners through reorganization of an entire semantic domain: The case of Chinese carry/hold verbs. *Scientific Studies of Reading*, 17(1), 71–88.

Sasanuma, S., Itoh, M., Mori, K., and Kobayashi, Y. (1977). Tachistoscopic recognition of Kana and Kanji words. *Neuropsychologia*, 15(4), 547–553.

Schatschneider, C., Fletcher, J. M., Francis, D. J., Carlson, C. D., and Foorman, B. R. (2004). Kindergarten prediction of reading skills: A longitudinal comparative analysis. *Journal of Educational Psychology*, 96(2), 265.

Scribner, S. and Cole, M. (1981). *The Psychology of Literacy*. Cambridge: Harvard University Press.

Seidenberg, M. S. (1985). The time course of phonological code activation in two writing systems. *Cognition*, 19, 1–3.

Sénéchal, M. and LeFevre, J. A. (2002). Parental involvement in the development of children's reading skill: A five-year longitudinal study. *Child development*, 73(2), 445–460.

Shen, D., Liversedge, S. P., Tian, J., Zang, C., Cui, L., Lei, C., Bai, X., Yan, G., and Rayner, K. (2012). Eye movements of second language learners when reading spaced and unspaced Chinese text. *Journal of Experimental Psychology Applied*, 18(2), 192.

Shen, H. H. (2005). An investigation of Chinese-character learning strategies among non-native speakers of Chinese. *System*, 33(1), 49–68.

Shen, H. H. (2008). An analysis of word decision strategies among learners of Chinese. *Foreign Language Annals*, 41(3), 501–524.

Shen, H. H. (2010). Imagery and verbal coding approaches in Chinese vocabulary instruction. *Language Teaching Research*, 14(4), 485–499.

Shen, H. H. (2011). *Teaching Chinese as a Second Language: Vocabulary Acquisition and Instruction*. Beijing: Beijing University Press.

Shen, H. H. (2013). Chinese L2 literacy development: Cognitive characteristics, learning strategies, and pedagogical interventions. *Language and Linguistics Compass*, 7(7), 371–387.

Shen, H. H. and Ke, C. (2007). An investigation of radical awareness and word acquisition among non-native learners of Chinese, *The Modern Language Journal*, 91, 97–111.

Shu, H. and Anderson, R. C. (1997). Role of radical awareness in the character and word acquisition of Chinese children. *Reading Research Quarterly*, 32, 78–89.

Shu, H. and Anderson, R. C. (1998). Learning to read Chinese: the role of metalinguistic awareness. In J. Wang, A. Inhoff, and H. C. Chen (eds). *Reading Chinese script: A cognitive analysis*. Hillsdale, NJ: Lawrence Erlbaum Associates.

Shu, H., Anderson, R. C., and Wu, N. (2000). Phonetic awareness: Knowledge of orthography–phonology relationships in the character acquisition of Chinese children. *Journal of Educational Psychology*, 92(1), 56–62.

Shu, H., Peng, H., and McBride-Chang, C. (2008). Phonological awareness in young Chinese children. *Developmental Science*, 11(1), 171–181.

Shu, H., McBride-Chang, C., Wu, S., and Liu, H. (2006). Understanding Chinese developmental dyslexia: Morphological awareness as a core cognitive construct. *Journal of Educational Psychology*, 98, 122–133.

Shu, H., Chen, X., Anderson, R. C., Wu, N., and Xuan, Y. (2003). Properties of school Chinese: Implications for learning to read. *Child development*, 74(1), 27–47.

Siegel, L. S. (1993). Phonological processing deficits as the basis of a reading disability. *Developmental Review*, 13, 246–257.

Simon, H. A. (1979). Information processing models of cognition. *Annual Review of Psychology*, 30(1), 363–396.

Sinclair, J. (ed.). (1995). *Collins Cobuild English language dictionary*. London: Harper Collins Publishers.

Siok, W. T. and Fletcher, P. (2001). The role of phonological awareness and visual-orthographic skills in Chinese reading acquisition. *Developmental Psychology, 37*(6), 886.

Siok, W. T., Jin, Z., Fletcher, P., and Tan, L. H. (2003). Distinct brain regions associated with syllable and phoneme. *Human Brain Mapping, 18*(3), 201–207.

Siok, W. T., Perfetti, C. A., Jin, Z., and Tan, L. H. (2004). Biological abnormality of impaired reading is constrained by culture. *Nature, 431*(7004), 71–76.

Siok, W. T., Niu, Z. D., Jin, Z., Perfetti, C. A., and Tan, L. H. (2008). A structural-functional basis for dyslexia in the cortex of Chinese readers. *Proceedings of the National Academy of Sciences, 105*, 5561–5566.

Siok, W. T., Kay, P., Wang, W. S., Chan, A. H., Chen, L., Luke, K. K., and Tan, L. H. (2009). Language regions of brain are operative in color perception. *Proceedings of the National Academy of Sciences, 106*(20), 8140–8145.

Sippola, A. E. (1994). Literacy education in kindergarten classrooms. *Reading Horizons, 35*(1), 4.

Siraj-Blatchford, I., Muttock, S., Sylva, K., Gilden, R., and Bell, D. (2002). Researching effective pedagogy in the early years. London: Department for Education and Skills, University of London.

Smith, F. (1992). Learning to read: The never-ending debate. *The Phi Delta Kappan, 73*(6), 432–441.

Snow, C. E. and Van Hemel, S. B. (eds). (2008). *Early childhood Assessment: Why, what, and how*. DC: The National Academies Press.

Snow, C. E., Burns, M. S., and Griffin, P. (eds). (1998). *Preventing reading difficulties in young children*. National Academies Press.

Snow, C. and Oh, S. S. (2011). Assessment in early literacy research. *Handbook of early literacy research, 3*, 375–395.

Sofou, E. and Tsafos, V. (2009). Preschool Teachers' Understandings of the National Preschool Curriculum in Greece. *Early Childhood Education Journal, 37(5)*, 411–420.

Stahl, S. A. and Hayes, D. A. (eds). (1997). *Instructional models in reading*. Routledge.

Stahl, S. A. and Miller, P. D. (1989). Whole language and language experience approaches for beginning reading: A quantitative research synthesis. *Review of Educational Research, 59*(1), 87–116.

Stevenson, H. W. and Lee, S. Y. (1990). Contexts of achievement: A study of American, Chinese, and Japanese children. *Monographs of the Society for Research in Child Development, 221*(55), 1–2.

Stevenson, H. W., Lee, S. Y., and Schweingruber, H. (1999). Home influences on early literacy. In D. A. Wagner, R. L. Venezky, and B. V. Street (eds), *Literacy: An International Handbook*. Boulder, Colorado: Westview Press.

Stevenson, H. W., Stigler, J. W., Lucker, G. W., Lee, S. Y., Hsu, C. C., and Kitamura, S. (1982). Reading disabilities: the case of Chinese, Japanese, and English. *Child Development, 53*, 1164–1181.

Street, B. (1984). *Literacy in theory and practice*. Cambridge: Cambridge University Press.

Street, B. (1995). *Social literacies: Critical approaches to literacy development, ethnography, and education*. London: Longman Press.

Strickland, D. (1994). Educating African American learners at risk: Finding a better way. *Language Arts, 71*, 328–336.

Strickland, D. S. (1990). Emergent Literacy: How Young Children Learn to Read and Write. *Educational Leadership*, 47(6), 18–23.

Strickland, D. S. and Morrow, L. M. (1989). Developing skills: An emergent literacy perspective. *The Reading Teacher*, 43(1), 82–83.

Stubbs, M. (1980). *Language and literacy: The sociolinguistics of reading and writing*. London: Routledge and Kegan Paul.

Sue, I. R. and Liu, I. M. (1996). Word and character superiority effects in Chinese (in Chinese). *Chinese Journal of Psychology*, 38, 11–30.

Sugishita, M., Ettlinger, G., and Ridley, R. M. (1978). Disturbance of cage-finding in the monkey. *Cortex*, 14(3), 431–438.

Sulzby, E. and Teale, W. H. (eds). (1988). *Emergent literacy: Writing and reading*. Ablex Publishing Corporation.

Sung, K. Y. and Wu, H. P. (2011). Factors influencing the learning of Chinese characters. *International Journal of Bilingual Education and Bilingualism*, 14(6), 683–700.

Sylva, K., Siraj-Blatchford, I., and Taggart, B. (2003). *Assessing quality in the early years: Early Childhood Environmental Rating Scale Extension (Ecers-E) four curricular subscales*. Trentham Books.

Taft, M. and Zhu, X. The representation of bound morphemes in the lexicon: a Chinese study. In L. B. Feldman (ed.), *Morphological aspects of language processing*. Hillsdale, NJ: Lawrence Erlbaum.

Tan, L. H. and Peng, D. L. (1991). Visual recognition processes of Chinese characters: A research to the effect of grapheme and phoneme. *ACTA Psychologica Sinica*, 23(2), 50–56.

Tan, L. H. and Perfetti, C. A. (1998). Phonological codes as early sources of constraint in Chinese word identification: A review of current discoveries and theoretical accounts. *Reading and Writing: An Interdisciplinary Journal*, 10, 165–200.

Tan, L. H. and Perfetti, C. A. (1999). Phonological activation in visual identification of Chinese two-character words. *Journal of Experimental Psychology: Learning, Memory, and Cognition*, 25(2), 382–393.

Tan, L. H., Feng, C. M., Fox, P. T., and Gao, J. H. (2001a). An fMRI study with written Chinese. *Neuroreport*, 12(1), 83–88.

Tan, L. H., Laird, A. R., Li, K., and Fox, P. T. (2005a). Neuroanatomical correlates of phonological processing of Chinese characters and alphabetic words: A meta-analysis. *Human Brain Mapping*, 25(1), 83–91.

Tan, L. H., Xu, M., Chang, C. Q., and Siok, W. T. (2013). China's language input system in the digital age affects children's reading development. *Proceedings of the National Academy of Sciences*, 110(3), 1119–1123.

Tan, L. H., Spinks, J. A., Eden, G. F., Perfetti, C. A., and Siok, W. T. (2005b). Reading depends on writing, in Chinese. *Proceedings of the National Academy of Sciences of the United States of America*, 102(24), 8781–8785.

Tan, L. H., Chan, A. H., Kay, P., Khong, P. L., Yip, L. K., and Luke, K. K. (2008). Language affects patterns of brain activation associated with perceptual decision. *Proceedings of the National Academy of Sciences*, 105(10), 4004–4009.

Tan, L. H., Liu, H. L., Perfetti, C. A., Spinks, J. A., Fox, P. T., and Gao, J. H. (2001b). The neural system underlying Chinese logograph reading. *NeuroImage*, 13, 826–846.

Tan, L. H., Spinks, J. A., Feng, C. M., Siok, W. T., Perfetti, C. A., Xiong, J., and Gao, J. H. (2003). Neural systems of second language reading are shaped by native language. *Human Brain Mapping*, 18(3), 158–166.

Tan, L. H., Spinks, J. A., Gao, J. H., Liu, H. L., Perfetti, C. A., Xiong, J., and Fox, P. T. (2000). Brain activation in the processing of Chinese characters and words: A functional MRI study. *Human Brain Mapping*, *10*(1), 16–27.

Tan, L. H., Spinks, J. A., Gao, J. H., Liu, A., Perfetti, C. A., Xiong, J., Pu, Y., Liu, Y., Stofer, K. A., and Fox, P. T. (2000). *Brain activation in the processing of Chinese characters and words: A functional MRI study.* Human Brain Mapping, 10, 16–27.

Tang, F. L. and Maxwell, S. (2007). Being taught to learn together: An ethnographic study of the curriculum in two Chinese kindergartens. *Early Years*, *27*(2), 145–157.

Tao, L. and Healy, A. F. (2002). The unitization effect in reading Chinese and English text. *Journal of Scientific Studies of Reading*, *6*(2), 167–197.

Taylor, D. (1983). *Family literacy: Young children learning to read and write.* Exeter, NH: Heinemann Educational Books.

Taylor, I. (1999). Literacy in China, Korea, and Japan. In D. A. Wagner, R. L. Venezky, and B. V. Street (eds), *Literacy: An international handbook.* Boulder, Colorado: Westview Press.

Teale, W. (1986). Home background and young children's literacy development. In W. H. Teale and E. Sulzby (eds), *Emergent literacy: Writing and reading.* Norwood, N.J.: Ablex Publication Corporation.

Teale, W. H. and Sulzby, E. (1986). *Emergent literacy: Writing and reading. Writing research: Multidisciplinary inquiries into the nature of writing series.* NJ: Ablex Publishing Corporation.

Teale, W. H. and Sulzby, E. (1994). Emergent literacy as a perspective for examining how young children become writers and readers. In E. M. H. Assink (ed.), *Literacy acquisition and social context* (pp. 7–20). New York: Harvester Wheatsheaf.

Tobin, J. (2007). An ethnographic perspective on quality in early childhood education. In J. X. Zhu (ed.), *Global perspectives on early childhood education* (pp. 131–143). Shanghai: East China Normal University Press.

Tobin, J. (2011). Implicit cultural beliefs and practices in approaches to early childhood education and care. *Asia-Pacific Journal of Research in Early Childhood Education*, *5*(1), 3–22.

Tong, X., McBride-Chang, C., Wong, A. M. Y., Shu, H., Reitsma, P., and Rispens, J. (2011). Longitudinal predictors of very early Chinese literacy acquisition. *Journal of Research in Reading*, *34*(3), 315–332.

Tse, S. and Li, H. (2011). *Early child Cantonese: Facts and implications* (Vol. 42). Walter de Gruyter.

Tso, R. V. Y., Au, T. K. F., and Hsiao, J. H. W. (2011). The influence of writing experiences on holistic processing in Chinese character recognition. *The 33rd Annual Meeting of the Cognitive Science Society*, Boston, MA, 20–23 July 2011. In conference proceedings, pp. 1442–1447.

Tzeng, O. J. L., Alva, I. C., and Lee, A. T. (1979). Meaning specificity in sentence processing. *British Journal of Psychology*, *70*(1), 127–133.

Tzeng, O. J. L., Hung, D. L., and Garro, L. C. (1978). Reading Chinese characters: An information processing view. *Journal of Chinese Linguistics*, *6*(2), 287–305.

Tzeng, O. J. L., Hung, D. L., and Wang, W. S. (1977). Speech recoding in reading Chinese characters. *Journal of Experimental Psychology: Human Learning and Memory*, *3*(6), 621.

Tzeng, O. J. L., Lin, Z. H., Hung, D. L., and Lee, W. L. (1995). Learning to be a conspirator: A tale of becoming a good Chinese reader. In B. de Gelder, and J. Morais (eds), *Speech and reading: A comparative approach* (pp. 227–246). Hove, Sussex: Erlbaum (UK) Taylor and Francis.

Tzuo, P. W. (2007). The tension between teacher control and children's freedom in a child-centered classroom: Resolving the practical dilemma through a closer look at the related theories. *Early Childhood Education Journal, 35*(1), 33–39.

Tzuo, P. W. (2010). The ECE landscape in Singapore: Analysis of current trend, issues, and prospect for a cosmopolitan outlook. *Asia-Pacific Journal of Research in Early Childhood Education, 4*(2), 77–98.

Vandervelden, C. M. and Siegel, L. S. (1995). Phonological recoding and phoneme awareness in early literacy: A developmental approach. *Reading Research Quarterly, 30*(4), 854–875.

Vellutino, F. R., Smith, H., Steger, J. A., and Kaman, M. (1975). Reading disability: Age differences and the perceptual-deficit hypothesis. *Child development, 46*, 487–493.

Vellutino, F. R., Steger, J. A., and Kandel, G. (1972). Reading disability: An investigation of the perceptual deficit hypothesis. *Cortex, 8*(1), 106–118.

Walker, K. (2007). Play Matters: Engaging Children in Learning. In *The Australian Developmental Curriculum – A play and project based philosophy.* Camberwell, Victoria: Australian Council for Educational Research.

Wang, J. and Leland, C. H. (2011). Beginning students' perceptions of effective activities for Chinese character recognition. *Reading in a Foreign Language, 23*(2), 208–224.

Wang, J. and Mao, S. (1996). Culture and the kindergarten curriculum in the People's Republic of China. *Early Child Development and Care, 123*, 143–156.

Wang, M. and Yang, C. L. (2008). Learning to read Chinese. In K. Koda and A. M. Zehler (eds), *Learning to read across languages: Cross-linguistic relationships in first and second-language literacy development* (pp. 125–153). New York and London: Routledge.

Wang, W. S. Y. (1981). Language structure and optimal orthography. In O. J. L. Tzeng and H. Singer (eds), *Perception of print: Reading research in experimental psychology* (pp. 223–236). Hillsdale, NJ: Erlbaum.

Wang, X., Han, Z., He, Y., Liu, L., and Bi, Y. (2012). Resting-state functional connectivity patterns predict Chinese word reading competency. *PloS One, 7*(9), e44848.

Wang, X. C. and Spodek, B. (2000, November). *Early childhood education in China: A hybrid of traditional, communist, and western culture.* Paper presented at the Annual Meeting of the National Association for the Education of Young Children, Atlanta, USA.

Weaver, C. (ed.). (1998). *Reconsidering a balanced approach to reading.* National Council of Teachers of English.

Weaver, C. (ed.). (1994). *Success at last!: helping students with attention deficit (hyperactivity) disorders achieve their potential.* Heinemann Educational Publishers.

Wells, G. (1985). Preschool literacy-related activities and success in school. In D. Olson, N. Torrance, and A. Hildyard (eds), *Literacy, language and learning: The nature and consequences of reading and writing.* Cambridge: Cambridge University Press.

Whitehurst, G. J. and Lonigan, C. (2001). Get ready to read. *An early literacy manual: Screening tool, activities and resources.* Columbus, OH: Pearson.

Whitehurst, G. J., Arnold, D. S., Epstein, J. N., Angell, A. L., Smith, M., and Fischel, J. E. (1994). A picture book reading intervention in day care and home for children from low-income families. *Developmental Psychology 30*, 542–555.

Williams, C. and Bever, T. (2010). Chinese character decoding: a semantic bias? *Reading and Writing, 23*(5), 589–605.

Winitz, H. (1981). *The comprehension approach to foreign language instruction.* Rowley, MA: Newbury House.

Winke, P. M. and Abbuhl, R. (2007). Taking a closer look at vocabulary learning strategies: A case study of a Chinese foreign language class. *Foreign Language Annals*, *40*(4), 697–712.

Wong, M. N. C. (2008). How preschool children learn in Hong Kong and Canada: a cross-cultural study. *Early Years*, *28*(2), 115–133.

Wong, N. C. M. (2003). A study of children's difficulties in transition to school in Hong Kong. *Early Child Development and Care*, *173*(1), 83–96.

Wong, N. C. M. and Rao, N. (2004). Pre-school education. In M. Bray and R. Koo (eds), *Education and society in Hong Kong and Macau: Comparative perspectives on continuity and change* (2nd edition) (pp. 15–34). Hong Kong: The University of Hong Kong.

Wright, B. D. (2009). Direct Assessment Methods – A Close-Up Look. *Western Association of Schools and Colleges*. Alameda, CA.

Wu, C. Y., Ho, M. H. R., and Chen, S. H. A. (2012). A meta-analysis of fMRI studies on Chinese orthographic, phonological, and semantic processing. *Neuroimage*, *63*(1), 381–391.

Wu, M. E. (1994). The relationships between concept of Chinese character and reading ability (in Chinese). In Taiwan Primary School Teachers Association (ed.), *Study on the Chinese Language Curriculum and Textbooks of Primary School* (Taipei) (pp. 47–59). Taipei: The Editor.

Wu, M. E. and Huang, Q. F. (1994). Young children's understanding of the functional literacy (in Chinese). In Taiwan Primary School Teachers Association (ed.), *Study on the Chinese Language Curriculum and Textbooks of Primary School* (Taipei) (pp. 28–35). Taipei: The Editor.

Wu, X. and Anderson, R. C. (2007). Reading strategies revealed in Chinese children's oral reading. *Literacy Teaching and Learning*, *12*(1), 47–72.

Wu, X. C., Li, W. L., and Anderson, R. C. (1999). Reading instruction in China. *Curriculum Studies*, *31*(5), 571–586.

Xiang, H., Lin, C., Ma, X., Zhang, Z., Bower, J. M., Weng, X., and Gao, J. H. (2003). Involvement of the cerebellum in semantic discrimination: An fMRI study. *Human Brain Mapping*, *18*(3), 208–214.

Xiao, X. Q. (2002). Analysis of character writing errors among foreign students. *Chinese Teaching in the World*, *2*, 79–85.

Xin, J. (2001). An experimental study of foreign learners' awareness of phonetic cues in pictophonetic characters. *Chinese Teaching in the World*, *2*, 2001–2002.

Xu, Y., Pollatsek, A., and Potter, M. C. (1999). The activation of phonology during silent Chinese word reading. *Journal of Experimental Psychology: Learning, Memory, and Cognition*, *25*(4), 838.

Yang, J. (2000). Orthographic effect on word recognition by learners of Chinese as a foreign language. *Journal of the Chinese Language Teachers Association*, *35*, 1–18.

Yang, J., Staub, A., Li, N., Wang, S., and Rayner, K. (2012). Plausibility effects when reading one- and two-character words in Chinese: Evidence from eye movements. *Journal of Experimental Psychology: Learning, Memory, and Cognition*, *38*(6), 1801.

Young, A. W., Hellawell, D., and Hay, D. C. (1987). Configurational information in face perception. *Perception*, *16*(6), 747–759.

Yu, B. L. (1989). Size effect of language units in short-term and long-term memory (in Chinese). *Acta Psychologica Sinica*, *1*, 1–7.

Yu, B. L. and Cao, H. Q. (1992). A new exploration on the effect of stroke-number in the identification of Chinese characters (in Chinese). *Acta Psychologica Sinica*, *2*, 120–126.

Yu, B. L., Jing, Q. C., and Si, M. H. (1985). Short-term memory span for Chinese words and phrases (in Chinese). *Acta Psychologica Sinica, 4,* 361–368.

Yu, B. L., Zhang, S. L., and Pan, Y. J. (1997). Effects of stroke type on identification of upright and tilted Chinese characters (in Chinese). *Acta Psychologica Sinica, 1,* 24–29.

Zang, C., Liang, F., Bai, X., Yan, G., and Liversedge, S. P. (2013). Interword spacing and landing position effects during Chinese reading in children and adults. *Journal of Experimental Psychology: Human Perception and Performance, 39*(3), 720–734.

Zhang, C., Zhang, J., and Zhou, J. (1998). A study of cognitive profiles of Chinese learners' reading disability. *Acta Psychologica Sinica, 30,* 50–56.

Zhang, H. C. and Shu, H. (1989). Phonetic similar and graphic similar priming effects in pronouncing Chinese characters (in Chinese). *Acta Psychologica Sinica, 3,* 284–289.

Zhang, W. T. and Feng, L. (1990). The visual recognition and capacity of short-term memory for Chinese disyllabic words (in Chinese). *Acta Psychologica Sinica, 4,* 49–56.

Zhang, W. T. and Feng, L. (1992). A study on the unit of processing in recognition of Chinese characters (in Chinese). *Acta Psychologica Sinica, 4,* 378–385.

Zhang, W. T. and Yang, D. Z. (1987). The effect of Chinese character's stroke numbers on the capacity of short-term memory (in Chinese). *Acta Psychologica Sinica, 1,* 79–85.

Zhang, W. T., Peng, R. X., and Simon, H. (1986). Short-term memory capacity for Chinese characters and phrases (in Chinese). *Acta Psychologica Sinica, 2,* 133–139.

Zhang, Y., Tardif, T., Shu, H., Li, H., Liu, H., McBride-Chang, C., Liang, W., and Zhang, Z. (2013). Phonological skills and vocabulary knowledge mediate socioeconomic status effects in predicting outcomes for Chinese children. *Developmental Psychology, 49*(4), 665–671.

Zhao, G. (2003). Character amount and vocabulary size among beginning European and American learners of Chinese. *Applied Linguistics, 3,* 106–112.

Zhao, J., Li, Q. L., Wang, J. J., Yang, Y., Deng, Y., and Bi, H. Y. (2012). Neural basis of phonological processing in second language reading: An fMRI study of Chinese regularity effect. *NeuroImage, 60*(1), 419–425.

Zhou, X. and Marslen-Wilson, W. (1999). Phonology, orthography, and semantic activation in reading Chinese. *Journal of Memory and Language, 41*(4), 579–606.

Zhou, X. and Marslen-Wilson, W. (2000). The relative time course of semantic and phonological activation in reading Chinese. *Journal of Experimental Psychology: Learning, Memory, and Cognition, 26*(5), 1245.

Zhou, Y. G. (1986). Modernization of the Chinese language. *International Journal of Social Language, 59,* 7–23.

Zhou, Y. Q. (1978). The efficiency of phonetization from phonetic radicals in nowaday Chinese characters (in Chinese). *Zhongguo Yuwen [Chinese Language Journal], 146,* 172–177.

Zhu, J. X. and Wang, X. C. (2005). Contemporary early childhood education and research in China. In B. Spodek and O. N. Saracho (eds), *Contemporary perspectives in early childhood education: Vol. 7. International perspectives* (pp. 55–77). Greenwich, CT: Information Age.

Zhu, J. X. and Zhang, J. (2008). Contemporary trends and developments in early childhood education in China. *Early Years, 28*(2), 173–182.

Zhu, Y. (2010). Rediscovering the impacts of digital flashcard on Chinese character memorization of beginning US learners. *Chinese Teaching in the World, 1,* 127–137.

Zhu, Y. and Wei, H. (2005). Effects of digital voiced pronunciation and stroke sequence animation on character memorization of CFL learners. *Journal of the Chinese Language Teachers Association*, *40*, 49–70.

Zhu, Z. P. (2002). Structural theory of Chinese character and Chinese character teaching. *Language Teaching and Linguistic Studies*, *4*, 35–41.

Zhu, Z. R. (1991). *Fundamentals and implements of language testing* (in Chinese) (pp. 100–107). Shanghai: Education Press.

曹传泳、沈晔（1965）：小学儿童分析概括和辨认汉字能力的发展研究 [J]。*心理学报*，*1*。

傅永和（1989）：漢字部件表的研製。載陳原編《*現代漢語定量分析*》。上海教育出版社。

傅永和（1991）：汉字结构及其构成成分的统计分析，载陈原编《*现代汉语定量分析*》（上海：上海教育出版社）。

彭瑞祥、张武田（1984）：速示下再认汉字的某些特征，心理学报，第1期，页49–53。

裘錫圭（1988）：*文字學概要*，北京：商務印書館，頁10–21。

沈德立（1988）：语言的直觉理解与表达，心理学杂志，第1期，页60–66。

徐仲舒（1995）：汉语大字典。武汉：湖北辞书出版社。

楊繼本（1987）：漢字心理在漢字信息輸入編碼上的應用，心理学报，1982，3。

叶重新、刘英茂（1982）：影响本国文字认识阈的因素，中华心理学刊，14卷，页271–279。

喻柏林（1986）：语音和语义编码在语词记忆中的相对效应，《心理学报》第2期，页140–147。

中國文字改革委員會（1965）：《印刷通用漢字字形表》。北京：文字改革出版社。

Index

Note: Page numbers in *italic* relate to figures; those in **bold** to tables.

accommodation–assimilation hypothesis 68
activation likelihood estimation (ALE) 36
activities: teacher-directed 52
adults: brain areas and writing 34; handwriting and reading studies on 41; spelling and rhyming by 35
analysis: skills 31; visual-orthographic 35–6
appreciation: of ideological content (New Standard) 128
Asher's learning hypotheses 76–7
assessment: age appropriate 119; criterion-referenced 122; in the early years 118–32; formative 118–20; multi-source approach to 119; norm-referenced 122; portfolio in SAIL 110–11; summative 118, 121–2; why and how? 118–19
attainment: assessment of 118–32
attitudes, skills, and knowledge (ASK) 62
auditory processing: and reading ability 30
awareness: phonological 29–30

Beijing 20; classroom observations in 88–90; early literacy education in 86–90; pattern of literacy development in 21–2; PPCLS in 125–6
belief–practice divide/gap 82–3, 100–1
big-book approach 89
bilateral fusiform gyrus 39
blood oxygenation 33
body movements: use in TPR 80
brain: activation and language 55; reading network 33–4, 68

brain areas (BA): BA6 38; BA7 28; BA8 35; BA9 28, 33, 35, 37, 44; BA10 35; BA39 28; BA40 28; BA45 28, 35; BA46 28, 46

Cantonese 19, 26; in Hong Kong 90–1; phonological processing of 30; and PPCLS 123; tones in 2, 112n
cerebral blood: flow and volume 33
character recognition: emergence of 21; and radicals 17
characters: clues to sound and meaning in 2; compound 3; forms of 3; graphic structure of 67; and handwriting skills 39; high frequency 2; ideographic 2; integrated 3; logographic 2, 56; modern corpus of 4; nature of 2–3; number of 2, 14; order of introduction 71–2; perception of 9; phonetic–semantic 4; pictographic 2; processing of 68; pronunciation–meaning correlation 69; recognition of 10; sensitivity to 70; simplified 2; spacing of 3; structure of 3–5, 10; traditional 2; typing of 75; units of 9; visual-orthographic 35–6; writing of 1, 37–8, 42
Child Appropriate Practice 60
childcare centers 15
children 106–7; awareness of orthography in 16–17; bilingual 30; dyslexic 43, *see also* dyslexia; grade 3 19; kindergarten 12, 15; learning freedom of 52; preschool 21–2, 30, 32; primary school 19–20, 25, 31; spelling and rhyming by 35

China: curriculum reform in 52–3, 100–3; early literacy education in 86–90; education reforms in 130; kindergartens in 19–20; Ministry of Education 87–8; National Education Council 88; official language of 1; pedagogical reforms in 52, 58; problematic policies/regulations in 83–4; simplified character use in 2; State Educational Committee 87; three practice gaps in 97–105

Chinese: age of 1; brain network of 28, 33–4; category of 5, 9; characters 1–6; cognition 9; common teaching pattern in 98–100; defining literacy pedagogy of 55–6; difficulty of learning 9; education in Hong Kong 90–2; education in Singapore 94–5; emerging pedagogical changes in 82–3; learning trend in 67; literacy 6–9, 87–8, 90–2, 94–5, 118–32; literacy acquisition in 14–24, 69–70; literacy modeling in 9–14; as logographic system 2; monosyllabism of 1–2; morpheme-syllable 2; morphographic 2; native speakers of 13; nature of characters in 2–3; neurological networks for 26–7; neuropsychological understanding of 25–44; new syllabus for 131; non-native speakers of 32–3; orthography of 1–2, 16–17; patterns of literacy development in 21–2; pedagogy 56–60; phonetic alphabet of 2; psycholinguistics of 1–24; reading literacy in 126–8; reading objectives in 130; reading studies in 25–9; reading tests in 129–31; role of writing in reading of 38–40; script level of 5; as second language (L2) 1, 23, 69–70; skills development in 16–20; strategies for learning as L2 70–1; structure of characters in 3–5; teaching in early childhood 86–117; teaching handwriting in 74–5; teaching in Hong Kong 90–4; teaching as L1 45–66; teaching as L2 67–85; teaching in Singapore 94–7; TPR approach to 75–81; traditional pedagogy for 52–3, 82; use of 1; writing system uniqueness of 5–6

chunk complexity: and STM capacity 13

classrooms: assessment of 119; comparison of 60, 88, 94, 97, 104; constraints in 54, 83, 101, 104; effective 50–1; inappropriate approaches in 52; observations in 120; sociocultural differences in 100; traditional pedagogies in 60, 81–3, 90, 97, 104; Western pedagogies in 52–4, 58, 60, 86, 99

cognition 9
cognitive learning strategies 70
cognitive skills 6
collaboration 15
commas 32
Committee on Early Childhood Pedagogy 51
communication linkages 105
comprehension-based teaching 76
Confucian heritage culture (CHC) 98
Contextually Appropriate Practice 60
continuity: child-centered (bottom-up) approach 103; comparison of patterns 104; holistic approach 102; horizontal 102; top-down approach 102–3; vertical 102
contour density theory 11
contour prior to content principle 11
copying exercises 54, 56, 58, 82, 91, 98, 101
correspondence: grapheme–phoneme 2; orthography-to-phonology 4; sound-to-script 4
cross-cultural studies 7, 59
crossword puzzles: use in TPR 81
cues: by phonetic radicals 4; by strokes 17
cultural influences 55, 59–60, 86, 100, 105
Culturally Appropriate Practice 60
culturally, contextually and child-individually appropriate practice (3CAPs) 60, 107, 112, 132
culture: Confucian heritage (CHC) 98

data: collection and analysis 121
development stage in SPA 63
developmentally appropriate practice (DAP) 58–9, 95, 101, 106
dialogic reading (DR) 56–7
difficulty 1
direct instruction 55; teaching by 57–8
direct-image hypothesis 23

documentation cycle: five stage 121
drama performances: in SAIL 109
dual-processing hypothesis 12
dyslexia 28–31, 34; markers for 35, 43

early childhood: teaching literacy in 86–117
early learning: and storybooks 61
ECE reforms 53
ecological systems theory 82, 100
education: bilingual 84; policy–practice gap in 101–2
emergent curriculum 58
emergent literacy 53, 57–8, 60, 92, 95, 97, 99, 108; vs. reading readiness 45–8
emotional security 16
encoding: and memory 14; phonetic 18; stage 11–13
England: visual skills in 19
English: brain networks in 28, 33–4; phonological processing in 30; in Singapore 94; teaching in Hong Kong 91–2
episodic buffer 43
error analysis: in literacy development 22–4
evaluation: of ideological content (New Standard) 128
event-related potential (ERP) 31, 33
executive functioning skills 32
Exner's area 26–7
extension activities: in SAIL 110
eye movements 13, 18; tracked 32

feedback: in SAIL 108–9
final sounds 48; list of Mandarin 49
first language (L1): alphabetic 9; Cantonese as 91; of children 76; Chinese as 45–66; English as 94; semantic divisions of 69
5W1H questioning skills 64–5
formative assessment *see* assessment, formative
French: neurological networks for 26–7
Full-time compulsory language curriculum standards (New Standard) 127–8
functional magnetic resonance imaging (fMRI) 25–6, 33, 35–6, 40
fusiform gyrus 43, 68

gestural system 27
global prior to part principle 11

goal identification 121
graphematic-processing hypothesis 11–13
graphemes 68, 72
grapheme–phoneme correspondence (GPC) 2, 17
grapheme–semantic association (GSA) 20–1, 23
graphic units: and spoken units 41
Guidance for Kindergarten Education 52, 88
Guide to the Pre-primary Curriculum (GPC) 53, 90–1, 107, 111

handwriting: and character/letter perception 38–9; and Chinese reading 38–9; skills 39; teaching in L2 74–5; as visual-motor coordination skill 38
Hanyu Pinyin 87
High/Scope method 52–4, 88
home literacy 15, 57
home–school connection 57, 91
homophones 1–2, 12, 32
Hong Kong 20, 23; actual practice in 59–60; child-centered continuity in 103; classroom observations in 92–4; 'Dos and Don'ts' list 91; Education Department 91; English teaching in 91; government of 90–1; Institute of Education (HKIEd) 47; literacy education in 55, 90–2; official language of 1; pattern of literacy development 22; pedagogical continuity in 104–5; pedagogical reforms in 52, 58; PPCLS in 125–6; practice gaps in 97–105; teaching approach in 51, 99; traditional characters use in 2; trilingualism of 90; visual skills in 18–19; Western pedagogies in 99
horizontal continuity *see* continuity, horizontal

identification with-phonology hypothesis 23
identification without-phonology hypothesis 23
immigrants: use of Chinese by 1
inferior frontal gyrus (IFG) 28, 34–7, 42–3, 68
inferior parietal lobule (IPL) 39–41
inferior parietal system 43
information and communication technologies (ICT) 66; use in teaching L2 73

information processing theory 9
initial sounds 48; list of Mandarin **49**
initiation stage in SPA 62
input stage 9–11
instructors *see* teachers
integration stage in SPA 63
International Association for Evaluation of Education Achievement (IEA) 128
International Research Centre (ISC) 128
Iran: literacy in 7–8
iTeach principles 53, 95

Japan: use of Chinese characters in 1

kindergartens 15; in Beijing 20; classroom observations in 88–90; cross-cultural study of 59; 'Dos and Don'ts' for 91; emergent literacy in 45, 47; pedagogical reforms in 52–3, 100
knowledge 106
Korea: use of Chinese characters in 1

language 50; and brain activation 55; etiological studies of 57; monosyllabic 1–2; neurological networks for 26–7; proficiency 84; tone 49; verb-biased 76, *see also* whole language approach
language transfer theory 69
learners *see* students
learning: activities in SAIL 113–17 Appendix; Asher's hypotheses 76–7; child-centered 55; Chinese as L2 67–71; and motor processing 39; multiple sensory modalities in 74; portfolios 120–1; strategies for L2 70–1; whole language 58
left inferior frontal gyrus (LIFG) 68
left inferior parietal lobule (LIPL) 68
left middle frontal gyrus (LMFG) 33, 39–40, 44; role of 28–9, 34–7; and working memory 43–4
letter perception: and handwriting 38
letter-to-phoneme correspondence 1
lexical coding 31
lexical constituency model 31–2
Liberia: syllabic writing in 7
lingual gyrus 68
Listen and read Approach to Chinese Literacy 89
literacy: acquisition of 14–24, 69–70; age of introduction 45; Chinese *see* Chinese, literacy; and classroom environment 16; and cognitive development 14; common sequences 20–1; common teaching pattern of 98–100; definitions of 6–9, 55–6; in the early years 118–32; education 87–8; emergent *see* emergent literacy; emerging changes in 82–3; error analysis in 22–4; five-stage document cycle 121; home 15, 45, 57; Hong Kong teaching practice 90–4; learning characters and 2; modeling Chinese 9–14; neuropsychological understanding of 25–44; patterns of development 21–2; pedagogy 56–60; preschool 15–16, 45; scale development 123–4; school 57; Singapore teaching practice 94–7; sociocultural approach to 6; stages of acquisition 14–15; studies 7–8; theories of acquisition 14–16; TPR approach to 75–81
literacy skills: development of 16–20; sequences in 20–1
logograms 23
logographs 98
long-term memory (LTM) 13

Malay: in Singapore 94
Mandarin 26; final sounds in **49**; initial sounds in **49**; tone markings 2, 24n; transliteration of 48
Manual of Kindergarten Practice 90
meaning 72; units 2
metacognition 31; learning strategies 70
metalinguistic awareness 19
middle temporal gyri 42
Min-nong (Pity on Farmers) 111
mirror neurons 40
Montessori Method 52, 88
morphemes 2; lexical 2; syllabic 1–3, 5
morphological awareness 4
morphological skills: role of 29–33
morphological training (MT) 56–7
motor processing 27; and learning strategies 39
motor programs 56
motor theory of speech perception 40
multiple-processing hypothesis 12–13

naming experiments 12–13
National Curriculum Guide (NCG) 88
nature–nurture controversy 57

neuroimaging 25, 33
neurological networks 26–7
neuropsychological understanding: of Chinese reading 29–37; of Chinese writing 37–44
neuropsychology: of Chinese literacy 25–44; of Chinese TPR 79
news sharing: in SAIL 109

observation 15
occipital gyrus 43
occipitotemporal region 68
onsets 4
Organization for Economic Cooperation and Development (OECD) 128
orthographic awareness 56
orthographic knowledge 32
orthographic representation: and writing 40–2
orthography: awareness of 16–17; character-specific 40; of Chinese 1–2
orthography-to-phonology correspondence (OPC) 4, 19
orthography-to-phonology transformation 28
orthography-to-semantics mapping 28

parafoveal previews 31
parents: as literacy teachers 15
pedagogy: child-centered 53; of Chinese literacy 55–60; emerging changes in 82–3; most effective approach to 56–8; shared by L1/L2 classrooms 81–5; teacher-directed 52; of teaching Chinese as L1 45–66; of teaching Chinese as L2 67–85; traditional 51–6, 58–60, 82, 98; Western 51–6, 58–60
peer evaluation 120
perception: of characters 9
performance 15
phonemes 1, 72; awareness of 19
phonetic-similarity errors 23–4
phonics-centered approach 48–51
phonological awareness 4, 18–20; importance of 29–30
phonological loop 43
phonological oddity task 43
phonological processing 11; hypothesis of 12
phonological sensitivity 32
phonological skills: role of 29–33
phonological training 55–6

phonology 23
picture shows: use in TPR 81
pinyin 2, 19–20, 24n; and brain activity 34; in L2 72–3; and phonics 48, 50; and reading success 30; typing in 39, 75; writing in 37, 39, 41–2
play 50–1, 57, 84, 92, 101, 103, 132; lack of 55, 81; learning through 53, 73, 87, 95, 100, 102–3
policy–practice gap 101–2
positron emission tomography (PET) 33
postmodernism 106, 112, 127
practice 15
prefrontal systems 43
preschool literacy 15–16
Preschool and Primary Chinese Literacy Scale (PPCLS) 122–6; analysis of variance of **125**; development of 123–4; final version of 133–205 Appendix 1A–E; scores 21–2; test–retest reliability of **125**; validation of 124–5
preschool–primary gap 102–5
Primary Chinese Reading Literacy Scale (PCRLS) 126–32; structure and content of **131**–2; text of 206–16 Appendix 2
priming effect 12–13
The Princess's Birthday Party 111
print exposure 31
processing: graphic-semantic 12; phonological 18–19; semantic errors in 22–3; of strokes 10
Programme for International Student Assessment (PISA) 126, 128–9
Progress in International Reading Literacy Study (PIRLS) 128
Project Approach 52–4, 58, 83–4, 95, 97, 99, 103, 107, 110; story-based 61–6
psycholinguistics: of Chinese literacy 1–24
Putonghua 87, 90, 92, 94; and PPCLS 123

quantity 1
questioning 16

radicals 3, 10; arrangement of 5; and character recognition 17; frequency of 10; number of 10; phonetic 3–6, 16–17, 70; semantic 3, 5, 16–17, 70

rapid automized naming (RAN) 32
read aloud approach 89
readiness view 88
reading: aloud 16; alphabetic 38, 40–1; brain network of 33–4; character 5, 9, 12, 17–18, 28, 40–1, 68; Chinese as L2 67–9; and cognitive skills 31; and configural processing 5; dialogic (DR) 56–7; and handwriting 38–9; holistic 4; interference in 12; L2 teaching approaches 71–4; and literacy 6; and LMFG 28–9, 35; modeling Chinese 9–14; neurological networks for 26–7; neuropsychological understanding of 29–37; pragmatics of (New Standard) 128; processes of 15; role of writing in 38–41; and working memory 36–7, 42–4
reading comprehension 31; in New Standard 127
reading literacy 126–8; current tests of 128–9
reading readiness 46, 57; vs. emergent literacy 45–8
reading retention (New Standard) 127
reading studies: etiological 57; themes and topics in 25–9
reading tests 129; 3-D structure of 131; new requirements for 130; problems and new directions of 129–31
reading wars 45, 48, 55
reading-through-writing hypothesis 41
Reggio Emilia 52–4, 88, 107
regularity 42
Regulations on Work in Kindergartens 87–8
research: definition of literacy in 7–8; themes 26; topics 26–9
Resolution of Reforming the School System 87
response time (RT) 10
rhyming tasks 35
rhythm and poem: use in TPR 81
rimes 4; awareness of 19, 30
role play 65, 81, 108, 116; use in TPR 81
rote learning 44, 53–4, 56, 73, 82, 88, 98, 101

school literacy 57
second language (L2): Chinese as 1, 23, 67–85, 94; English as 92; mother tongues as 94

see and say: use in TPR 81
self-evaluation 120
self-generated elaboration 73
semantic processing errors 22–3
semantic skills: role of 29–33
semantic-similarity errors 24
sensorimotor cortex (SMC) 42
sensorimotor theory 77
Shenzhen: actual practice in 59–60; classroom observations in 88–90; common L1 and L2 pedagogies in 81; early literacy education in 86–90; language proficiency in 84; literacy pedagogy in 55; pedagogical continuity in 104–5; pedagogical reforms in 52; problematic policies/regulations in 83–4; teaching in 99; traditional pedagogies in 83; Western pedagogies in 99
short-term memory (STM) 13–14
simulationist framework 40
sing and say: use in TPR 81
Singapore 20; actual practice in 59–60; bilingual education in 84–5; class observations in 95–7; common L1 and L2 pedagogies in 81; language proficiency in 84; literacy education in 94–5; literacy pedagogy in 55; multilingualism of 94; official language of 1; pattern of literacy development 22; pedagogical reforms in 52–3; PPCLS in 125–6; problems in L2 classrooms 84; simplified character use in 2; teaching in 99; three practice gaps in 97–105; Western pedagogies in 99
single-cell recording 40
skills 31–3, 129–32; cognitive 6; comprehension 76; handwriting 38–9; importance of 31–3; learning 63; literacy 6, 8, 16–20, 47–8, 59, 82, 84, 101; morphological 29–33; motor 27, 38; oral 56–7; orthographic 12, 18–19, 30–1, 42, 57; phonological 19, 23, 29–33; processing 35–6, 43, 127; reading 14–15, 46, 50, 54, 56–7, 89–90, 105, 127; semantic 29–33; transfer of 68–9, 129; visual 12, 17–19, 29–33, 38; writing 14–15, 54, 56, 58, 98, 105
socioeconomic status (SES): and phonics 48; and reading 30

sound-to-script correspondence 4
Soviet Union 87
spacing effects 13
specificity 26
spelling: errors 30; tasks 35
spoken units: and graphic units 41
stages: encoding 10–13; input 9–11; of literacy acquisition 14–15; retrieving 9; storage 13–14
step on: use in TPR 81
storage stage 13–14
Story Approach to Integrated learning (SAIL) 61, 66, 94, 97, 106–12; example of 111–12, 113–17 Appendix
Story-based Project Approach (SPA) 61–6; five activities of 64; four delivery steps of 63–4; seven post-project activities for 65–6; six questions in 64–5; three stages of 62–3
storybooks: characteristics of 61; and early learning 61; and teaching 61–2
storytelling: in SAIL 108–9
stroke and radical number effect 10
stroke-number effect 9–10; in L2 72
stroke-type effect 10
strokes 3, 9; frequency of 5; number of 3, 10, 17; patterns of 3, 17; and STM capacity 13–14; used to distinguish homophones 2
students: difficulties of 73; ELL 57; L1 2, 26, 38, 44; L2 2, 4, 26, 30, 38, 44; literacy of 2; roles in TPR 78; using L1 to learn L2 69
sublexical processing 12–13
summative assessment *see* assessment, summative
superior frontal gyrus (SFG) 37
superior parietal lobules (SPLs) 34, 39–40
syllables 1, 3; awareness of 19, 32; deletion of 32; elements of 48; number of 2; segmental elements of 2; special Mandarin 49
symbol-to-sound rules 1
symbols: written 1
syntax knowledge 14, 31

Taiwan 19; official language of 1; traditional character use in 2; visual skills in 18–19
Tamil: in Singapore 94
tap and say: use in TPR 81

teacher-instructed elaboration 73–4
teachers 56; assessment by 120; belief–practice divide/gap of 58, 82–3, 100–1; and policy–practice gap 101–2; priorities of 98; roles in TPR 78; training of 101
teaching: child-centered 53; Chinese as L1 45–66; Chinese as L2 67–85; Chinese philosophy of 52; common pattern of 98–100; comprehension-based 76; by direct instruction 55, 57–8; in early childhood settings 86–117; effective approaches in L2 73–4; handwriting in L2 74–5; helpful methods in L2 74; Hong Kong literacy practice 90–4; outcome-oriented 48; practice 86; process-oriented 48; reading 71–4; revision 121; Singapore literacy practice 94–7; and storybooks/storytelling 61–2, 108
teaching plans: evaluation of 121
test questions: objective and subjective 132
text spacing 33
text-decoding ability (New Standard) 127
theme exploration: in SAIL 109
theory of multiple intelligences 61–2
tones 2, 48; Mandarin 49
toss up: use in TPR 81
Total Physical Response (TPR) 75–7; Chinese 78–81; common activities in 77–8; five-step teaching model of 79–*80*; learner roles in 78; neuropsychological mechanism of *79*; teacher roles in 78; ten common activities in 80–1
trace theory 76
training: literacy methods 56; morphological (MT) 56–7
transparency 1; phonological 4
twin studies 57

unit size 13
United States of America (USA): literacy in 8
universal reading process 32, 68
universality 26–7

VAD test 125–6
validity 42
verb-based L2 teaching 76
verbal memory 31

vertical continuity *see* continuity, vertical
visual grapheme–semantic associations 23
visual memory 31
visual skills 12, 17–19, 38; role of 29–33
visual system 27
visual word-forming area (VWFA) 26
visual-orthographic processing skills 30–1
visual–auditory discrimination 20–1, 23
visuospatial sketchpad 43
vocabulary knowledge 32

whole language approach 15, 45, 53, 57–60, 83, 92, 95, 99, 108; vs. phonics-centered approach 48–51

word identification 32
word segmentation 3, 13
working memory: and LMFG 43–4; and reading 36–7, 42–4
writing: alphabetic 5, 11, 26; character 39–42, 44, 70; and literacy 6; logographic 98; neuropsychological understanding of 37–44; and orthographic representation 40–2; processes of 15; role in reading 38–41
writing systems 27; uniqueness of 5–6

Zhuyin Fuhao 19

For Product Safety Concerns and Information please contact our EU
representative GPSR@taylorandfrancis.com
Taylor & Francis Verlag GmbH, Kaufingerstraße 24, 80331 München, Germany

www.ingramcontent.com/pod-product-compliance
Lightning Source LLC
Chambersburg PA
CBHW062128300426
44115CB00012BA/1854